Ghost Channels

Bernadette Marie Calafell, Marina Levina,
and Kendall R. Phillips, General Editors

GHOST CHANNELS

Paranormal Reality Television and the Haunting of Twenty-First-Century America

Amy Lawrence

University Press of Mississippi / Jackson

The University Press of Mississippi is the scholarly publishing agency of
the Mississippi Institutions of Higher Learning: Alcorn State University,
Delta State University, Jackson State University, Mississippi State University,
Mississippi University for Women, Mississippi Valley State University,
University of Mississippi, and University of Southern Mississippi.

www.upress.state.ms.us

Publication of this work was made possible in part thanks
to a generous donation from Dartmouth College.

Parts of chapter 1 were originally published as "Paranormal Survivors:
Validating the Struggling Middle Class" in *Journal of Popular Film
and Television* 45, no. 4 (2017): 219–30.

All photographs in chapter 5 were taken by Terry Lawrence.

The University Press of Mississippi is a member
of the Association of University Presses.

Copyright © 2022 by University Press of Mississippi
All rights reserved

First printing 2022
∞

Library of Congress Control Number: 2022930665

Hardback ISBN 978-14968-3810-0
Paperback ISBN 978-1-4968-3811-7
Epub single ISBN 978-1-4968-3812-4
Epub institutional ISBN 978-1-4968-3813-1
PDF single ISBN 978-1-4968-3814-8
PDF institutional ISBN 978-1-4968-3815-5

British Library Cataloging-in-Publication Data available

Contents

Introduction: Viewer Discretion Advised 3

1 Paranormal Survivors: Validating the Struggling Middle Class 25

2 Ghost Hunters: Men on the Edge 51

3 My Favorite Medium: Women's Work 86

4 Confronting Evil: A Short Trip to the Dark Side. 117

5 Abandoned Institutions: "It's in the Walls". 133

6 In America There Is Real Evil: Excluded Americans 161

7 The Next Generation: Children of the Paranormal 199

Notes 219

Bibliography 247

Index 253

Ghost Channels

Introduction

Viewer Discretion Advised

"America has *always* been a land of ghosts, a nation obsessed with the spectral."[1]
—Jeffrey Weinstock

Throughout American history there have been periodic outbreaks of obsession with the paranormal. Often arising in times of crisis, this persistent undercurrent has found expression in rituals public and private and across all forms of media. From the somber weight of the seventeenth-century Salem witch trials to the birth of Spiritualism in the 1840s, the lighthearted amusements of newspaper horoscopes in the 1930s or twenty-first-century television's *Long Island Medium*, it is clear that this cyclical "preoccupation" with the paranormal reflects "deep-seated aspects of the American character."[2]

Between 2004 and 2019, over six dozen documentary-style series dealing with paranormal subject matter premiered on television in the United States. Combining the stylistic traits of horror (carefully crafted scenes of suspense punctuated by jolts of fear) with earnest accounts of what are claimed to be actual events, "paranormal reality" incorporates subject matter formerly characterized as "occult" or "supernatural" into the established category of reality TV.[3] In these series, "paranormal" refers to phenomena that cannot be accounted for by rational means, including ghosts, poltergeists, apparitions, shadow figures, light anomalies, shape-shifters, and various "negative

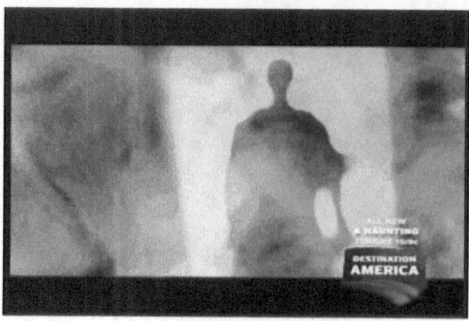

entities" that are said to coexist with the living.[4] Their presence is demonstrated by unexplained, often terrifying events that are either communicated directly through people who possess special psychic abilities or detected by technological devices such as radio-frequency samplers, digital voice recorders, or infrared "night-vision" cameras. As is typical of reality television in general, paranormal reality shows represent their human subjects as ordinary, everyday people, albeit people who regularly take part in paranormal investigations, who have seen spirits all their lives, or who happen to have had personal encounters with ghosts.

Despite the number of programs produced and their evident popularity (some running for over a decade), paranormal reality programming has received little critical attention. This may be due partly to the scorn with which the subject is routinely greeted. The world of the paranormal is often dismissed out of hand, those who deal in it branded as con artists, their customers superstitious and irrational. At the end of the nineteenth century, noted psychologist William James declared that if people believed it possible to communicate with the dead, it was because of their own "soft-headedness and idiotic credulity."[5] At the beginning of the twenty-first century, another scholar warned that "the recent dignification of Spiritualism as a subject of serious enquiry" risks leading people to forget "the shrieking silliness of the whole business."[6] At best, interest in the paranormal elicits a sigh, the entire subject regrettable proof of how obstinately people cling to outmoded beliefs.

Abandoning debates about whether or not the paranormal is "real," modern scholars have accepted that "proving or disproving the existence of ghosts is a fruitless exercise."[7] Once ghosts are no longer viewed as "a literal phenomenon requiring empirical verification," it becomes possible to shift the focus to "the persistence of the *trope* of spectrality."[8] Writers such as

María del Pilar Blanco and Esther Peeren (prompted by Marx and Derrida) argue that it is more productive to think of the paranormal as "a conceptual metaphor capable of bringing to light and opening up to analysis hidden, disavowed, and neglected aspects of the social and cultural realm, past and present."[9] In other words, instead of asking whether audiences believe that paranormal shows are "real," it is more fruitful to ask what these texts can tell us about contemporary cultural concerns. Which issues preoccupying contemporary culture are being addressed in these programs and why are they being expressed in paranormal terms? Why the resurgence of interest in the paranormal at this historical moment and why in this form? By exploring the social tensions, contradictions, and fissures that are raised across multiple programs we begin to see the "various ways in which the occult and the paranormal force us to re-describe" and reconsider "the aesthetic and political ramifications of the popular."[10]

Adding to the overall disdain for paranormal reality television is its adoption of reality TV's style and methods. As in much of reality television, people who are not professional performers look directly into the camera to speak as themselves about their own experiences. In some programs, a less polished visual style implies lower budgets and a do-it-yourself approach as amateurs take "television" into their own hands, using consumer-grade cameras and sound recorders to provide "objective" proof of their subjective experiences. The adoption of such well-established documentary techniques situates paranormal series firmly within the category of reality TV—a form whose own relation to reality is hotly contested.

As Misha Kavka notes, "reality TV sits at the devalued end of the cultural spectrum," with viewers, participants, individual programs, and the genre as a whole held in contempt.[11] Combining reality television techniques with paranormal subject matter creates a uniquely bad object. In 2009, a critic in the *New York Times* characterized the entire swath of paranormal series as "repetitive" and "not the least bit frightening," equating their appeal with that of "soft-core cable porn" and "professional wrestling."[12] Class bias is made explicit when the programs are described as appearing only on "the more populist environment of basic cable."[13] But if, as June Deery argues, reality TV is "worth analyzing" on the grounds of its "impact, tenacity, and cultural resonance," the same can be said for paranormal reality television.[14]

While numerous works have been written describing the economic, legal, and industrial factors underlying the development of reality television, few mention programs that feature paranormal subject matter.[15] Kavka's *Reality TV* (2012), Deery's *Reality TV* (2015), and Laurie Ouellette's *A Companion to Reality TV* (2014) and *Lifestyle TV* (2016) offer detailed discussions of structured competition shows like *Survivor*, *American Idol*, and *The Amazing Race*, "docusoaps" (*Beverly Hills Housewives*, *Keeping Up with the Kardashians*), as well as series about "cooking, travel, fitness, fashion, etiquette, dating, shopping, home decorating, sex, health, finance, parenting, . . . weight loss, makeover, property and self-help"—but not a single reference to any of the dozens of paranormal reality programs broadcast during the same period.[16] One major exception is Annette Hill's *Paranormal Media* (2011). Taking a primarily sociological approach, Hill studies how audiences in Great Britain view paranormal-based reality programs.[17] Given paranormal reality's disreputable position in popular culture, Hill finds that regular viewers (even self-styled fans) approach these programs "from a position of distrust." "No one wants to be seen as uncritical, gullible and naive when it comes to paranormal matters."[18] Using their knowledge of genre conventions, she argues, viewers question the existence of paranormal phenomena represented in specific episodes, critique the techniques used to construct effects like fear and suspense, and describe themselves as maintaining a critical distance.[19] Skepticism, however, does not constitute a wholesale rejection of either content or style. As scholars have noted elsewhere, "Belief in the veracity of what you are watching is not a prerequisite to engagement and pleasure."[20] As historian Simone Natale points out, nineteenth-century producers of "magic shows and spiritualist séances" found that "a degree of uncertainty about the authenticity of an attraction would contribute to the arousal of interest in the public and the popular press."[21] Audiences "wavered between acceptance and skepticism but were nonetheless drawn."[22] Evidently, the chance to walk this tightrope of simultaneous belief and unbelief is part of the pleasure supernatural entertainments provide.

Karen Williams describes paranormal reality television as a form that "harbors two intentions: one of earnest authenticating and the other of spectacle and effect."[23] Embracing spectacle as a means and entertainment as a goal does not in itself preclude paranormal reality from addressing substantive cultural issues. Folklorist Diane Goldstein, for example, asserts that even though "ghost stories" may be "subject to forces of commercialization," it does not mean they are "necessarily made trivial or meaningless."[24] For Williams, the true "power of reality TV lies as much in its depiction of the *experience* of reality as it does in the depiction of reality itself."[25] Such shows "may not render the ghost, but they do render the subjective experience of haunted spaces and haunted people." In the process, they give voice (in admittedly highly mediated ways) to those who find their lives and experiences outside the mainstream.

Like a thrill ride, paranormal reality television attempts to transform the fear caused by a sudden perception of precariousness into a form of entertainment. The *frisson* of flirting with disaster, though, is only pleasurable if contained. Every paranormal reality show I shall discuss relies on familiar narrative structures and generic conventions to limit what could otherwise be a disturbing glimpse of the fundamental instability at the heart of America. The recent resurgence in "occult" practices such as astrology and reading tarot cards signals a widespread desire to find alternate routes back to a sense of control. But like wartime surges in patriotism, bull markets, or religious revivals, belief in these inverted images of mainstream hegemonic institutions eventually wanes as they too fail to establish a firm foundation upon which one can manage the present and reliably predict the future.

The instability underlying the lives of Americans applies to the medium of television itself. The paranormal reality series discussed here are the product of what can be characterized as the cable television era. The term "cable television" is shorthand for the period that saw a decisive shift away from analog/"broadcast" television to digital formats (including cable as well as satellite services). This technical and regulatory change (mandated to be completed in the US by 2009) restructured television and the way viewers interacted with it, shifting costs directly to consumers in exchange for a dramatic increase in stations, hours of operation, and targeted viewing options ("niche" programing).

As the accompanying list shows, the trend in paranormal reality programming began around 2004 with the debut of *Ghost Hunters* on the SciFi Channel.[26] By its fifth year, the show had become "the channel's flagship reality show," attracting "three million viewers, more than half in the 18–49 demographic."[27] A deluge of imitators followed, leading the *Hollywood Reporter* to proclaim in 2009 that "the ghost-hunting genre shows no signs of slacking on cable" TV.[28] In fact, the paranormal reality trend was picking up steam. Over the next ten years, more than fifty new series debuted. As new series appeared, the earlier ones did not pass away. Like the undead, programs that were no longer producing new episodes stayed in circulation, feeding cable television's endless appetite.

SERIES BY YEAR

2004
Ghost Hunters (Syfy)
Psychic Detectives (TRA)

2005
A Haunting (DISC)
Ghostly Encounters (A&E)

2007
Paranormal State (A&E)
America's Psychic Challenge (LIF)

2008
Ghost Adventures (TRA)
Ghost Hunters International (Syfy)
Psychic Kids: Children of the Paranormal (A&E)
The Real Exorcist (Syfy)

2009
Celebrity Ghost Stories (BIO)
The Haunted (AP)
Ghost Lab (DES)
Ghost Intervention (TLC)
Ghost Hunters Academy (Syfy)
Ghost Stories (TRA)

2010
My Ghost Story: Caught on Camera (BIO)
Paranormal State: The New Class (A&E)
Fact or Faked: Paranormal Files (Syfy)

2011
The Dead Files (TRA)
Long Island Medium (TLC)
Paranormal Witness (Syfy)
Haunted Collector (Syfy)
Paranormal Challenge (TRA)

2012
Haunted Highway (Syfy)
The Haunting of... with Kim Russo (BIO)

2013
My Haunted House (LMN)
When Ghosts Attack! (DES)
Haunted History (A&E)
Ghost Inside My Child (LMN)
Ghost Mine (Syfy)

2014
Ghost Asylum (DES)
Ghost Stalkers (DES)
Amish Haunting (DES)
Psychic Intervention (BIO)
Hauntings and Horrors (DES)
Angels Among Us (TLC)
Who Was I? My Past Lives (LMN)
American Supernatural (WEA)
Ghost Adventures: Aftershocks (TRA)

2015
Ghosts in My House (DES)
Paranormal Survivor (TRA)
Psychic Matchmaker (TLC)
Demon Files (DES)
I Was Possessed (LIF)
Alaska Haunting (DES)
Project Afterlife (DES)
Answered Prayers (TLC)

2016
Paranormal Lockdown (DES)
Ghost Brothers (DES)
Deadly Possessions (TRA)
Monica the Medium (FREE)
Ghosts of Shepherdstown (DES)
Haunted Case Files (DES)
Kindred Spirits (TLC)
Ghosts in the Hood (WE)
Hollywood Medium with Tyler Henry (E!)

2017
Fear the Woods (TRA)
Haunted Towns (DES)
The Healer (TLC)

2018
Seatbelt Psychic (LIF)
Haunted Hospitals (TRA)
Mama Medium (TLC)

2019
Destination Fear (TRA)
Paranormal 911 (TRA)
Paranormal Caught on Camera (TRA)
Paranormal Emergency (TRA)
Portals to Hell (TRA)
Ghost Bait (TRA)
Psychic Kids (A&E)
Ghosts of Morgan City (DISC)
Ghost Hunters (A&E)
Ghost Brothers: Haunted Houseguests (TRA)
Ghost Loop (TRA)
Ghost Nation (TRA)
The Holzer Files (TRA)
Famously Afraid (TRA)
Trending Fear (TRA)

Cable stations:		
A&E: Arts and Entertainment	FREE: Freeform	TRA: The Travel Channel
AP: Animal Planet	HIS: History Channel	TRU: TruTV (formerly Court TV)
BIO: Biography	LIF: Lifetime	WE: We TV
DES: Destination America	LMN: Lifetime Movie Network	WEA: The Weather Channel
DISC: Discovery Channel	SYFY: Syfy (also Sci Fi)	TLC: The Learning Channel
E!: Entertainment Television		

Where "quality" (i.e., scripted) dramas with paranormal subject matter have been occasionally welcome on major networks (e.g., *Ghost Whisperer* on CBS [2005–2010] and *Medium* on CBS and NBC [2005–2009]), paranormal reality series are found almost exclusively on the more obscure, non-premium cable channels. Several cable channels have dedicated the majority of their programming to reality series about the paranormal.[29] During one week in 2015, for example, Destination America broadcast sixty hours of paranormal shows arranged in multi-hour blocks. Monday featured eight hours of *Ghost Asylum*; Tuesday and Thursday each aired eight hours of *A Haunting*; and Wednesday and Friday were set aside for *The Haunted* (eight hours and eleven, respectively). That same week another fifty hours of paranormal reality programs were available spread across Lifetime (six hours of *My Haunted House*), The Travel Channel (five hours of *Ghost Adventures*), Syfy (ten hours of *Paranormal Witness*), and History 2 (eight hours of *Haunted History*).[30] In a single week, a dedicated viewer could binge watch or record over one hundred hours of paranormal reality programs.

At the height of its appeal, cable channels with no obvious connection to the supernatural found ways to incorporate paranormal subject matter into their existing brand identities. With its focus on actors, comedians, and other pop culture figures, A&E (Arts and Entertainment) and E! Entertainment Television developed programs such as *Celebrity Ghost Stories* and *Hollywood Medium with Tyler Henry*. The Travel Channel's *Ghost Adventures* and *The Dead Files* center on visits to allegedly haunted destinations across the United States. Even the Weather Channel got into the act, suggesting that atmospheric disturbances can disturb the spirit world (see the series *American Super/Natural* or *Tornado Alley*'s "Twisted Believers").[31]

Because no trend lasts forever, investing in paranormal reality is not a guarantee of continuing audience interest or financial stability. But whether interest in the paranormal stays strong or begins to fade, the medium in which these series flourished is crumbling. As part of an ever-changing medium/technology/business model, cable television at the end of the 2010s is itself becoming obsolete due to the popularity of streaming, on-demand viewing, and social media.[32]

If every word of the phrase "paranormal reality television" is unstable, open to question, and subject to changes brought on by increasing social and economic pressures, we must remember that what is really being questioned, investigated, and tested at the heart of this genre is what passes as "normal." As we will see, these shows tell us two things: "normal" is not what we thought it was, and normal, everyday life can be terrifying.

Title Sequences: Introducing Horror

Across the genre, paranormal reality series begin the same way: with a disclaimer. At first this seems to signal producers' and programmers' awareness of paranormal reality television's dubious status in the popular imagination. Designed to protect the broadcaster from complaints and/or legal action, disclaimers call attention to these programs' shaky status within a corporate system. For instance, A&E begins each episode of the series *Paranormal State* (2007–2010) with the following: "The views of the occult and supernatural documented in this show are not necessarily those of A&E Television Network." While the legalese of such language establishes distance between the channel's ownership and potentially controversial content, disclaimers also serve as a kind of advertising. Balanced between caution and come-on, appeals for "discretion" acknowledge that texts can be read differently by different audiences. While parents might be comforted when The Travel Channel warns that an episode of *Ghost Adventures* contains "adult situations and mature content that may be not be suitable for younger audiences," younger viewers might be enticed, encouraged to test their ability to handle forbidden material.[33]

Even for a single viewer, the push/pull, attraction/repulsion of such disclaimers requires a divided viewing position. Having been alerted to be on guard against fear or flim-flammery, one is immediately assured that the people appearing on the program are genuine and therefore worthy of emotional and intellectual investment. After posting a "Warning!" (spelled out in large red letters), MSNBC's *My Ghost Story: Caught on Camera* proclaims: "What you are about to see are Haunted Events Encountered by Real People."[34] *When Ghosts Attack!* states: "The victims you are about to see are real. These stories are their personal accounts." By fashioning their subjects as victims (people who have suffered), the producers elicit sympathy, promote viewer identification, and deter overly critical readings of the witnesses' truth claims. *Paranormal Survivor* is even more insistent: "You are about to see *real people* reliving horrifying paranormal encounters."

As the title sequences proper begin, the carefully worded warnings, reality-claims, and equivocations are suddenly left behind as the viewer is plunged into the realm of horror. A stentorian-voiced narrator begins each episode of *When Ghosts Attack!* with the statement, "There are ghosts that haunt—ghosts that hunt—and ghosts that kill." A fast-paced montage rushes us through a landscape of violence, signs of death, and things barely seen. Canted shots of cemeteries, stone angels, damaged dolls, skulls, and crosses punctuate views of Gothic buildings silhouetted against the sky. Jagged, handheld camerawork lurches through dilapidated corridors. Back-lit figures waver in and out of focus, struggling to emerge from haloes of white light. Disturbing music (often low tones pierced by sudden noises or sharp cries) accentuates suspense. Technical "glitches" (scratched frames; the sound of static; the jerky, unnatural motion of time-lapse photography) suggest that televisual technology is not quite under control. Even the graphic design of the letters in each title follows a distinct stylistic pattern. The "N" in the title of *A Haunting* is slashed through as if the screen has been torn by a mythic beast. The white letters of *My Ghost Story: Caught on Camera* form themselves out of a mist. The childlike drawing of a house that frames the title of *My Haunted House* has a blood-red roof, with the "H" in "House" dripping down the screen. Red drops also slide from the letters of *Ghost Stories*, while the white liquid that forms the words *Paranormal State* seems to drip upward, violating the laws of physics.[35]

Sensational and gory, these stylistic flourishes signal that we are entering the realm of horror, a destabilizing genre that disturbs assumptions about family, identity, bodily integrity, the reliability of perception, the security of the domestic sphere, and the predictability of time and space, upending the natural order. In doing so, horror challenges our deepest beliefs in ourselves and how the world works, or (even more unsettling) exposes how unstable those assumptions have been all along. Over time, though, what a culture fears changes.[36] As the previous generation's ghouls and monsters lose their power to terrify, the horror genre evolves. Classic themes of threatening forces

somewhere "out there" (Old World monsters like Dracula, Frankenstein, or The Mummy) give way to modern tropes where it is the benign surface of everyday life that hides the most profound threats.[37] Instead of taking place in a castle or a manor house out on the moors, the modern paranormal narrative occurs in urban apartments (*Rosemary's Baby* [1968]), suburban ranch houses (*Poltergeist* [1982], *Nightmare on Elm Street* [1984]) or the manicured milieu of the country club (*Stepford Wives* [1975], *Get Out* [2017]).

By locating horror within the everyday, paranormal reality television side-steps the expensive special effects, costumes, and set construction needed for classical Gothic horror while suffusing domestic space with the unnerving potential to house limitless evil. Household chores, for instance, become fraught with suspense. Doing the dishes allows someone (or some*thing*) to sneak up behind you when your back is turned; taking the laundry to the basement makes you vulnerable to having your ankle grabbed or being pushed down the stairs; glancing in the bathroom mirror suddenly reveals a terrifying figure close by. The riskiest thing you can do is sleep in your own bed. Because reality TV as a genre makes it "difficult for outside observers to tell what has been manipulated and what hasn't," the use of its

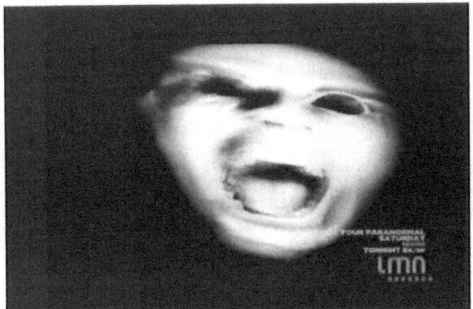

Shock cuts: *Celebrity Ghost Stories*   Shock cuts: *Ghost Asylum*

tropes is particularly effective when it comes to undermining the viewer's sense of security.[38] In its depiction of encounters with the metaphysical (the nonhuman, ghosts, unspecified "forces beyond our comprehension," etc.), paranormal television joins reality with horror to lay bare the fears of a particular cultural moment. Based on the dozens of paranormal reality series on television in this period, nothing is more horrifying than daily reality.

By far the most disturbing paranormal reality programs are the ones based on firsthand accounts. In programs such as *Paranormal Witness*, *Paranormal Survivor*, and *A Haunting*, people who are neither celebrities nor TV stars provide eyewitness accounts of their traumatic experiences with the paranormal. The people on these shows find themselves in a constant state of fear, immersed in situations they did not choose, trapped in houses they cannot escape. If the paranormal is a way to express the inexpressible, the haunted houses featured in these series serve as an apt metaphor for the 2008 housing crisis (chapter 1). In these first-person narratives, victims are given a voice and the nightmare they have been through is recognized and validated.

First-person programs interweave the truth claims of eyewitness testimony with reenactments staged and shot like fictional horror films. Dramatizations propel viewers into the scene, keeping the audience off balance by drastically limiting their ability to see. Obscured, under-lit, or out-of-focus figures lurk in the shadows until a shock cut reveals something too hideous to look at. Perspective continually shifts as characters are stalked by tracking shots from the point of view of malignant presences. The soundtrack fosters a sense of dread regarding what might be lingering just outside the frame, leaving the audience in the position of wanting to see and not wanting to see at the same time.

More than simple horror shows, it is the scenes of testimony that set the first-person paranormal reality shows apart.[39] Individuals look into the camera and speak directly to the viewer. A classic documentary technique, direct address is fundamental to this kind of program. When witnesses state unequivocally, "This happened to me," their credibility hangs on the assumptions that they are who they say they are and that what they say can be trusted. The witnesses' authenticity is established by the distance between them and the polished performers usually featured on television. They also vary in terms of age, class, and body type. Hailing from small towns and rural areas outside the major media centers of New York and Los Angeles (places often mocked as "flyover" country), they speak with regional accents and unorthodox grammar.[40]

Describing their experiences, contemporary Americans are in a position similar to that of nineteenth-century Spiritualists. For those early proponents of the supernatural, "testifying was a risky act."[41] Declarations of contact with spirits were met with "disbelief," "ridicule, even diagnoses of madness."[42] When people (then and now) look to be believed, despite the fact that nothing supports their testimony but a personal appeal, it lends a sense of urgency to their accounts, a sense that there is a great deal at stake. Those earlier "testimonies" were also "*self*-assertions: demands for a public recognition of the value of personal experience, no matter how extraordinary or idiosyncratic it might be."[43] As Hill points out, paranormal events are "real to the people who experience them."[44] At heart, first-person programs are about validation. People present themselves as ordinary Americans whose experiences must be acknowledged. And those experiences are grim.

Across dozens of first-person programs, in episode after episode, people tell about finding their dream home only to see it turn into a nightmare. Not being experts or authority figures, these witnesses struggle to define something they cannot explain, describing phenomena they have only glimpsed, dimly perceived, and partially understood. Knowing they might be dismissed as crazy, they nevertheless insist on being heard. Marginalized partly because of class (how they look, dress, or speak), and partly because of their insistence on configuring their experience in paranormal terms, the people on these shows are convinced that their sufferings have been overlooked, their pleas for help ignored, and their lives undervalued. Terrified and desperate, they do the only thing they can. They run for their lives.

The picture painted of life in America by first-person programs is bleak, the fissures exposed disturbingly deep. Not only is the American dream of social mobility and financial security through home-ownership shown to be a myth: it could kill you. And there is no one who can help. Experts of all kinds—psychics who verify the presence of spirits, investigators who document the haunting with advanced technology, even priests who perform official exorcisms—fail to resolve the problem. It is an understatement to suggest that what our current obsession with ghosts and hauntings ultimately reveals is "the insufficiency of the present moment," the inability of existing social institutions to address the conditions that have made daily life unendurable.[45]

Other paranormal reality programs strive to make the supernatural manageable, fitting it into more familiar (potentially more commercial) narrative formats. Built around ghost-hunting teams (chapter 2) or mediums who claim contact with the dead (chapter 3), these programs provide a reassuring sense of predictability. Rather than being prey to the unknown, ghost hunters and mediums engage with the paranormal when and where they choose. Unlike the people victimized in first-person shows, paranormal investigators and mediums make their encounters with the paranormal serve them, validating their methods and expertise in episode after episode. The presence of recurring characters offers the audience the chance to build an emotional connection with the show's cast. Depicted as ordinary in every way *except* their connection to the paranormal, the stars of these programs invite identification. You too could get together with friends and form a ghost-hunting team as people did in *Ghost Adventures*, *Ghost Lab*, *Ghost Asylum*, *Ghost Brothers*, *Destination Fear*, etc. You might meet or even become a reality TV personality yourself, an opportunity made explicit in the series *Ghost Hunters Academy* and *Paranormal Challenge* (both 2011) where members of the public were invited to try out for a slot as a cast member on a paranormal show.[46]

Constructing programs around "ordinary" people-turned-television-celebrities offers the audience the fantasy of celebrity as a solution to the economic and personal crises depicted in first-person shows. It also mitigates financial risk for the producers by providing a more reliable foundation for marketing and expansion. A hit show can generate numerous spin-offs and variations. The SciFi series *Ghost Hunters* (2004), for example, led to *Ghost Hunters International* (2008) and *Ghost Hunters Academy* (2009). When the original series ceased production, team members Amy Bruni and Adam

Berry created *Kindred Spirits* (2016) for the family-friendly TLC. In 2019, a new *Ghost Hunters* debuted on A&E opposite The Travel Channel's *Ghost Nation*, both shows featuring cast-members from the original *Ghost Hunters*.

As is the case with fictional television, the same performers appear in multiple series, providing continuity across the genre. In 2016, Destination America's *Paranormal Lockdown*, for example, joined Nick Groff (former star of *Ghost Adventures*) with Katrina Weidman from *Paranormal State*. In its first season, the series featured a steady stream of guest stars who had become known to audiences from appearances on other paranormal programs, including investigators Amy Bruni, Adam Berry, and Grant Wilson from *Ghost Hunters*, John Tenney (*Ghost Stalkers*), and psychics Lorraine Warren and Michelle Belanger (frequent guests on *Paranormal State*). John Zaffis alone ("Founder of the Paranormal Demonology Research Society of New England") has made guest appearances on *Paranormal Lockdown*, *Ghost Hunters*, *A Haunting*, *Ghost Adventures*, and *The Demon Files* (2015), in addition to helming his own series, *Haunted Collector* (2011).[47]

Paranormal investigators balance demonstrations of expertise with claims of ordinariness. *Ghost Hunters*, *Ghost Adventures*, *Ghost Asylum* (2014), etc., routinely begin each episode with scenes of men hitting the road in their SUVs. By establishing that potentially otherworldly phenomenon exist within driving distance, these programs make paranormal investigation into a kind of weekend getaway, one that affords team members opportunities for male bonding, risk-taking, and the chance to prove themselves through personal challenges. As in sports, the ghost-hunting format is built around a climactic encounter with the paranormal that is scheduled to happen within a previously determined timeframe. On *Paranormal State*, for instance, the investigation takes place during "dead time"—late at night when all the lights are off. The *Ghost Adventures* team puts itself on "lockdown" (being locked inside a haunted building) for an entire night, while *Paranormal Lockdown* increases the stakes by confining its stars in a location for three full days.

Daring to spend the night in a haunted house has been a common feature of paranormal investigations dating back to at least 1882 when the Society for Psychical Research was founded.[48] Like the SPR, reality television's paranormal investigators present themselves as evidence-based realists, hoping to make ghost-hunting a legitimate scientific pursuit by "affirming standards of precise measurement, rigorous controls, and experimental consistency."[49] Unlike the SPR's founders—renowned doctors, psychologists, authors and philosophers who had reputations to protect—ghost hunters on American television are not "men of status."⁵⁰ In her work on British ghost hunters, Michelle Hanks found that most were either underemployed or trapped in jobs that left them feeling alienated and unfulfilled. As a consequence, they chose to define themselves by their hobbies which they pursued out of interest, not necessity, and where they were accompanied by like-minded friends.⁵¹ Ghost hunting on American television provides working and middle-class men with similar opportunities for self-affirmation.

Representations of male social support networks fused with fantasies of empowerment counter a strain of hopelessness that characterized segments of the US population between 2000 and 2019. These years saw a dramatic "increase in suicide and alcohol-related deaths" for middle-aged white men—what researchers Anne Case and Angus Deaton identified as "deaths of despair."⁵² This trend was particularly acute for "those with a high school degree or less" whose opportunities were limited due to "a long-standing process of cumulative disadvantage."⁵³ Democratic, egalitarian, requiring no training, and available to all who wish to participate, ghost hunting on reality television rescues working-class men from despondency by re-fashioning them as heroes: they handle terrors that have rendered others desperate and take on the "big questions" that have mystified scholars for centuries.⁵⁴

Refusing to cede authority to experts, ghost hunting teams take control of technology. As the stars of *Ghost Adventures* announced in the series' original title sequence, there are "no big camera crews following us around." By presenting an assortment of image-styles, each with distinctly different visual qualities, paranormal reality makes it possible to see television technology and its effects. Daylight interviews with local witnesses are contrasted with grainy "night-vision" scenes. Color-drained, static long takes from security cameras are juxtaposed with amateur footage on VHS, complete with dates and time-stamps. The "evidence" television's ghost hunters produce is marked by visible and audible signs of technological mediation. Voices captured on digital recorders are played back while fragments of speech are spelled out in subtitles as we see graphs charting sound frequencies—visual, objective "proof" that we hear what we think we hear. At the same time, we see technology fail. Cameras die, batteries are drained, monitors go dark, or communications are cut. The televised image itself is disrupted.

Because these series bind masculinity to presumptions of technological competence, the men's sense of identity is threatened in scenes of technical

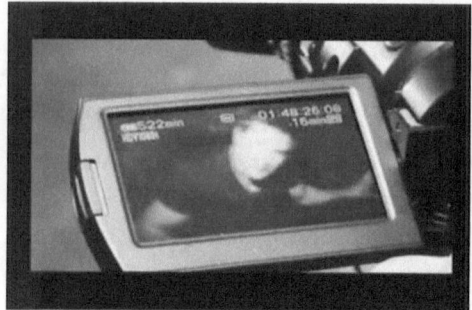
Ghost Adventures

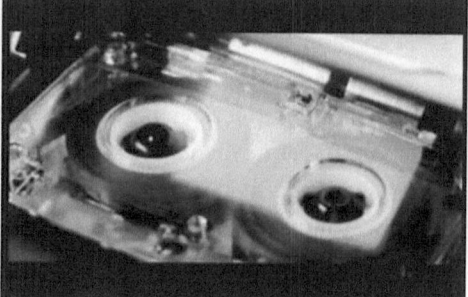
Celebrity Ghost Stories

malfunction. When technology fails—as it frequently does—it may shake the audience's confidence in more than the digital equipment. In narrative terms, each show's climax comes at such moments, when technology and masculinity are pushed to their limits.

Series built around psychic mediums (chapter 3) replace the "hard" knowledge produced by investigators' scientific methods with soft or "feminine" ways of understanding that foreground relationships, intuition, and emotional/psychic sensitivity. Fitting seamlessly into TLC's lineup of shows built around families, *Long Island Medium* offers scenes from the day-to-day life of an average middle-class family in Hicksville, New York.[55] A long-married couple, the Caputos, worry about their children going to college, discuss whether to have the bathroom remodeled, and carry out daily errands (such as visiting the hairdresser or dry-cleaner). As Laurie Ouellette says, like most families featured on US television, the Caputos are "people who are 'just like us,' but spectacularly different."[56] In this case, Theresa Caputo talks to dead people. Inserting the paranormal into the everyday life of middle-class America with its well-lit domestic spaces, backyard pools, and SUVs, series about psychic mediums balance the extraordinarily specialized skills of their central characters with ordinary qualities to which audiences may relate. In the process, traditional assumptions are reaffirmed, especially the value of family, a resilient and elastic institution that evidently can accommodate the most arcane occult phenomena.

But where first-person and ghost hunting series bolster groups that feel socially marginalized, series about mediums evince a fear that women have too much power. From the nineteenth century, when female mediums stepped onto public platforms for the first time, to the sitcom *Bewitched* (1964–1972),

Technical failure: *Ghost Adventures*

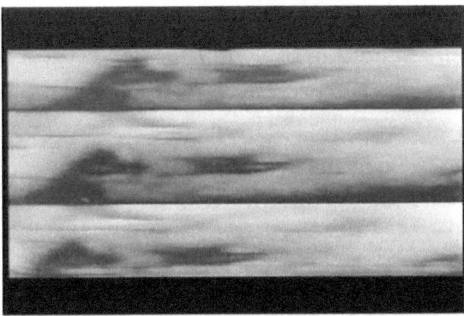
Technical failure: *Ghost Adventures*

Paranormal Survivor

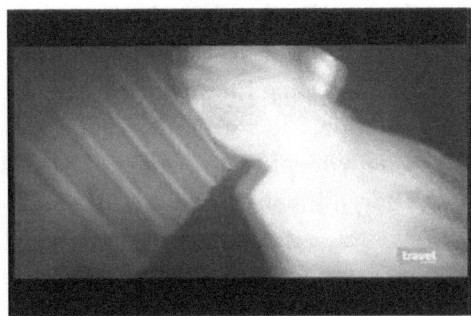
Ghost Adventures

American popular culture has allowed that women may possess amazing abilities as long as those powers are used to reaffirm traditional assumptions about gender.[57] Depicting female psychics as naturally domestic and selfless, paranormal reality television series continue this pattern. "Sensitives" (in the emotional as well as psychic sense) Theresa Caputo (*Long Island Medium*), Kim Russo (*The Haunting of . . .*), Rosie Cepero (*Angels Among Us*), and Jennie Marie Cancelmi (*Mama Medium*) are presented as nurturing figures, healing broken hearts in this world while helping troubled spirits move on to the next. These series spend more time reassuring audiences and less time trying to frighten them as they try to downplay potentially disturbing images of female power.

Because the psychic's claim of unearthly knowledge challenges reason, science, and every post-Enlightenment empirical method for understanding the world, this figure can also function as a site of resistance. Series that capitalize on the subversive potential of the medium-as-outsider willingly disrupt the domestic certainties and traditional definitions of gender that other shows use to contain those with uncanny powers. Older women, for instance, are neglected or absent from most forms of television programming. On *Psychic Detectives*, however, freed from domesticity and from being defined exclusively as wives and mothers, they confront violence and murder, exposing the limits of a male-dominated police force by providing answers when the professionals are stymied.

Resisting pressure to conform to standardized identities and behaviors, psychic mediums since the nineteenth century have "used mediumship to skew codes of normative gender and sexuality."[58] As a supernatural metaphor, psychic ability was seen to offer "new possibilities" by which gender, class, and racial power could be "subverted and remade."[59] Male psychics like Phil Jordan (*Psychic Detectives*), James Van Praagh (*Monica the Medium*), and Chip Coffey (*Paranormal State*) shed restrictive definitions of masculinity by embracing the supposedly "feminine" traits of empathy, sensitivity, and intuition. Shows featuring male mediums—including a new generation who openly identify as gay (e.g., Tyler Henry [*Hollywood Medium with Tyler Henry*], Thomas James [*Seatbelt Psychic*], and investigator Adam Berry [*Ghost Hunters, Kindred Spirits*])—provide a platform where "difference" is championed. On *Psychic Kids: Children of the Paranormal* (2008), for example, young people coming to grips with being "different" (i.e., psychic) rely on medium Chip Coffey to advocate on their behalf, even if that requires him to question the authority of their parents or defy the institution of the family itself (chapter 7). As such, series about psychics can be some of the most progressive *and* the most reactionary programs on paranormal television.

The sunny view from *Long Island Medium*'s Hicksville darkens appreciably when mediums and ghost hunters come face to face with negative spirits. The so-called demonic (chapter 4) constitutes a threat of such magnitude that even television-based paranormal professionals can only sound the alarm and retreat. Instructing audience members to bow to a "higher authority" when faced with evil, they warn viewers explicitly and repeatedly not to toy with spirit-summoning paraphernalia such as Ouija boards. Instead, people must cede control to specialists trained in established religious traditions. Whether reinstituting the hierarchy of expert over amateur alienates audiences or if demonic possession and the work of exorcists is simply too esoteric, no series on this subject has lasted more than a handful of episodes. Nevertheless, the persistence of the subject across the genre foregrounds the religious undercurrents on which much of the popular understanding of the paranormal rests. In the end, however, there is a different explanation of negative spiritual phenomena that dominates paranormal reality.

Ghost Adventures *Paranormal Survivor*

"In America There Is Real Evil"

> "If we want to study social life well . . . we must learn how to identify hauntings and reckon with ghosts."[60]
> —Avery Gordon

Serene aerial perspectives introduce us to picturesque towns nestled in beautiful landscapes—a postcard version of America that is soon revealed to be littered with the empty hulks of failed institutions (chapter 5). Tucked into forests and surrounded by rolling hills, abandoned hospitals and prisons emerge as modern exemplars of hauntedness. Behind these monumental façades, cameras wander down empty corridors, past the decaying walls and peeling paint that attest to discredited ideologies that sought to subject the individual to a totalizing vision of social order. Paranormal investigations of these architectural anachronisms alternate between reassurances that society has overcome its past mistakes and the lingering suspicion that there is something these decrepit spaces have yet to tell us.

In paranormal reality television, "America" is figured as an ideal and a problem. Self-consciously addressing the concept of "America" as both a nation and an identity, these programs figure temporal and physical space as haunted. There is no piece of land left untouched or undefined by (often conflicting) historical narratives; no individual is free from the impact of repressive institutions. Confronting the tortured legacies of the past, paranormal reality programs cloak themselves in the guise of history by citing dates and statistics, interviewing local witnesses, and documenting stories about the people who died in these buildings. It is here that we find the limits of paranormal-programs-as-history as accounts of the past are repeatedly

Ghost Asylum

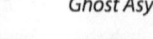

Ghost Asylum

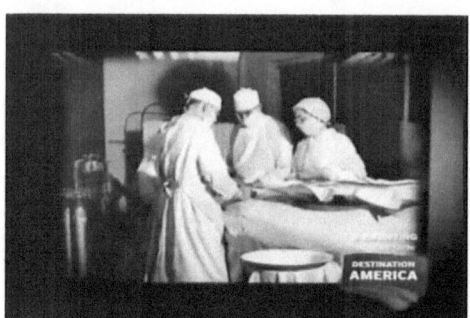

Ghost Asylum

Ghost Asylum

shunted aside in favor of a different story—the exploits of the contemporary ghost-hunting team. Reduced to exposition or backstory, history merely establishes the ominous setting into which our heroes boldly go. Yet, through the use of historical documents, photographs, and even moving images, the past is made vivid. Such well-established documentary techniques insure that the faces and names are read as "real," as remnants of actual people who were confined (often against their will), treated cruelly, and died. The images and stories of the dead are a stark reminder of the consequences of social powerlessness, whether due to mental illness, disability, poverty, or racial and ethnic difference.

Images of the dead raise the question of who speaks and who is silenced. Who is telling these stories and to what purpose? Exploitation—of the living *and* the dead—is a perennial concern in regard to the paranormal. Mediums, for example, are routinely accused of exploiting the grief-stricken. Investigators of abandoned institutions find themselves in a different ethical quandary, dealing with victims who number in the thousands—none of whom consented to being represented on television. Some programs proceed in full sensationalistic mode, providing lurid accounts of lynching, judicial murder, and sexualized violence. The few voices raised in protest often come from female psychics. Amy Allan on *The Dead Files* frequently speaks of the dead in terms of their rights and feelings. Visiting a former sanitarium, she declares, "Let the dead have it. I don't think living people should be here."[61] On an episode of *Paranormal State*, Michelle Belanger fervently suggests that everyone who works in paranormal television has an ethical responsibility to the spirits of the dead. "If you really believe these things exist," she insists, then "they're not just something there for your entertainment."[62] Having opened the door to doubt—of their own processes, their place in America's troubled history—paranormal programs at times interrogate the premises on which they are built.

Episodes about abandoned institutions become exemplars of the same legacy of injustice that is said to have provoked hauntings in the first place. For example, the overwhelming percentage of regular cast members on paranormal programs are white—a fact that goes unremarked as whiteness as a construct is left unexplored. (First-person anthologies consistently present a more diverse population.) The homogeneity of the casts, however, does not mean that these programs have nothing to tell us about race and ethnicity in America's past and present. In chapter 6 we see how whiteness, like one's identity as an American, is (and has been) defined time and again in terms of exclusion—bringing to mind Avery Gordon's description of the "seething absences and muted presences" at the heart of American history and identity.[63] Native Americans and African Americans—despite very different historical experiences—are restricted to a similar function in paranormal narratives where they are relegated to serving as signifiers of a distant past. Present as an idea but absent as individuals, they are allowed to haunt white popular culture while being denied the chance to speak for themselves as contemporary figures. When, on occasion, living Native Americans and African Americans are invited to take part in specific episodes, they call out the most blatant examples of exploitation or try to break through the sentimental complacency that is sensationalism's opposite.

Because it can be neither proved nor disproved, the paranormal is a slippery subject. Nevertheless, the paranormal-as-conceptual-metaphor provides an opportunity for people who are (or feel) marginalized, dismissed, or ignored to say things they could not express by other means.⁶⁴ When what they experience as individuals, however, is rooted in decades-old injustices, individuals find themselves face to face with the horrors of history, a legacy inseparable from their identity as Americans. Paranormal reality exposes the precariousness of deeply held beliefs about who Americans are, what the country stands for, the distance between what the nation promises and how it works, and who must pay for the past. By attending closely to the dozens of paranormal reality TV programs produced between 2004 and 2019, we can see how television in the first decades of the twenty-first-century constructs entertainment from the intersection of "paranormal" and "reality," and in the process gives us a glimpse of what is haunting America.

1

Paranormal Survivors
Validating the Struggling Middle Class

"Those who live in the most dire circumstances possess a complex and oftentimes contradictory humanity and subjectivity that is never adequately glimpsed by viewing them as victims."[1]
—Avery Gordon

Individuals address the camera with the urgency of testimony. "Words can't describe everything that we experienced. But all of it was real."[2] Often depicted in bare settings (spotlit against black backgrounds), the speakers are not anonymous. Openly identifying themselves, they defy disbelief. "My name is Lori Settle and people may find that my story is very unbelievable," a woman says in *When Ghosts Attack!*, "There's No Place Like Hell" (2013). "But it is very real," she concludes, "and it happened to me." Declaring their names (which are also frequently printed on-screen throughout each episode) reinforces the sense that these are witnesses taking a stand, stating something for the record. Sincerity is all they have to support their credibility but it is a powerful tool because there is much at stake. "My name is Katherine Driver," a woman says in another episode. "I felt like I was going to die [and] it was going to be at the hands of something I couldn't see."[3]

Reality programs based on firsthand accounts of paranormal experiences use these scenes of testimony to anchor complex structures that intertwine

documentary techniques with those associated with fiction. Voice-over narration accompanies establishing shots of cities, landscapes, and neighborhoods, as it provides narrative hooks that begin and end each segment. Reenactments staged in full "horror movie" mode (dramatic lighting, canted angles, blurred vision, sudden cuts to figures in gory make-up, scary music, etc.) are corroborated by these shots of firsthand testimony, bringing us back to each show's ultimate guarantor of truthfulness, its privileged source of evidence—personal experience.

The primary goal for the witnesses on these shows is validation. Presenting themselves as "ordinary Americans" (neither psychics nor investigators), people who might otherwise be overlooked put themselves forward, demanding a forum in which to tell their stories. Because of the complexity of their emotional, economic, and familial problems, it is often difficult for them to articulate the pressures they have been under. What is clear is that they have been traumatized, their basic assumptions about how the world works severely shaken. Confronting this new order, a few overcome the unwelcome challenges they find themselves facing but most are lucky simply to survive. Either way, it is crucial that they tell their stories and that someone listen.

Between 2004 and 2019, close to a dozen programs focusing on "first-person" accounts of the paranormal spread across cable television with offerings on A&E, Syfy, Biography, Discovery, The Travel Channel, Lifetime Movie Network, and Destination America. Programs such as *A Haunting*, *The Haunted*, *Ghostly Encounters*, *When Ghosts Attack!*, *Paranormal Survivor*, and *Paranormal Witness* are grounded on "the authority of everyday lived experience."[4] A title card at the beginning of *A Haunting* claims that "the events depicted" are "based on eyewitness accounts," while episodes of *Paranormal Witness* are "based entirely on eyewitness testimony." Except for A&E's *Celebrity Ghost Stories*, the witnesses

The house: "There's No Place Like Hell," *When Ghosts Attack!*

on these programs lack an established public persona. Each episode features "unknown" figures whose testimony we must take on faith.

At the same time, it is clear that these witnesses do not control the way their stories are told. Previously established film and television conventions are used to package their accounts as entertainment—most obviously by including elements from the horror genre such as foreboding comments from off-screen narrators or dimly lit reenactments punctuated by shock cuts and music spikes. As anthologies that introduce new central characters with each episode, these shows rely heavily on convention to make them predictable from episode to episode. In fact, if not for their title sequences, these shows would be hard to tell apart given their pronounced similarities in style, narrative structure, and recurring themes. Therefore, rather than examine a single series, we can look at examples across the genre to see what these shows are telling us. One thing is clear: despite these programs' highly codified representations of each witness's account, in the last decade "average" Americans think they have been through hell.

It begins with a house.

The American Dream

"The new dwelling is not the last solution."[5]
—Siegfried Kracauer

At first, the house seems ideal—"too good to be true." In *When Ghosts Attack!*, "There's No Place Like Hell," Lori Settle, a newly married twenty-seven-year-old with a young daughter, works as a hairdresser. "What was missing in my life was a home of my own. Something to be proud of," she recalls. The family feels fortunate when they move to Fayetteville, West Virginia. "The house fell into our laps." "It was wonderful in the beginning," Lori reports, "but that did not last long." Lori's mother, Beverly, keeps an eye on her new son-in-law: "After a while Donny started to change." Donny becomes depressed and withdrawn. He wasn't volatile toward the family, Lori insists, "but he was so angry." One day, Lori finds him dead in their bathroom. "There was so much blood it completely covered the bathroom floor." Using medical terms, the autopsy concludes that "his aorta ruptured." Lori, however, uses more vivid language, explaining what it is like to be under more pressure than a person can bear: "His heart had exploded." Despite the trauma of this event and her conviction that her husband was killed by a supernatural force, Lori reports that she "still didn't want to leave" the place she considered her home. Lori's mother, on the other hand, decides to leave the moment she sees claw marks appear on her daughter's face: "At that instant I really became a believer." But it was not ghosts or poltergeists she blamed: it was the house. "It was a bad place."[6] Nevertheless, Lori and her daughter stay until one day Lori is pushed down a flight of stairs. "We left with the clothes on our backs," she reports. "That was it."[7] Though they lost everything, they feel lucky to have gotten out alive. "That house is pure evil through and through," Lori concludes. She can even pinpoint the location of evil: "It's in the walls."

For many the phrase "the American dream" refers to home ownership, which, in turn, serves as a sign of financial and domestic stability. The episode "There's No Place Like Hell" (the very title supplanting "home" with "hell") illustrates how reluctant people are to relinquish this ideal. Yet episode after episode replays the same narrative:

- "A Texas family sees their dream house turn into a nightmare when their animals begin to die one after another." (*The Haunted*, "Land of Misery," 2010)
- "A family's dream home turns into a nightmare when a demonic spirit possesses their son." (*Paranormal Witness*, "The Real Haunting in Connecticut," 2012)
- "A Virginia family finally finds their dream home. But it quickly turns into a nightmare when an unknown presence targets their children." (*When Ghosts Attack!*, "Voices of the Dead," 2013)[8]

The ultimate symbol of achievement and belonging is revealed to be the site (even the source) of the greatest threat to these witnesses as, step by step, their dream is dismantled.

Paranormal shows like *A Haunting*, *The Haunted*, and so on are a perfect inversion of the cable channel HGTV (House and Garden Television), on which consumers obsessively shop for the perfect home.[9] On programs such as *House Hunters*, *Property Virgins*, and *Hawaiian Life*, the ideal home is always available as individuals, couples, or families find "the one" out of an abundance of options. On *Property Brothers*, *Fixer Upper*, *Love It or List It*, and *Income Property*, the added adventure of home renovation increases the pool of possible ideal homes in a way that satisfies both buyers and sellers. Shoppers come and go as the realtors, designers, and hosts of these shows become television stars, the recurring characters that can be relied on each week to ease the path of consumers in the real estate market. The good-looking couple with the perfect marriage, family, home, and business featured on *Fixer Upper* or *Flip or Flop* are the opposite of the couples we meet on paranormal TV, where families are at risk—stressed, struggling, driven to the breaking point, with their increasingly dire circumstances represented by a house that overwhelms them.[10] Paranormal shows present a counternarrative to HGTV, telling us what happens when a good house goes bad.

Faith in the American dream exemplified by HGTV's upbeat attitude became increasingly difficult to sustain with the collapse of the housing market in 2008.[11] (Except for *A Haunting* and *Ghostly Encounters*, which debuted in 2005, all the shows discussed here premiered after 2008). In an economic report titled "Nightmare on Main Street," Lori Trawinski borrows her title from the 1980s film series *A Nightmare on Elm Street*, locating horror in the heart of suburbia.[12] She lays out the numbers. "As of December 2011, approximately 22.8 percent—one in five—of mortgage loans nationwide were underwater."[13] "From 2007 to 2011, more than 1.5 million older Americans lost their homes as a result of the mortgage crisis."[14] Although her study was designed to evaluate the effect of the housing crisis on people over fifty, Trawinski concludes that "no age group, race, or ethnicity [was] spared from the effects of declining home values and the financial difficulties caused by the Great Recession and continuing economic weakness."[15] For those over fifty, foreclosure rates increased 873 percent, while the rate increased for those under fifty by 729 percent .[16] In fact, Trawinski concludes, it was not those struggling financially but "middle-income borrowers [who had] borne the brunt of the foreclosure crisis."[17] In other words, it was the people who felt safe, for whom the system had seemed to work, who had the most to lose.[18]

It takes a great deal to persuade homeowners that their dream home is a threat. As Lori says on *When Ghosts Attack!*, "I never thought in a million years this house would take one of our lives."[19] Even after finding her husband's body, she resists leaving. "I became a prisoner in my home. I was still trying to hang onto our dream." Even those who manage to separate the idea of "house" from "home"—defining the physical structure in terms of a financial rather than an emotional investment—are stymied by unseen forces. A woman tries to sell her father's house, left vacant for years. It is littered with dead mice and described as smelling like "death." Cleaning ladies are hired, but they don't last a day.[20] When a man tries to fix up his great-great-grandfather's house, the narrator tells us, "the renovations seemed to unleash something terrifying. Construction workers were terrorized by apparitions, unexplained noises, and overwhelming feelings of dread. They stopped work and fled."[21] These first suggestions of paranormal activity are seemingly innocuous breakdowns in social/work relations. As in horror films, the true extent of the threat initially goes unrecognized.

Most house-hunters are looking for more than financial security. For many, a new home signals a new beginning, a means to overcome some kind of setback that has already disrupted their lives. "Three brokenhearted women renting an old house together seek a fresh start, but instead get what they believe is a supernatural tormentor" (*Paranormal Witness*, "When Hell Freezes Over," 2015).[22] "A stroke victim and her family seek a fresh start in a new country home, but instead end up fighting for their lives and sanity" (*Paranormal Witness*, "Sacred Ground," 2015). Men and women relocate following divorce (*Paranormal Witness*, "The Visitors"; *My Haunted House*, "Vow of Silence" and "The Closet," 2014). Most often, emotional needs and financial pressures overlap, as when families relocate as "a method to cut down family expenses" (*Paranormal Witness*, "The Coven," 2013). Some take foolish risks to save money—for instance, leasing a house where a violent murder took place because the rent is cheap (*My Haunted House*, "Cryptic," 2014). Others are taken by surprise, unaware of their home's bloody history, as when the couple in *My Haunted House*, "The Nursery" (2013), find out too late that a woman murdered her child in their new home.

Despite the occult subject matter, these shows are surprisingly direct about the effect economic realities have on a family: daily struggles that predate the housing crisis. *A Haunting*, "Nightmare in Bridgeport" (2012), begins in the speaker's childhood, during which he was raised by his mother and grandmother because his father was away much of the time, working two jobs. In *A Haunting*, "Back from the Grave" (2012), marital conflicts arise because husband Aaron works the night shift, leaving his pregnant wife home with their little boy. When she calls him at work because she is afraid that someone is in the house (she hears footsteps and heavy chains being dragged), he counters that it could be "something in the heating system." His practical, mechanical explanation clashes with her need to be listened to, their emotional disconnection exacerbated by his absence. She feels abandoned and he feels unfairly accused and caught in a bind.

Financial concerns raised early in many episodes become a reason to stay even as the hauntings intensify. Time and again, people explain simply that they could not afford to leave. When Lori Settle finally decides to flee her house, her desperation is expressed in financial terms: "I started over a hundred percent—with nothing." Another woman declares, "I didn't care if I lost the security deposit."[23] Both stories in "There's No Place Like Hell" involve single mothers renting freestanding, detached houses. Although they are not technically homeowners, renters often consider their dwellings home. The distinction between renters and so-called homeowners is for the most part imaginary. The majority of people who think of themselves as owners have in fact financed the purchase of their house and thus share ownership with the mortgage-holder until the loan is repaid—often decades later. By thinking of themselves as owners, they are engaged in a socially condoned (long-term) fiction. Like renters, they are allowed to stay in their homes on a month to month basis. This is what the 2008 housing crisis exposed. People had mortgages (and lost houses) before 2008, but the breadth of the crisis brought widespread awareness of just how tenuous the homeowners' claim to that status was. A third woman (a single mother like Lori and Marcia but one with a mortgage) walks away from a home in which she had invested everything, recognizing that it was never truly hers to begin with. "I let the bank take it back," she declares. "The bank can have it" (*The Haunted*, "The Possession of Cassie," 2010).[24] By 2011, financial advisers were publicly recommending exactly that.

An article posted on a site discussing bank rates announced in October of 2011 that financial advisers were publicly advocating "strategic default," i.e., borrowers "turning in the keys to their homes and refusing to make any more payments."[25] Although such a practice "has long been . . . viewed as highly irresponsible," the author notes, "in the wake of a collapsed housing market and sluggish economic recovery, a few noted finance authorities, including Suze Orman, have actually come out and recommended" it.[26] Although it results in "a nasty mark on your credit profile," "many strategic defaulters" (like those living in haunted houses) "would rather live [with] those consequences" than stay. Not only that, "Orman says . . . you shouldn't feel bad" about "purposely ruining your credit and reputation as a borrower." Consider your home as simply "an investment that is no longer worth it" and proceed to make the most logical business decision. Another expert also dismisses the tendency to "feel bad" when you find yourself unable to uphold your financial obligations. "Moral qualms," he points out, are a "barrier [that] was constructed by . . . the government, the financial industry, and social control agents like banks and media."[27] In this analysis, terms like "guilt" and "responsibility" are deployed by interested parties to confuse financial calculation with personal morality thus insuring high rates of repayment.[28]

The witnesses on first-person paranormal reality shows, however, do not express a sophisticated understanding of their place in a larger financial market. Instead, they testify to the emotional, psychological, and even physical toll experienced by those living within such a system. As relationships break down, these witnesses come to recognize and assert that they are at the mercy of large, unseen forces they can neither control nor understand. As one expert explains, what these shows lay out is the process by which people come to realize that they live in a "world which does not seem to admit the possibility of control, where life is subject to capricious external forces which strike indiscriminately, exposing people to radical changes of fortune and unanticipated disruptions to the everyday world."[29] Rather than mounting a political critique, the witnesses configure these forces in metaphysical language, using spectral metaphors to stand in for issues and effects they cannot articulate otherwise.

In her influential work *Ghostly Matters*, Avery Gordon describes how the use of spectrality—seeing and describing the world in paranormal terms—becomes a way to express aspects of modern life that are ignored (or purposely omitted) from other forms of discourse. "In haunting, organized forces and systematic structures that appear removed from us make their impact felt in everyday life in a way that confounds" the usual ways we explain the world to ourselves.[30] Caught between the abstract logic of economic systems and a punishing lived reality (a reality that is "partial, coded, symptomatic, contradictory and ambiguous"), people turn to an archaic and seemingly irrational system to explain what is happening to them.[31] According to Kevin Glynn, "occulted knowledges" (such as belief in the paranormal) "persist despite (or perhaps because of) their constant disavowal and marginalization by the truth-producing institutions of official culture."[32] People who belong to "alienated and relatively disempowered social formations" embrace these alternative knowledges because they provide them with "a way to escape bonds of/express resistance to scientific rationalism which seems . . . hostile and inadequate when it comes to explaining people's daily lives/lived experience."[33] For Glynn, it is tabloid media, with its taste for sensation and disdain for conventional standards, that creates "space for the circulation" of these alternative knowledges. As part of tabloid media, paranormal reality TV affords a valuable opportunity for both the witness and audience. People who do not expect to be listened to have the chance to tell their story in the terms they have chosen on "a cultural terrain on which their agency can be maximized"—and recognized.[34] The audience also has the opportunity "to recognize and listen to voices and knowledges that would likely be considered simply irrational or apolitical."[35]

Despite the risk of being labeled irrational, the witnesses on these programs insist on using terms they know can be used to discredit them. They do so because these terms are truer to their experience than those offered by science, social science, or economics. The election of, and adherence to, such alternate systems of knowledge can be seen as a kind of resistance, a political act.[36] In this light, "the ghost" can be seen as a figure "with a specifically ethical and political potential."[37] As Gordon asserts, the use of spectral metaphors cannot be dismissed as either "pre-modern superstition nor individual psychosis; it is a generalizable social phenomenon of great import."[38] (It should be noted that some theorists of the spectral are careful to distinguish between the usefulness of spectrality as a metaphor and "believing in actual ghosts.")[39]

While spectral metaphors would seem ideal as a means for expressing things amorphous and ineffable, we should be careful to recognize that the witnesses in these shows are not speaking in a theoretical vein. Nor should we simplify their experience by reducing it to financial or economic pressures. There is more than money at stake when one loses not only a home but faith in the concept of "home" itself as well as the belief that one understands the world we live in. What these witnesses are trying to describe is more than the details of an experience. "Being haunted draws us *affectively*, sometimes against our will and always a bit magically, into the structure of *feeling* of a reality we come to experience, not as cold knowledge, but as a transformative recognition."[40] In other words, the world suddenly *feels* different, one's place in it utterly changed in ways people know at a level deeper than they can consciously formulate. Their sense of conviction—the certainty that what they now know is true and was there all along but hidden—is best expressed by the attempt to merge the occult and the esoteric (the paranormal) with what is empirically verifiable (in the witnesses' terms, "real"). As witness Marcia Eden asserts, "Words can't describe everything that we experienced. But all of it was real—and it happened to us."[41]

Ordinary Americans

For a long time, American English lacked a term for the class position occupied by those on the cusp of the middle class but in danger of falling out of it. "Working class" failed to acknowledge material and educational achievements while "petit bourgeois" sounded pejorative and was never commonly used for self-identification. Since the Great Recession of 2008, "struggling middle class" has become the term du jour for those who see themselves as middle class but at risk or in danger of losing ground and of failing their children, who are allegedly doomed to do less well than their parents. Nearly every witness in the programs featuring firsthand accounts can be identified as a member of this class, dealing with a problem that is available only to those who already have an economic foothold but find it becoming increasingly precarious—a condition exemplified by the possibility of losing a house. How they deal with the ground shifting under their feet is laid out in episode after episode.

The speakers present themselves as "ordinary." Although they are presented in a manner consistent with professional television (good lighting, static camera position), their hair, clothes, and make-up (its excess or absence) set them apart from professional media personalities. The men do not wear suits and ties or even tailored jackets. Their hair is longer or more unusual in its style than that of reporters or news anchors, for example. The women are often older and heavier than the actresses cast in commercials or on scripted television, their skin less perfect, make-up too emphatic, hair less coifed. Telling their stories, they make grammatical mistakes and reveal accents common to underrepresented regions of the country. These elements establish class difference in terms of economic or educational status. This can be used to deflect identification for audiences seeking to distance themselves from figures they disdain as gullible, but it provides many viewers with a rare opportunity to see people "like themselves" being given a platform to tell their own stories.

The houses we see are equally unpretentious. Occasionally an imposing Victorian appears, complete with turret and wrap-around porch, or a quaint Queen Anne farmhouse with a dollop of gingerbread (*Paranormal Survivor*, "Haunted Objects," 2015), but most paranormal witness shows are set in 1960s-style ranch houses.[42] Architecturally undistinguished, suburban, and ubiquitous, these dwellings pose a greater danger *because* there is no backlog of classic horror references to warn the unwary house hunter. Even houses featured on multiple paranormal shows such as "Sallie's House," the subject of episodes on *A Haunting* (2006), *Paranormal Witness* (2013), and *Ghost Adventures* (2015), and often hyped as one of the "most haunted" houses in the country, have deceptively benign façades. As one investigator describes the site of a modern haunting: "The house was a normal, everyday American home until you realize the terror that's going on behind the walls."[43]

But while paranormal investigators might identify these houses as "nothing out of the ordinary," as being "just like any kind of cookie-cutter home that you might find in Anytown, USA," each story is situated in a precise geographical context. Every episode of *Paranormal Survivor* begins with white text being "typed" onto a black background: "1975, Taylor, Michigan" or "1979, Chester, CT."[44] Many of these towns are the kinds of places that rarely appear on television, such as Kingsville, Missouri; Wellington, Kansas; Carthage, Mississippi; Hastings, Nebraska; or Liberty, Arizona. (These five appear in one episode of *My Ghost Story: Caught on Camera* [2013].)[45] Their obscurity testifies to the everyday, all-American quality of the witnesses who live and work in the town, the neighborhood, or the target house itself. By naming the town and state, these shows literally ground insubstantial phenomena by locating the witnesses' accounts in actual physical locations that can be found on a map. The fact that the towns exist supports the veracity of the witnesses' testimony by implying that "you could go there and see for yourself." *A Haunting*, "Angels and Demons" (2012), begins with the narrator stating, "Arnold, Maryland, just outside of Annapolis" (we see a highway sign that reads "Arnold").[46] "Cathy and her son, Michael, are at a crossroads, preparing to start a new chapter in their lives." They are shown driving, mobile yet looking to put down roots. They are in Arnold, Maryland, and "at a crossroads," poised between the past and "a new chapter." The characters are placed (and displaced) temporally as well as geographically. Cathy and her son arrive in Arnold "in the fall of 2010." Pinpointing an exact date provides the illusion that these events could be documented. We could go to the local newspaper and "look it up." Of course, if we consulted local records—newspaper archives, libraries—we would not find official accounts. As Buse and Stott argue, these stories are about people and "practices [that are] otherwise silenced or neglected by the mainstream historical record."[47]

The only way we can actually "see" what happened is through the dramatizations where the events the witnesses describe are reenacted. The use of reenactments makes visible—in lurid and memorable form—what we are being told. This reinforces a witness's story for the audience, especially when other characters express doubt about something they did not see themselves. At the same time, reenactments make visible the artifice involved in their production. By dividing a character into a "real" person and an actor playing a part, a distance is established between the witnesses (seen speaking to the camera in direct address) and the actors who often do not resemble the people they play. In "Angels and Demons," for instance, Cathy Sheets has dark, carefully coiffed, chin-length hair, and sounds like actress Elizabeth Ashley, with a deep voice and a Southern drawl. She is dressed like a professional and wears carefully applied, attractive make-up. The actress who plays her in the reenactments has stringy blonde hair, pays little attention to her clothes (jeans and floppy shirts), and wears little or no make-up. The discrepancy is never addressed. Cathy's son, on the other hand, looks so much like the actor playing him that it is difficult to tell whether there *is* an actor or if he is both a witness and playing himself.[48]

Cutting back and forth between testimony and reenactments (or accompanying a staged scene with a witness's voice-over) stresses not only the fictional status of the staged scenes but the subjective nature of the witness's account. When the speaker tells us "this happened," we see a version of what is described, presumably the best approximation low-budget special effects can provide. (For instance, when Jeannie recounts being attacked in her bed in *Paranormal Witness: Pure Terror*, "Voodoo Preacher," the darkness is pierced by occasional flashes of light, allowing the briefest glimpse of someone in

Cathy Sheets, "Angels and Demons," *A Haunting*

red make-up with prosthetic horns and a stringy wig.) An attempt is made to counter the subjectivity of one character's version of events by supplying multiple witnesses to corroborate the main character's story. But each witness appears on camera alone, the separation from others emphasizing that each person has a partial perspective. Everyone knows only part of the story. Just as knowing the location and date does not tell us what happened, often the testimony of these supporting witnesses cannot actually verify what the main character experienced. As a consequence, the central witnesses on these programs often tread carefully, beginning by acknowledging the unbelievable nature of what they are about to say.

Initially aligning themselves with reason, many witnesses report that they were at first skeptical of the possibility of supernatural or paranormal phenomena, their knowledge of which comes primarily from the media. A young woman states, "I never believed in ghosts. I never watched ghost shows. I never was really interested in scary movies that had anything to do with that."[49] They present themselves as reluctant to attribute events to paranormal causes. Their first experiences consist of "small things, things that you could easily dismiss," such as a door slamming or an object not being where one left it.[50] A man who wants to become a property developer ignores the signs: "I didn't believe in ghosts so I just kinda, like, brushed it off."[51] The subjects themselves think they might be dreaming or hallucinating. "I thought it was all in my head," another woman states.[52] As rational explanations fail to account for their experiences, many witnesses report that they were afraid that people would think they were crazy, that no one would believe them.

It is clear that these are people who do not expect to be listened to. Many of them are women, struggling to describe a vague sense of unease that is difficult to define. (Ghosts aren't the only invisible figures that nevertheless exist in the shadows, unattended.) Lori Settle says that in her new house, "I felt like I was never alone. I was always being watched." Not surprisingly, the most disturbing locations are those associated with "women's work": the kitchen, the laundry (especially if it is in the basement), and the bedroom. Historically women have been dismissed as hysterical when they resist or are unable to adapt themselves to life in a confined domestic space. When Cathy Sheets is rushed to the hospital after becoming ill in her kitchen (her hands turn blue and her head becomes numb), she is diagnosed as having had a panic attack.[53] Medical science identifies her problem as psychological, her anxiety the product of self-generated excess. In other words, what she fears is in her head, not in the world around her. In *When Ghosts Attack!*, "There's No Place Like Hell," Marcia Eden states unequivocally, "None of this was in my head. It was completely real." Her defensiveness is understandable, given how such stories are often received. "I don't have to try to convince anybody," she insists, "'cause I know it was real."

Seeking Validation

The first part of each episode shows how the witnesses come to accept the paranormal, learning to privilege their own experience over socially condoned, "rational" explanations. The second half shows how they deal with it.

When the witnesses come to accept that they are being haunted, they blame themselves for not having realized it sooner. In their view, holding onto the socially acceptable (but inadequate) explanations of scientific rationalism caused them to fail to fulfill their proper social roles. Cathy Sheets says she feels like a bad mother because her teenage son did not feel he could tell her about the ghostly things he had seen in their new house. When he wakes her one night, afraid that there is something in his room, she tells him dismissively, "You're a man. Deal with it." When her daughter tells her there is a man in her room, Lori Settle tells her it was only a bad dream and she should go back to bed. "I don't know what I was thinking," Lori declares, looking back on it. "I should have never have left her alone in that room." A man explains how it makes him feel when his family is subject to paranormal harassment. "I'm the husband, I'm the protector, and here something's attacked your wife and your kid. It makes you feel like crap."[54]

Spouses fail each other. In *Paranormal Witness*, "The Harpy" (2013), the tensions between a husband and wife are expressed in their different responses to the paranormal—responses that expose the difficulty of maintaining traditional gender roles. When Tony and Deb move into an old house, Deb enthusiastically pursues contact with spirits while Tony begins to decline physically and psychologically. His greatest fear is of his own feelings of hostility toward Deb which he attributes to paranormal influence. "It wanted me to hurt my wife," he states. Tony's concept of masculinity requires stoicism and a brave front. "Being her husband and man of the house," he says, "I wasn't all the time admitting how scared I was." It is also Tony's job as a man to make sure that his family is safe. Although Deb wants to stay, eventually Tony puts his foot down, insisting they leave immediately. As soon as they drive away, he reports, "The heaviness, the bad thoughts, just instantly gone.... No matter how much *it* wanted me to hurt my wife, *I* wasn't gonna let it." Although it is implied that Deb's interest in the paranormal blinded her to Tony's physical and emotional deterioration, Tony still concludes, "How could a guy not be protective of his wife in that situation?" Left unaddressed (though evident throughout) is the fact that it was Tony himself who needed to be protected. He was in the greatest danger and, simultaneously, posed the greatest threat to his wife.

No longer doubting themselves, the witnesses turn their attention outward, looking for validation from those closest to them. This is when they begin to see that they are being failed by others. When Cathy, recently married, tells her husband what she has seen, he does not believe her. "Maybe this thing is in your head," he says during a fight. Another foundational assumption about how the world works shifts beneath her as she considers his lack of support. "Whatever was going on, you're there for your spouse," she insists. "For better or worse, richer or poorer, in sickness and in health. That was not happening and I felt it."[55] Husband Brian's emotional absence is underscored by the way his face remains hidden in shadow during his testimonial scenes. The narrator explains that "for professional reasons Brian only consented to be interviewed under the condition of anonymity." In this situation, because the husband's name has been clearly stated, "anonymity" is redefined as facelessness.

As the witnesses recount, when they finally begin to realize the danger they are in, they seek help from experts in the paranormal. Both Tony in "The Harpy" and Cathy Sheets consult psychics. When he asks for help from Peter, a psychic/paranormal investigator, Tony is given a man-to-man pep talk about asserting dominance. "You people are in control. . . . This is your house and you set the rules. . . . Comfortable with that?" Tony: "I have to be, right?" Peter: "Yes, you do." When Cathy consults a friend who is a practicing psychic-medium, she is also told that she needs to learn to control her fear. (In other words, it is her problem.) In these cases, women and men who fail to dominate find themselves being diagnosed rather than helped.

On those occasions when psychics or investigators confirm the presence of the paranormal, the witnesses feel supported. "You feel such a sense of relief to hear that from someone else—to say that there is something there. That you're not going crazy. That this is real" (Rachel Pinkerton, *My Ghost Story: Caught on Camera*).[56] When Cathy's husband does not believe her accounts of paranormal activity, she calls in a male investigator, "a former naval intelligence officer," whose use of technology impresses her—at first. "I don't know anything about technology," she says. "I don't know anything about paranormal. I don't know anything about any of this. *He does*." The investigator's technology validates Cathy's experience. "All these horrific things that confirmed, confirmed, confirmed, confirmed exactly what I had seen and heard." It also serves to convince husband Brian. Listening to the swirling voices captured on tape, he turns to Cathy and says, "I am so sorry that I didn't believe you." "Wow," Cathy says, remembering that moment. "Finally, he understands. It was a relief."

Despite the moments of reassurance, the witnesses find that experts cannot fix their problems. As the narrator points out, Cathy's high-tech paranormal investigator "offers no solutions. He's a scientist, not a soothsayer." A medium might confirm the presence of a spirit but cannot "cleanse" the house; the investigators might capture evidence of paranormal activity but have no answers about what to do next. A woman on *The Dead Files*, "Battlefield: Flint MI" (2013), describes how asking for help ended up making her feel worse. She has had "investigators come in. We've done cleansing. We done sea salt [sic] around the yard." She has even had "an exorcism [done] on me." Although every authority she has called on has let her down, she turns the blame on herself: "I feel like I'm a bad mother." Despite her conclusion, this woman's summary begins the shift each episode takes from the witnesses' tendency to blame themselves to an incipient critique of larger social structures as the people they turn to for help repeatedly let them down.[57]

As scientific reason fails (even the applied science of paranormal research), witnesses turn to what they see as the ultimate authority on matters spiritual and metaphysical—the Church. In *Paranormal Survivor*, "Don't Invite Them In" (2015), for example, Dustin calls a priest to have his house blessed—without telling the priest about his experiences with troubling, unexplained phenomena. The priest seems distracted during his visit, and when he leaves, Dustin listens to the tape he made of the ceremony. He hears unintelligible responses to every statement the priest made while blessing the house, as if "someone's talkin' back to him and doesn't want him here." As conditions worsen in *A Haunting*, "Angels and Demons," Cathy calls in a priest. The family has high hopes. Husband Brian says in voice-over, "When the priest arrived at our house, this was like our salvation. We couldn't get him in the house fast enough. We felt like this was what we needed. This was the answer. This would take care of all our problems." But the Church will fail them as well. The narrator intones, "In a matter of seconds Father John knows something is here. Something very dark." Cathy notices the priest shudder as he enters the haunted basement. "He was scared. His hands were shaking." The priest prays in a quivery voice then tells the family, unpersuasively, "You'll be safe now." Plagued that night by "a horrific dream," Cathy wakes to the sound of chanting and a dark figure "looking straight in the face of me. Boy, what a way to wake up." A disappointed customer, Cathy reports that "as soon as the sun came up, I got on the phone with that priest."

The attitudes expressed in these episodes echo positions taken by Spiritualists in the nineteenth century. According to Andrew McCann, Spiritualists mounted a campaign of resistance against "the would-be monopolists of all knowledge, in religion, science, and literature."[58] Actively resisting the "condescension" of men in authority, people who "felt browbeaten, unable to speak with authority of their own experience," used accounts of the paranormal as a way to mount "imaginative criticism" of social hierarchies of knowledge.[59] By "raising into prominence unlettered Americans, hysterical girls, charlatans" and other kinds of "shady characters" who were "expected to remain in the background of society," they effectively put "conventional forms of authority into question."[60]

How to End It

Perhaps the most surprising aspect of first-person paranormal programs is the number of episodes that refuse to end happily. Problems are not solved, the evil spirits do not vanish, and the main characters are terrorized, attacked, and driven out of their homes. In *When Ghosts Attack!*, "There's No Place Like Hell," the families in both segments incur significant financial losses as they abandon their homes. In *A Haunting*'s "Nightmare in Bridgeport," paranormal investigator Bob Baker tries to resolve otherworldly issues in his parents' house after his father's death. But even after asking for help from fellow investigators and having priests perform a spiritual cleansing, a dark, overwhelming force attacks and almost kills him. He, too, runs for his life.

Rather than depict these characters as defeated, paranormal TV celebrates their escape. Seen through a paranormal lens, what might be seen as a failure becomes a victory, a heroic tale of survival against unimaginable odds. After a period of relentless, escalating tension, the characters find a welcome sense of relief as when Tony and Deb drive away from their haunted house: "The heaviness, the bad thoughts, just instantly gone." When Cathy calls the priest back, he tells her, "Get out of the house. Immediately." "It felt great leaving the house," Brian assures us, but Cathy is not satisfied. As in any classic horror film, she insists on going back one last time.

If it is not possible to defeat the amorphous "dark forces" (a capitalist financial system, the housing crisis, spirits, and demons), in these shows it is possible to win symbolically. A few characters even manage to keep their homes. Having been let down by her spouse, friends, mediums, doctors, paranormal investigators, and the Church, Cathy is on her own. But before she can reestablish a sense of stability in the face of "the dark forces trying to destroy her," she must reassess who she is and how she relates to the world—and, as the narrator reiterates, "she must do it herself." Although she returns to the house accompanied by her husband and son, she defines herself as being alone. "I felt so alone and so scared but I couldn't give up," she states. In this statement, "alone-ness" describes a feeling rather than the absence of others. Because Cathy privileges her inner experience over external factors, she directs her attention to her own emotional state. "I had to keep myself calm," she says. "They want you mad. They want you upset. They want you crying. They want you to be fearful. You do the opposite. Have no fear. No fear." "You have to be strong," she concludes. Preparing to confront the Devil, Cathy reembraces her religious faith—but on her own terms. "I gotta pray," she says. "I gotta focus, and I gotta close this thing."

Across reality television, belief in the paranormal is frequently intertwined with traditional religious faith. In the episode "Refuge in Rosaries," the half-hour Canadian series *Ghostly Encounters* presents two stories where paranormal events are accommodated within traditional Roman Catholic doctrine.[61] Witness Alex Roman tells about his experience as a child when he and his brother were terrorized when heavy furniture began moving around in their bedroom. One night, convinced he was about to be smothered, Alex looked at an image of the Virgin Mary on his wall and silently prayed for help. The activity stopped. "It was almost as if there was some spiritual hand saying, 'Thus far and no further,'" he recalls. Because her parents were deeply religious, a bubbly young woman named Susan Flores tells us that she was well-prepared when "a devil from hell" crawled into her bedroom one night and jumped onto the ceiling. Although she struggles to describe this inhuman entity, she knew nevertheless exactly what to do.

> So I went to get the candle, rosary, holy water. Of course, I put rosary first on myself just in case [laughing] and I put holy water on me first, then I bless, and I said, "In the name of the Father, the Son and the Holy Spirit, I command you to leave right now. You are not welcome in this house."

Expelling a demon is not that easy, she explains. It took all the holy water she had to get it out. "And then it was gone. It was gone."

Though Christianity is by far the dominant theological system represented in the paranormal genre, prayers from any tradition are welcome.[62] The most common non-Christian tradition invoked involves Native American spiritual beliefs, with episodes from every kind of paranormal series featuring scenes where sage-smoke is used to chase away negative energy. Different religions, however, do not offer a better success rate when it comes to saving your house. An American family living in Taiwan, for example, calls in a Daoist priest to address the bad *feng shui* of their Vegas-style mansion (*A Haunting*, "Hungry Ghosts," 2006). He tells them the house was designed to kill them and performs a ritual cleansing. Because ultimately no amount of incense or chanting can counteract bad design, he urges them to move out as soon as possible. They do.

Throughout *A Haunting*'s "Angels and Demons," Cathy has accepted established Catholic ritual as long as it helped her. When her teenage son was afraid, Cathy told him to "say a 'Hail Mary' and you'll be fine." Later, when she has a demonically induced seizure in her car (starting when the crucifix is ripped off the rosary hanging from her rear-view mirror), she begs her son to say the Lord's Prayer, crying out, "Say it again, say it again, say it again." After her disappointing encounter with the priest, though, she spurns the need for institutional sanction and returns to the house despite his advice. Not submissive to the Church but demanding, it is Cathy's conviction that she has a direct connection with otherworldly figures (angels and saints) that fuels her perseverance and enables her success. Describing herself modestly as "just an ordinary girl," she laughs—"What am I? Joan of Arc? No. I'm just Cathy. I am not a priest. I'm not a nun. I don't know how to do an exorcism. I don't fight demons. I am just a regular girl that works."

Even though Cathy explicitly denies the comparison, her identification with the female warrior-saint is telling. Like Joan, Cathy's religious beliefs become more self-directed over time. According to her own testimony, Joan was sustained by a personal connection to the Divine—a position she held even though it put her at odds with the Church. It was the belief that she received messages directly from saints and archangels that enabled her to reject the constraints of gender, put on men's clothes (which the Church also objected to), and become a soldier—a role Cathy is about to fill. Comparisons with Joan are not entirely positive, however. While Cathy's faith gives her the courage to fight powerful demonic forces, by comparing herself to Joan she is citing someone who was herself abandoned by the Church and executed as a heretic. As Cathy returns for the final confrontation, the narrator announces, "The time has come for [Cathy] to become a heroine or a victim." Saint Joan, of course, was both.

There is no ambiguity when Cathy prays for help from St. Michael the Archangel.[63] Not only is he "the strongest angel in heaven," she explains. "He's a warrior." The martial terminology is reiterated when the narrator announces that "control of [Cathy's] home and her soul has come down to one final battle." As hell breaks loose in the master bedroom (crashing music, howling wind, moving furniture), Cathy holds up a crucifix and prays to St. Michael until white light blinds the image and a sense of peace is restored. The episode ends with an idyllic scene of a family once again safe in their home as husband, wife, and son play outside on the grass on a sunny day. Her psychic friend comments approvingly, "Cathy's learning how to be a fighter."

When specialists and experts fail to find a resolution, the ordinary American is left to deal with matters on her own. If tabloid media celebrates "victories of those who rise above victimization to strike back,"[64] paranormal television's depiction of the average person as more resourceful than experts validates the individual as it indicts established institutions. However, there is still a tension between reading the figure of the witness as a person and seeing them as characters constructed within a text. As Ouellette points out in reference to reality television in general, "While it may seem as if television is now bursting with ordinary people 'speaking for themselves,' they are following the roles, conventions and 'scripts' that popular reality formats require of them."[65] Inserted into "an industrial context that offer[s] little control to its subjects," the witnesses who offer first-person testimony in paranormal reality programs find their failure, terror, and loss packaged as entertainment. I would argue that what makes the result appealing rather than appalling is the *illusion* these shows give that ordinary Americans are speaking for themselves. Ouellette insists that even though their images and stories are "mediated and controlled at every stage," "when ordinary people express the constraints within which they operate," "small but powerful moments" seep through.[66] Calling for a "more complex understanding of how subjective experience can be communicated" through such highly mediated forms, we must, as Ouellette suggests, move beyond "claims to the real."[67]

What is not an illusion—what we might call real—is the way these shows give the disempowered members of the *audience* the chance to imagine what it would be like if you could commandeer time on television and make people listen: make them see what you see, take you seriously, and understand the full extent of what you have lived through. The women and men featured as witnesses on these programs stand as models of success against overwhelming forces no one could seriously be expected to overcome. Demanding recognition for the unfairness of their situation and the inadequacy of the institutions they were taught to depend on, these ordinary citizens can say, "I did nothing wrong. I believed in the American dream, I bought my own home and look what happened. I went through hell, but I struggled, I fought back, and I endured."

In the process of telling their story, they become heroic. Not victims, but survivors.

There is a third possibility. They could become celebrities.

Television Is the Answer

In the larger realm of reality TV as a whole, being on television is itself a form of validation. As Graeme Turner argues, if "the media occupies the social center of our culture," "it helps explain the attractiveness of making the transition from being an 'ordinary person' to being . . . someone who has been given access to the media center." "Fame operates as a validation of the self," "the process of celebrification" legitimizing the individual by providing a "sense of affirmation."[68] In the nineteenth century, Spiritualism had already shown how people could leverage a connection to the paranormal to improve their social and economic status. Historians describe how Spiritualism's "practices and processes gave" marginalized populations such as women and members of the working class "unprecedented access to cultural power and validation."[69] Performing a séance or appearing in a public lecture hall not only provided a source of income, it gave Spiritualists a platform from which to speak. When they channeled the voices of the dead, all eyes were on them. In the twenty-first century, paranormal reality television offers a similar opportunity, promising "ordinary people" a chance at celebrity based on their interactions with the paranormal. There is also the implied promise that fame means material success. Though, as Laurie Ouellette points out, "while the vast majority of people who appear on reality shows become neither rich nor famous, the specter of transforming ordinariness—and the spectacle of difference—into personal fame and fortune looms large."[70]

Studies of reality television focus on the distinction between "ordinary celebrities" ("non-actors . . . turned into media content") and "real" celebrities.[71] "Real" celebrities have "accumulated intertextual capital"—in other words, credits. Lists of accomplishments (in media, art, sports) detail the ways they have "earned" their status as public figures.[72] "Professionally networked," they have people and companies within the media industry (agents, managers, press agents, lawyers, "contacts," and so on) who are invested in promoting and maintaining their careers.[73] Yet, even with an established track record and support system, the "real" celebrity does not have a firmer hold on financial or social status than the "ordinary" Americans who tell their stories on paranormal reality shows. As it does with the dream of home ownership, paranormal reality exposes "celebrity" as a tenuous, unsustainable condition. If "reality television celebrity is allegedly open to us all," paranormal reality places the limits of celebrity in plain sight.[74]

Celebrity Ghost Stories (Biography) is structurally identical to other shows based on eyewitness testimony. Like *My Ghost Story: Caught on Camera*, every episode has three to five segments per hour, each of which illustrates what Glynn calls "television's close proximity to oral popular cultures."[75] A single person sits alone on an empty, well-lit set and begins to tell a story. Polished dramatizations are intercut with the guest's dramatic recitation.

The first move is to establish that the celebrity, already set apart, is as "ordinary" as the rest of us. The title sequence tells us "75 percent of Americans believe that there are events that take place that cannot be explained" and that "over half" of the 75 percent "believe they have experienced paranormal events themselves." Rather than being singled out, celebrities are situated within the overall population, as susceptible as anyone to being caught up in things they do not understand. While the program's title signals that the "average" Americans of other first-person anthology shows have been replaced by people who have a special claim to achievement, status, and (it is implied) financial success, like other first-person witnesses, the celebrity "guest stars" present themselves as, if not average, having been ordinary once. By telling stories of their childhoods (before they had money) or of their years of struggle before they achieved professional success, the celebrity guest invites identification from other "average" viewers.

Former child actress Linda Blair, for example, best known for the film *The Exorcist* (1973), recalls the time when she was little and exploring an abandoned house with friends.[76] When they run away, leaving her trapped in the house (the door won't open), she is terrified. Hearing footsteps, she turns to see a ghostly family covered in blood slowly moving toward her. They get closer and closer, reaching out to grab her, when suddenly the door opens and her sister pulls her to safety. Victoria Rowell (an actress on a long-running day-time drama) had a similar experience visiting her grandparents' house in the country. This time, the danger is outdoors as the little girl and her sister run from zombie-like figures marching toward them from a graveyard. Such childhood fears (being caught somewhere you are not supposed to be, being menaced by strangers) are common to everyone, making the celebrity seem less distant and more relatable. (All the stories in the Blair/Rowell episode of *Celebrity Ghost Stories* involve childhood experiences.) Seeing where now-famous people lived as children also has a leveling effect when those locations are economically undistinguished. These segments are also testaments to class mobility by showing that someone from an "ordinary" rural or working-class background went on to become famous.

The supposed glamour of show business is demystified in other stories when the performers tell about being unknown, working late nights, spending hours on the road in unfamiliar hotel rooms or short-term rentals. After the public has gone home, performers left alone in empty dressing rooms or recording studios suddenly realize that they are not alone (Nathan Morris of Boyz II Men, 2014). Staying in a fancy old hotel is less appealing when the lady who passes you in the hall is a jilted bride who committed suicide decades earlier (Michael Imperioli, 2010). Taking advantage of the chance to learn about new places can backfire, as when an actor Patrick Muldoon (*Melrose Place*), shooting a film in Charleston, South Carolina, is attacked in bed by the spirit of a Civil War soldier he "picked up" while exploring an historic cemetery (2010).

Not all encounters with spirits are negative. Actress/singer Lainie Kazan appreciates having one more chance to tell her late husband she loves him when she hears his spirit one night playing the piano in their living room (2012). Actress Dot Jones ("Emmy-nominated" and "known for her work on *Glee* and *Lizzie McGuire*") recalls her father's death when she was a child and how she came to know that he was always with her in spirit (2012). "It's pretty awesome," she beams. Some spirits are downright helpful. A ghost saved actor Joe Pantoliano (2010) from a bad relationship by scaring off his would-be fiancée. (The ghost knew she wasn't right for him.) Comedian Carlos Mencia's life is saved by his late brother who appears in the nick of time to save him from being killed in a drive-by shooting (2012).

Something more frightening than ghosts haunts *Celebrity Ghost Stories*. While celebrities demonstrate that it is possible to improve one's social and financial status by working in show business, they also show how precarious that move can be. When the title sequence proclaims that "the identity of some of these people ... may surprise you," the surprise is often that you have never heard of them. Ignorance of the performer's credits unleashes a cascade of scorn for those claiming to be famous.

Like any member of the struggling middle-class, the celebrity stands on unstable economic ground. Long-entrenched aspects of show business such as ageism, perpetual underemployment, and job insecurity are problems the general public have only recently come to recognize apply to them as well. Employment, financial security, and upward mobility are shown to be—like celebrity—achievable but not sustainable. As the struggling middle class is all too aware, downward mobility is as likely as its opposite. Given capitalism's unrelenting pressure to succeed, fleeting or temporary success becomes another name for failure. In the harsh world of capitalism (as manifested in popular culture), those who move up are blamed for not staying up. Critics and viewers often sneer at the "formerly famous" as "has-beens" or "wannabes." The audience's urge to distance themselves from these "so-called" celebrities is primarily defensive. It shields them from recognizing that social mobility is a slippery slope on which it is nearly impossible to gain a firm footing. If celebrities are people who had the ambition, skill, and luck to attain success, then what conclusions can we draw when even they cannot hold onto what they have achieved? The very category *"former* celebrity" undermines hope, ambition, and faith in the system by calling attention to the trap door built into social mobility, the treachery underlying American capitalist culture. It is taboo to say such things but they can be whispered, or glimpsed, in the shadowy corners of low-status genres like horror and paranormal reality television shows.

Staring down potential ridicule and repudiation, the guests on *Celebrity Ghost Stories* risk more than witnesses on other first-person shows. Compared to "unknown" Americans, the celebrity guests are unusually exposed. They speak as themselves with only a title card to verify (remind us) who they are. Each storyteller is the only witness, staking everything on personal credibility. Unlike the other first-person shows, no friends or family members appear to back up their accounts. Considering the circumstances, the celebrity guest exemplifies an admirable resilience and, in the process, tells us one more thing about the relationship between American society, popular culture, and the paranormal. On *Celebrity Ghost Stories*, encounters with the paranormal are analogous to success. Like an encounter with the paranormal, success may not last long but that does not mean it did not happen. Even if you only met a ghost once (or for a short time experienced fame or financial security), once is something. It did happen. And you will always have a good story to tell. As a skeptic notes, "Just because I don't believe in ghosts doesn't mean I don't want to hear a few ghost stories."[77] Transforming experience into entertainment, the guests on *Celebrity Ghost Stories* are in their element, offering viewers the simple pleasure of listening to someone tell a story. It is something professional entertainers do exceptionally well.

There are certain limitations to first-person paranormal programs. The frightening instability of the world depicted in these programs is underscored by the fact that the audience does not know from week to week who they will see or how the story will turn out. If, occasionally, a story ends well (Cathy Sheet in "Angels and Demons"), the sense of victory feels temporary at best.

Who knows what the next episode will bring? Series that have multiple stories per episode, like *Celebrity Ghost Stories*, reopen the chasm every time a new guest appears. Once again, a world we hoped might be safe turns out to be filled with the potential for terror.

While the unpredictability of first-person-based programs works well in the horror genre by keeping audiences in the dark, shows built around a cast of recurring characters have a strong appeal for producers and programmers. Giving audiences the chance to develop an ongoing relationship with characters they expect to see on a weekly basis can help build a regular fan base. Being able to lean on a genre-specific "star system" minimizes risk and works well with established marketing techniques. As is true of the reality genre as a whole, costs are reduced (at least initially) as producers develop their own celebrities instead of relying on established stars. At the same time, the introduction of a consistent format and regular cast makes the material less unsettling and the overall effect more reassuring. The construction of leading characters as experts with special skills—whether as ghost hunters or psychic mediums—threatens to undermine their identification as "ordinary" people. How paranormal reality navigates these issues will be the focus of the next chapters.

2

Ghost Hunters
Men on the Edge

Fundamentally conservative, shows built around ghost-hunting teams shift viewer identification away from witnesses and toward male-dominated teams that utilize reason, scientific methods, and specialized technology to verify or debunk accounts of paranormal activity. Compared with first-person programs, ghost-hunting shows offer a series of reliable, repeatable pleasures including recurring characters and an easily reproducible format that rarely varies from episode to episode. Predictability minimizes the risk for producers and cable channels by making the shows easier to market, especially when capitalizing on the popularity of the personalities around whom these series are built. Nevertheless, shows about paranormal investigations have at least three central areas of contestation they must navigate: ordinariness versus celebrity, masculinity under stress, and the association of technology with reason.

First, the investigators are not victims suffering from paranormal events. Outsiders called in to fix what is defined as someone else's problem, the investigator-as-(amateur)-expert stands at an emotional distance from the witnesses who have called for help. By depicting paranormal investigators as potential heroes, these shows attempt to mollify the antipathy toward "experts" demonstrated in first-person programs. At the same time, ghost-hunting shows go to great lengths to maintain the ghost hunters' status as "just folks," ordinary people who put themselves in extraordinary situations.

Ghost Adventures

This becomes more challenging when the "ordinary people" who anchor a hit series become television stars.

A second issue concerns the presentation of white, middle- and working-class masculinity. The men at the center of these series are consistently under threat: physically, psychologically, and, at times, spiritually. The suspense of each episode, the lead-in to each commercial break, rests on the depiction of men in peril. At the same time, each show presents the means by which these dangers can be met. The existence of a team, a figurative (sometimes literal) brotherhood, is shown to sustain men, enabling them to face down any menace.

The teams are supported in their efforts by technology which has been specially designed or adapted to document the existence of the paranormal. Running the gamut from cutting-edge scientific equipment to repurposed, consumer-grade gadgets found around the house (cell phones, flashlights), technology serves several purposes in ghost-hunting series and has multiple, at times contradictory, meanings. In place of the inchoate sensations people report as signs of a paranormal presence, here night-vision cameras, electromagnetic field detectors, and electronic voice recorders are presented as objective ways to document "what's really there." Television itself becomes a way for ghost hunters to document their experiences as the teams set up cameras that can be monitored off-site for multiple hours of surveillance. They carry their own cameras/recorders so that we can see the investigation through each team member's (technically enabled, mediated) point of view.

The reliance on technology becomes a way of relating to the world. Because the "evidence" produced by these devices is presumed to be subject to proof through scientific experiment, technology becomes synonymous with reason which is, in turn, linked to masculinity. The "hard evidence"

Ghost Hunters

technology provides is equated with the "hard" bodies on display as various team members adopt highly self-conscious militarist or macho styles of posture, speech and dress. But, like masculinity (vulnerable and unstable), technology routinely fails. Recuperating these failures becomes a key project of every series about paranormal investigators as encounters with the paranormal reveal fissures within reason, technology, and masculinity.

Average Guys in the *New York Times*

On Halloween in 2002, an article appeared in the *New York Times* about a loosely organized group of about twenty-five people who pursued paranormal investigations as a hobby.[1] Calling themselves the Atlantic Paranormal Society (TAPS), the members carried out investigations of paranormal phenomena that could be found within driving distance of their home base in Rhode Island. Despite its dismissive tone, the article garnered immediate interest in the world of reality television. Two veteran producers—Tom Thayer (the former president of Universal Television) and Craig Piligian (*Survivor*, 2000–2002)—sent the article to Mark A. Stern, an executive at what was then the SciFi Channel.[2] Stern sent the article on to "the team in New York," where the series was officially greenlit and Piligian's Pilgrim Studios began production on a series that would run for twelve years.

Ignoring the article's patronizing tone, the producers detected strong indications of potential audience appeal. Where the *Times* saw a bunch of amateurs getting together every Saturday at Starbucks, TV executives saw a team that had formed organically. The group's provincial identity (their territory was described as ranging from Maine to New Jersey) indicated a valuable connection to small-town America. Their established presence online, getting "about 6000 hits a day from around the world," demonstrated their ability to attract and sustain an audience interested in paranormal subjects. The most important quality, though, was authenticity. "There were two things that really rang true to me," Stern recounts. "One was how authentic these guys were." They were doing the "things they'd do whether there were cameras on them or not."

Authenticity matters across reality television but it has a special meaning in relation to the paranormal. If the people featured on these programs can be trusted to be who they say they are, then the audience is more likely to trust their claims about the supernatural. The producers did. "I believed in them," Stern reports. "I really did believe that these guys were sincerely exploring this. I wasn't being manipulated. They weren't manufacturing." Nor did it seem that they were in it for the money or the fame. An executive at Pilgrim Studios insisted that the team had higher goals: "This isn't just a TV show for them to be on. It's a life-calling to help people resolve either anxiety or fear, [to] try to help explain something odd that's going on in these folks lives."[3] "They go in to help," another executive said. "That's the core, that's the essence of it. That's their mission statement."[4] The sense of responsibility the members of the team felt to their clients had been mentioned in the original *Times* article in which it was noted that even when the team did not find proof of the paranormal, they were careful to respect their clients' feelings. According to Jason Hawes, who was to become one of the leads on *Ghost Hunters*, "the group had a duty to bring comfort" to those who sought their help. "You're investigating, but you're also like a psychologist," Hawes said. To assuage any suspicion of base financial motives, the *Times* also pointed out that the team "works strictly pro bono." As Hawes asserted, "the rich and poor both need help."

Another aspect that appealed to Stern was what he called the team's "rigor." "The surprising, counterintuitive part of that show that none of us could have predicted was that 95 percent of the time they didn't find anything." "They were skeptics" who were eager to explain things away. For the producers, scenes where the team matter-of-factly exposed the mundane cause behind a sudden noise or trick of the light made it all the more powerful when the team came across phenomena they could not explain. For Pilgrim Studios founder Craig Piligian, this was key to the show's appeal. If the team "said there was something going on, that was rare, so it meant something was going on." More important, the team earned the audience's trust "because we never lied to them. That was our big deal." When the *Times* article acknowledges an occasion where signs of the paranormal were fabricated, it was "a client [who] faked evidence." (The author notes with amusement Hawes's "robustly disapproving language" when he recalls finding that someone had hidden speakers in the walls.) On this point, the production company, the SciFi Channel, and the TAPS team were adamant: "Don't fake anything. Don't muck it up. Don't pretend."[5] "It became a template," Stern recounts. When people came to SciFi after the success of *Ghost Hunters* with proposals for similar paranormal reality programs, Stern told them, "You don't have to find a ghost every time. We won't cancel you if you don't find a ghost. We *will* cancel your show if you pretend to find something."

Perhaps the most surprising choice the producers made was to emphasize something that the *Times*' article had mined for humor. Firmly putting the idea of paranormal phenomena in its place, author John Leland notes that 75 percent of the alleged hauntings the ghost-hunting club has investigated have "turn[ed] out to be nothing more than noisy pipes, creaking boards or overactive imaginations." As a consequence, he concludes, team member Jason Hawes's "plumbing expertise comes in handy." The article's title—"Don't Say Ghostbuster, Say Spirit Plumber"—directly cites the 1984 comedy that parodies groups like TAPS. Juxtaposing the metaphysical with the prosaic for comic effect, the term "spirit plumber" implies that spiritual pursuits (literally pursuing spirits) are laughably incongruous with down-to-earth practical trades such as plumbing. The producers of *Ghost Hunters*, on the other hand, rely heavily on the figure of the plumber as a way to bolster the team's credibility, integrity, scientific rigor, and authenticity.

By trimming the Atlantic Paranormal Society from its original twenty-five members to just six, and presenting Jason Hawes and Grant Wilson as the team's *de facto* leaders, the producers made plumbers central to the series' brand identity. Although Wilson is never mentioned in the 2002 *Times* article, he and Hawes share equal standing in the television series, literally shown standing beside a Roto Rooter truck in the title sequence, wearing company uniforms. Some scenes of Hawes and Wilson at their day job are simply the prelude to an investigation. In *Ghost Hunters*, "Inhuman Entity" (2009) and "A Ghost of a Marine" (2012), for example, Jason and Grant are fixing a sink or a toilet when they receive news of a possible haunting; in "Eastern State

Penitentiary" (2004), they muse on a recent investigation while replacing a faucet. In other episodes, the investigation depends on their specialized skills. In "Angel of Death," for example, a gas fireplace is reported to turn itself on and off. "Let's take a look at the fireplace," Hawes cautions, "'cause, as a plumber, I've worked on these things before."[6] Examining it, he determines there "could be a faulty switch." More to the point, he declares, "I don't think there's anything paranormal with this." Steve, his teammate on this investigation, eagerly concurs: "I think we disproved that claim." "A hundred percent," Jason reiterates. In this scene, practical knowledge functions as a sign of the characters' level-headed pragmatism, demonstrated by their eagerness to seek concrete, scientifically verifiable explanations. Displaying a healthy dose of skepticism, they are eager to accept non-paranormal causes for unexplained phenomena.

Secondly, identifying the men as plumbers solidifies their authenticity as ordinary members of the working class. The dual identity indicated by the condescending term "spirit plumber" tracks with an assumption about working-class attitudes identified by Michele Hanks in her sociological study of British ghost-hunting groups. Many members of these groups are "either underemployed or partially employed. . . . [and] struggled to find long-term, meaningful employment." Having "day jobs," as do the members of TAPS, they consider their paranormal work a hobby rather than a potential source of income. Nevertheless, "their identities as paranormal researchers figure prominently in their senses of self."[7] "Engagement with paranormal research" provides people who find little fulfilment in work with a source of satisfaction, a way "to craft meaningful identities grounded in emergent expertise."[8]

As "ghost hunters," Hawes and Wilson mirror the lives of other working-class and middle-class men, "average Joes" who are defined primarily by interests that are separate from their professional status or income. However, rather than being representatives of "alienated labor" whose work life is a form of "drudgery" that can only be offset by the satisfaction of side interests (living for the weekend), these ghost hunters celebrate both their professional lives *and* their free-time pursuits.[9] Although the show documents the men's weekend exploits, their skill in the paranormal realm rests on their expertise in the overlooked parts of this world, things normally hidden in the walls or buried underground and routinely ignored until it acts up. By integrating their working-life as plumbers with their spirit-pursuing, weekend interests, Jason and Grant reconcile what are assumed to be socially contradictory positions. In this way, they perform the function of celebrities or stars as defined by Richard Dyer.[10]

A third issue arises at this point that is common across reality television: how to maintain one's authenticity as an "ordinary" person once one has become the star of a hit television series. In *Understanding Celebrity*, Graeme Turner lays out the "highly contradictory and ambivalent" ways the media presents reality television stars. Either they are thought to be "extraordinary or they are 'just like us,'" Turner writes. "They deserve their success or they 'just got lucky.'"[11] Respected when they are thought to be "genuine down-to-earth people," reality stars thought to be inauthentic are dismissed as "complete phonies," and subject to withering "derision and contempt."[12] In 2009, when *Ghost Hunters* had become "Syfy's most popular show," the *Times* published another piece attacking the cast on exactly this point.[13] "They've pulled a fast one," author Mike Hale announced. "The plumbers of *Ghost Hunters*" merely "play the part of working-class heroes." Lacking authenticity in these realms (playing a part), the identity of "ghost hunter" has nothing to support it. No longer "real" plumbers or genuinely members of the working class, "they've created a new career—the paranormal investigator—that requires neither good looks nor any discernible skill beyond the ability to walk through an old building waving a flashlight."[14]

Denouncing every form of work/identity claimed for Hawes and Wilson in *Ghosts Hunters*, Hale also discounts television work as itself a form of labor. In her work on celebrity, Milly Williamson has a more nuanced assessment of how all three identities—worker, hobbyist, television celebrity—prop each other up. Even when their "personas as 'ordinary' . . . hide the fact that they are highly paid" television personalities, reality TV stars can be seen not as simply fraudulent but as models of a different kind of success.[15] "The type of self lauded in this context is one in which both the self-as-entrepreneur and the self-as-branded-commodity takes center stage."[16] In other words, by working with producers to create a series that parlays their actual experience in one field and interest in another into material suitable for weekly television, these working-class heroes have found a way to assume agency by capitalizing on, and selling a version of themselves. Unlike the witnesses beset by the paranormal, ghost hunters are not victims of social or economic forces beyond their control. Navigating three identities/three kinds of work—and making it pay—they have learned to play the game.

While regularly appearing cast members become celebrities and are clearly paid for their participation, remuneration for those appearing in a single episode takes a less obvious or direct form which again raises the issue of exploitation.[17] The witnesses or victims featured in first-person shows are sidelined in series focused on ghost-hunting teams, their accounts made fodder for the teams' investigative exploits. The most obvious benefit for the "ordinary" people who appear in any specific episode accrues to the owners of the restaurants, hotels, and small businesses the ghost hunters explore. Publicity is gold. The owner of the Myrtle Plantation (featured on multiple paranormal reality series) reports that "rather than hurting the business, as I feared, stories of the hauntings brought people by the droves.... Ghosts turned out to be the greatest possible attraction."[18]

This Week's Case

For its producers, *Ghost Hunters* is the model of how a series based on paranormal investigations should work.[19] "You can legitimately say it started that whole trend," Stern states. "It was such a breakout hit, everyone started to copy it." Except for the notable absence of plumbers, every investigation-based series that followed *Ghost Hunters* is strikingly similar in terms of format, style, and cast, so I shall discuss them as a group.

Where anthology-style first-person programs were unpredictable, with some episodes being more successful than others, *Ghost Hunters* established a format that would provide guaranteed pleasures week after week, in this series and all those that followed. According to the producers of *Ghost Hunters*, each episode followed a "natural progression": "First was the information, then there was the investigation, then there was the reveal."[20] The basic structure is procedural: the team learns about a problem someone is having with what they suspect is paranormal phenomena; the scope of the problem is laid out and the stakes set as the investigators interview their clients, investigate, and gather evidence. A mainstay of police dramas and mysteries, procedural narratives attempt to tame or control the chaos of disorder by foregrounding the existence of a method or routine that in itself institutes a sense of order and sometimes solves a finite problem by explaining a mystery.[21]

When we first meet them, ghost hunters are doing ordinary things like driving and talking. Their cars are middle-class-average, mostly vans and SUVs. *Ghost Hunters* begins with Jason Hawes riding shotgun, explaining the background of the case to his partner who drives and asks questions. Other

Ghost Asylum

Ghost Hunters

team members follow in a small caravan of black SUVs, communicating through walkie-talkies. *Ghost Adventures* can fit its three-man team into a single car, while the duo in *Ghost Stalkers* heads out in a small camper they call "the RV" (which also doubles as their headquarters during the course of the investigation).

The scenes of driving make clear that in these shows the paranormal is "out there," situated as something you go *to* as opposed to a thing that makes an unwanted appearance in your home or personal space. This literal distancing is a key difference between investigator programs and other kinds of paranormal shows. Here there is no deep personal connection between the investigators and the places they visit or the spirits they encounter. The investigators are not haunted or compelled like the first-person witnesses, or grief-stricken like those who consult mediums. They pursue the paranormal of their own free will and on their own terms.

Because they are not personally connected to the hauntings they investigate, the teams must supply a reason for why they pursue the paranormal. As in *Ghost Hunters*, some depict themselves as providing a service. *Paranormal State* and *Haunted Collector* open each episode with the team's leader explaining that they have been called in to help the owners of properties that are reputedly haunted.[22] Others describe themselves as "seekers" (*Paranormal State*), Parsifals searching for a greater truth as they roam the country on what *Ghost Adventures* calls "our ghost adventures quest."[23] Despite the high ideals (and redundancy) of an "adventure quest," in many programs the stated motives are ultimately beside the point. At times, the investigators seem to be engaged in what Hanks calls "ghost tourism," looking for a way to do something fun in one's leisure time.[24] On *Haunted Highway*, for example, the two-person teams stay outdoors overnight at a location that is rumored to be haunted in order to gather evidence to prove the matter to their own satisfaction (and to provide material for a television show). In this formulation, ghost hunting is like any other hobby: a chance to get away from work/family/domestic space, stay up late, and hang out with friends. While the ostensible goal of every investigative show is to prove that the paranormal is real, the major source of drama comes when the clients are left behind and the team confronts the dark alone. Ultimately, what matters in a ghost-hunting show is the contest: men subjecting themselves to a trial and seeking out a challenge, eager for the chance to prove themselves. The ghost hunter must be a master of technology, bond with members of a team, and demonstrate courage in the face of a threat that exceeds the bounds of reason. The world paranormal investigators confront can be filled with dread but, as one character tells us, that's part of the thrill. Turning to the camera while approaching a location at night, Zak Bagans of *Ghost Adventures* declares, "It's cold. It's dark. And it's exciting as hell."[25]

Stylistically, ghost-hunting series are a mix of documentary and horror. As the team members arrive at their destination, titles identify the time and place. In the *Ghost Hunters* "Angel of Death" episode (2016), a title card reading "TAPS Case: The Inn at Aberdeen, Valparaiso, Indiana" introduces a documentary-like formality that is reinforced by a portentous male voice-over. After obligatory social rituals (meeting the clients, shaking hands, introducing themselves), Jason and Steve Gonsalves begin to interview the locals, listening to eyewitness accounts of ghost sightings and other paranormal phenomena. "Paula Siecker: Housekeeper," for example, is afraid to pick up laundry from the basement. Once, she delivered all the neatly folded linens to the rooms only to return to the basement to find a sheet splayed over a chair.

The disquieting effects of the clients' stories are made vivid through dramatic reenactments that make the paranormal's unsettling intrusion into daily life something we can see and hear for ourselves. When the inn's owner tells about the ghost of a little girl, we see a transparent image of a young girl flicker then disappear at the top of the inn's central staircase. As the witnesses identify specific spaces as being ominous, the camera moves unsteadily through the inn, making every perspective unstable. Wide-angle lenses make rooms appear distorted and unnatural. The soundtrack also endows the space with a sense of uncanny presence. As we pass through one room, we are told this is where "a door opens and closes on its own." In another, Jason

Paranormal State

tells us in an authoritative voice-over that "visitors report hearing someone screaming and seeing a large shadow figure lurking about." Listening for a far-off echo of terror makes the silence pregnant with menace. Other shows, like *Ghost Adventures*, use music to keep the audience on edge while we gaze at empty rooms or hallways where nothing is happening. Because these spaces are empty, the apparitions fleeting, the screams unheard, and, according to witnesses, the occurrences of paranormal phenomena fundamentally unpredictable, narrative, image, and soundtrack become focused on *potential*, what might have happened and what might happen again on this very spot. Ordinary spaces are imbued with possibility. What follows is a sustained state of suspense.

Where witnesses are confused, frightened, and hesitant about "the scene of the haunting," the ghost hunters are eager to rush in. In the preliminary stages of the investigation, they actively pursue information, poring over newspapers, maps, deeds, and land records at the local library or interviewing local historians about scandals, epidemics, natural disasters, or sudden deaths associated with the subject location. Despite its status as part of the historical record, this kind of evidence proves to be no more than a suggestive morsel, an illusion of confirmation. Intriguing correlations, however, can be very enticing, beguiling the audience with possibility. What if the ghost of the girl *is* little Belinda Hancock who fell down the stairs in 1901? Posing the question invites the audience to explore the parallels and, in the process, participate in creating a story.

The appeal of imagining a connection increases dramatically when we are supplied not only with names and dates but faces. Antique photographs from newspapers or snapshots from family albums contribute precisely this jolt of "the real," the sudden realization that we are looking at an actual person who lived. As Barthes writes, "Photography's inimitable feature . . . is that someone has seen the referent (even if it is a matter of objects) *in flesh and blood*, or again *in person*."[26] What had been a mere construction of words, a story told, is suddenly made vivid (in its root sense), surprising, and teeming with unpredictable detail. Historic photographs provide the raw material out of which the "apparitions" we see are built, resulting in a complex visual text that is part made-for-TV fictional construct and part genuine historical document.

As newer programs try to differentiate themselves from the earlier ones, the use of photographic evidence becomes more lurid. In episodes of *Ghost Asylum*, original documentary footage of mental hospital patients is presented to encourage us to imagine that their spirits still occupy the abandoned buildings described on the soundtrack as "home to the deranged, mutilated, and diseased."[27] Although neither investigators nor witnesses know the people in the photographic images (or their spirits) personally, on those occasions when historical figures are featured we see images of people we *do* know—in a manner of speaking. For instance, when *Ghost Adventures* visits a house that they claim to be the site where the so-called Black Dahlia was tortured and murdered in the 1940s, studio photographs of the living Elizabeth Short alternate with crime scene images from the tabloid press showing her corpse. Although a visual "blur" obscures the gruesome center of the black-and-white photo showing where the woman's body has been cut in half, nothing is done to block the view of her hideously damaged face. Often, paradoxically, the attempt to corral the "realism" effect of photography accompanies a shift toward sensationalism.

Historical documents, photographs, coincidence, and the correlation of names and dates are strongly suggestive and make up a major part of the first half of a televised paranormal investigation. Despite the attention given to this kind of material, however, the shows themselves do not consider it any more definitive than firsthand accounts. For ghost hunters, the ultimate proof of the paranormal can only be achieved in person, using technology.

Boys and Their Toys

If ghost-hunting teams present themselves as amateurs in relation to the paranormal, they take equal pains to distinguish themselves from professional filmmakers. In the first years of *Ghost Adventures*, the title sequence featured Zak Bagans bragging that there are "no big film crews following us around." By disavowing expertise in television production, the teams maintain their status as ordinary citizens while offsetting suspicion that they are capable of technical trickery or faking evidence of the paranormal. Consumer-grade cameras are frequently featured, reinforcing the do-it-yourself ethos familiar from fictional horror films like *The Blair Witch Project* (1999), *Cloverfield* (2008), and the *Paranormal Activity* films (2007, 2010, 2011, 2012).[28]

As they set up their equipment, the teams lay out their methodology, especially as it pertains to the use of electronic media. Like a game with rules, there are strict parameters to the investigation. First, there is a time limit. The investigators announce that they will stay at the location overnight (*Ghost Hunters*, *Ghost Adventures*). Some stay longer. On *Ghost Asylum*, the first night is an initial exploration of the space which allows the team to plan more pointed encounters with entities the second night. The duo on *Ghost Stalkers* alternate over two nights, with one person being "inside" each night while the other monitors the situation from a digital command post. *Paranormal Lockdown*'s two-person team adds the physical challenge of staying on-site for seventy-two hours straight.

In addition to temporal limits, there are physical boundaries. "Lockdown" refers to a period of time within a confined space. It is a term permeated with concerns about security. On the one hand, a "lockdown" is a technique for keeping civilians in a safe place in order to protect them during mass shootings. It can also mean the opposite, containing outbreaks of violence (i.e., riots) by keeping prison inmates in their cells. In both cases people are confined in a specific location for an indefinite period, held in a state of suspense, not knowing whether the walls can hold at bay a threat of unknown and unpredictable proportions. In a paranormal "lockdown," rather than secluding themselves from the danger, the investigators voluntarily put themselves in peril in an enclosed space like fighters in a cage-match or gladiators entering the arena. The announcement that the time has come for "lockdown" serves as a boast as the investigators display their willingness to endure a prolonged state of suspense, late at night, in a location suffused with risk. Although the time limit means that there will be an end to the contest, we and the investigators know that, no matter what happens, they must stay and see it through.

As part of their observational-documentary approach, paranormal investigative programs make a particular point of foregrounding the conditions of filming. On *Ghost Adventures*, the team is its own crew with each of the three members carrying a camera. They take turns filming each other as subtitles identify the image's source (e.g., "Zak cam" or "Nick cam"). There are also two technical assistants ("audio tech" Jay and "audio/video tech" Billy) who monitor the equipment and communicate with the team members via walkie-talkie. Though they are occasionally incorporated into events, the technical crew is usually shown staying off-site during the investigation itself. This sense of taking the audience "behind the scenes" serves the dual purpose of demythologizing the show's production (*a lá* cinema verité) and validating the trustworthiness of the participants—a move comparable to a magician showing you that there is nothing up his sleeve.

Setting up the technology for the night's investigation involves aspects of science and ritual. In *Ghost Hunters*, "Angel of Death," we see a montage of team members setting up tripods, aiming cameras, and unwinding cable. One person explains the reasons for a particular camera placement while the scene cuts to a shot drained of color. Subtitles appear at the top of the screen ("DVR Camera: 1st Floor Hallway") and at the bottom ("Claims: Shadow figure, apparition, screaming"). The next shot is taken from behind that camera, showing it in harsh, bright light as it points down a hallway toward a closed door. Meanwhile, "Dave Tango: Tech Manager" stands in front of a monitor featuring a split-screen divided into multiple parts. He explains that the visual feeds come from six cameras stationed around the property. One of them is "thermal," he points out, indicating a highly colored, cartoon-like image that represents any unexplained changes in temperature.

As the technical set-up is completed, the crew receives an order through a walkie-talkie to "lock it down." The lights go out and the image changes to "night vision" with color and lighting effects to suggest that we will now see in a new way as technology transforms the conventional photography of the earlier scenes. Once the technology is in place, the investigation can begin. On *Ghost Hunters*, this moment is marked by having the screen split horizontally into three images with team members moving toward the main building in the center in blue-tinged black-and-white. This section of the image expands as we move with them into the investigation proper.

Paranormal reality TV's investigators flaunt their use of technology—evidence of their "scientific" process—by making the technology (often some kind of digital media) extra-visible. Something is added to the image, an excess to mark technology's presence: the green hue of "night vision"; the

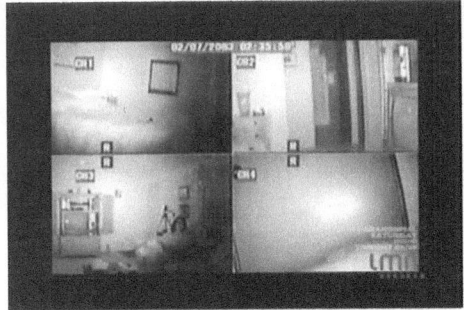
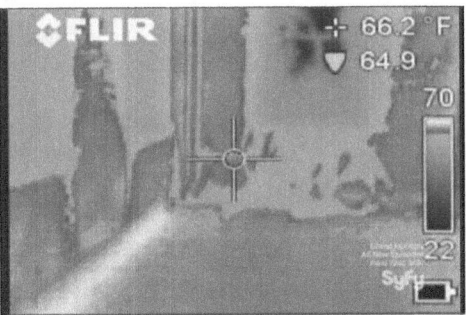

Paranormal surveillance split-screen, *My Ghost Story: Caught on Camera*

Paranormal heat-sensing imagery, *Ghost Hunters*

use of split-screen or shots on surveillance monitors; the addition of graphics (arrows, timestamps) that call attention to specific areas of an image; the visual tracks of soundwaves depicting volume or a sudden noise; the sound of static or filters during the playback; the use of subtitles to tell us we are hearing "enhanced audio," "unexplained noises," "footsteps," "a man's voice," or to spell out what a spirit has said (something that is seldom as clear to the audience as it is to the investigators).

The vast number of technological devices employed unleashes a barrage of specialized terminology. On *Ghost Adventures* alone, we are introduced to digital recorders for capturing "EVPs" (electronic voice phenomena—"class-A EVPs" if you're lucky), cameras that provide "HD night vision," "full spectrum still photography," a "regular vision X camera," as well as a "thermal imaging camera" that provides mapping of body heat and cold spots.[29] A "K-2 meter" or "electromagnetic detector" measures "geo-magnetic anomalies," spikes in EMFs (electromagnetic frequencies) or sudden unexplained variations in the EMS (electromagnetic spectrum). A "frequency analyzer" provides voice-prints that visually display sounds captured by the Ovilus, the SB7 Spirit Box, or the new-and-improved SB11 that (we are told) combines two SB7's plus a temperature sensor. Not to mention the "REM pod," a 3D Connect Motion tracking system, and an "ultraviolet camera" that captures "a whole new spectrum of light seen for the first time."[30] New technologies require elaborate descriptions, for example when a split-screen image presenting an overexposed black-and-white image on the left and a graph showing various "real-time" measurements on the right is explained to be the product of a "structured light sensor camera with skeleton image tracking which maps

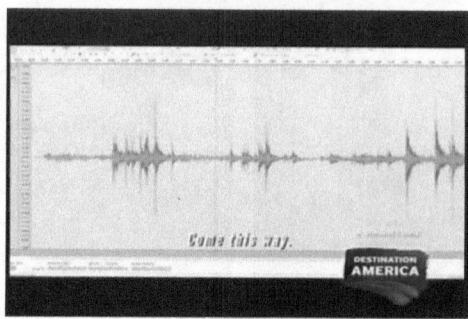

Paranormal sound technology, *Ghost Asylum*

objects by using an infrared laser grid system along with motion connect technology."[31] On an episode of *Ghost Stalkers*, we are introduced to a man known for his "scientific methods and state of the art technology" who has created a "worm-hole detector" that reveals when a "portal" or "vortex" is opening from "the other side."[32] (When that happens, wavy green lines meet on a computer monitor.)

It is important for every series that focuses on paranormal investigation to be seen as being on the cutting edge. According to Pilgrim Studios vice president Gretchen Stockdale, the *Ghost Hunters* team was "encouraged to let us know if there's new technology" so that they could be seen using "the very best stuff." The team would call the production company "and say we gotta get some new piece of equipment." *Ghost Hunters* executive producer Mike Nichols recalls that Grant Wilson, in particular, "was really very into the science end of it—electromagnetic fields and a lot of those theories." Although paranormal investigators revel in technology, their access to specialized or expensive equipment threatens to undermine their status as "regular guys." Consequently, on *Ghost Asylum* the Tennessee team play down their technical expertise as they promise to "combine modern scientific method with some serious backwoods Southern know-how." When they use special devices, the mastery conveyed by streams of technological specifications is offset with a heavy dose of "good-old-boy" unpretentiousness.

"Dude! Two hundred and forty-six milligaus!"
"246?!"
"Two-forty-six. Then it drops straight back down to zero. Holy crap, dude!"

Helpful subtitles explain that the "Gauss Meter" is an "Analog Meter with an audio tone that measures Extremely Low Frequency Radiation," but the actual function of the device is not as important as the juxtaposition of verbal sophistication with slang.[33] For example, Chasey Ray (identified as the "engineer") reports at one point that they have "started gettin' proximity hits with our mel-meter and stuff." (A semi-comic character, Chasey Ray stands apart from the others due to having the heaviest Southern accent, a trait highlighted in the show's second season when his dialogue is occasionally subtitled.)[34]

Displays of technology are not restricted to the devices featured within the narrative. Sophisticated techniques demonstrate the technical possibilities of television itself. Images seen earlier in an episode are brought back repeatedly so they can be explored through slow motion, freeze frames, split-screens, and by zooming in on details. The frozen or slowed image is often altered— e.g., by diagraming over it (circling the area the audience should focus on) or using soft focus to frame a significant area as a "vignette." As with cinema verité, poor image or sound quality is presented as proof that the images were not staged by professionals. Amateurishness confirms spontaneity, for instance when someone drops the camera when frightened or produces a shaky image by running with a handheld camera.

The "surveillance" aesthetic of the static-camera footage shown on monitors attests to the technology's objectivity. At times the multiple images displayed on a surveillance monitor show us nothing happening. *Ghost Adventures* frequently fast-forwards these images while Zak points out in voice-over that nothing happened for several hours. In the episode "Haunted Savannah," Zak tells us that despite investigators asking the spirits "countless questions," "no audio evidence through EVPs is captured here."[35] When investigators on *Ghost Hunters* have what Jason Hawes calls "a quiet night," it establishes their perseverance and integrity.[36] They are not inventing false excitement. The impact is all the greater then when unmanned surveillance cameras (recording automatically in empty rooms) capture something no human is present to see. *Ghost Stalkers* has a particularly chilling example when split-screen is used to show an inset image of investigator Chad in the basement while on the larger screen, in an upstairs room, a doll is seated on a chair; slowly, that chair begins to rock.[37] Whether the time spent in "lockdown" is terrifying or becalmed, the cameras have it covered.

There are moments where investigators, like mediums, sense the paranormal without the aid of any electronic device. On *Ghost Adventures,* "Mackay Mansion," Billy shouts out that someone has just touched him. He needs repeated reassurance that it wasn't Zak, behind him with the camera, poking him in the back. Elsewhere team members tell us that the air feels heavy around them or that the hair on their arms is standing up. Unlike mediums, though, the investigators rely on technology to verify that they have made contact with the paranormal world. It is not enough to announce the existence of a cold spot when a close-up of a temperature sensor can show how quickly the temperature has dropped.[38] In the same episode, Zak announces that he's "grabbing the EMF detector to see if I can measure the energy that's passing through me at this moment." Capturing an image or a voice on a recording device not only makes it possible to prove its existence to others, it also proves it to oneself. As Zak breathlessly declares in another episode, "This mel-meter just documented what I saw with my own eyes."[39]

The preference for electronic evidence over human perception rests on the assumption that technology is more sensitive to the paranormal, its ability to register electronic or atmospheric phenomena far exceeding human sensory capacity. Introducing the SLS (Structured Light Sensor) camera, Zak explains that "this device maps a figure that we cannot see with our own eyes."[40] In "Angel of Death," two members of the *Ghost Hunters* team explain that they will try to attract the ghost of a little girl by setting a teddy bear next to a "Rem-pod" so that it can function "as a trigger object." As a storm begins outside, a high-pitched electronic tone suddenly sounds. "We got Rem-pod action," K. J. declares, reiterating the assumption that the device is signaling an otherwise imperceptible paranormal presence. "Please do it again," Dustin asks, and the device sounds again. Repetition on demand is used to demonstrate that the sounds or the lights were a response and not a coincidence. The sound of a knock on the wall or a flashlight turning itself on immediately after a question has been asked is presented as proof of an "intelligent" response.

An "intelligent response" is the gold standard of paranormal investigations because it means communication is taking place between the investigators and the spirit world. As far back as 1882, groups such as the Society for Psychical Research began "a program of pragmatic experimentation focused squarely on verifying the act of communication itself."[41] In his book *Haunted Media,* Jeffrey Sconce traces the way some Americans, introduced to wireless forms of communication such as radio, began to believe in "the capacity of electronic media to create" (or, in paranormal terms, reveal) "displaced, absent, and parallel worlds."[42] Despite a "nervous ambivalence" about contacting "the other side," the climactic scenes of every ghost-hunting program center on these moments of contact, interactions simultaneously enabled and verified by technology.[43]

When the equipment beeps or dials light up, it is left to the investigators to decipher what the signals actually mean. While psychic mediums assert knowledge based on their own authority, the spiritual investigators' work is primarily interpretive as they attribute meaning to events whose cause is otherwise unknown—a loud bang from an unseen source, perhaps, or an open door that used to be closed. The explanations ventured are often couched in what could be called "the rhetorical suggestive": "Is this light anomaly the same spirit that caused our equipment to fail earlier?" "Could this be evidence of spirit energy?" Because these questions cannot be answered, and their hypotheses neither proved nor disproved, the question of the paranormal is kept open. As former Syfy executive Mark Stern commented, "In a world with quantum physics, you have to hold open the belief that there is stuff out there that is too weird for us to explain."

Because team members make no claim to psychic skills or esoteric training in mystical matters, it is technology that serves as the ultimate test, "objective proof" of any phenomena. Digital cameras, recorders, temperature sensors, and other specialized devices are situated within, and equated with, scientific methodology. The idea of bringing scientific practices into the world of metaphysical exploration is not new. "In the late nineteenth and early twentieth centuries," Sconce points out, "research into psychic phenomena became more empirical and systematic" as it became "increasingly informed by the doctrines of scientific rationalism."[44] According to Steven Connor, Spiritualism at this time attempted to appease skeptics by sharing "with its opponents the language of investigation, evidence, exhibition and exposure."[45] For instance, on *Ghost Adventures*, we can find Zak pointing out the team's "strict investigation protocol" (in this case, searching the location thoroughly to make sure it is empty).[46] They are also shown testing the acoustics to make sure that voices from outside the location will not be recorded accidentally—what they call "spill-through" that might "contaminate" their recordings.[47] All the teams make a point of showing false readings as proof of their objectivity and scientific skepticism. If the ghost hunters in "Angel of Death" announce that the mysterious gas fire kept starting because of a faulty switch, *Ghost Adventures* is sure to be more emphatic. In "Old Licking County Jail," when suspicious thumping sounds turn out to be nothing but a piece of plywood flapping over a window, a big red stamp appears on-screen that declares the sounds to be "DEBUNKED."[48] Such scientific methods shore up not only the investigators' credibility but that of the technology. As Zak reiterates, the "*Ghost Adventures* crew" "take extra measures to show you the validity of the equipment."

Ghost hunters justify the use of increasingly specialized equipment by pointing to the range of paranormal phenomena they encounter—all of it phenomena presumably best revealed through technology. During lockdown, ghost hunters might find themselves dealing with "residual energy" (leftover, unconscious echoes from the past as opposed to the "intelligent" spirits who interact with investigators in the present); "orbs," or balls of light that embody spirit energy; objects that are cursed or carry evil energy; ley-lines (magnetic fields connecting spiritually active sites around the globe); and more. The kinds of spirits they encounter are also depicted as potentially dangerous. In addition to partial and full-bodied apparitions (what people traditionally call "ghosts"), investigators face "dark" energy, shadow figures, a "siren spirit" that's "wanting to entice us" (*Ghost Asylum*), shape-shifters, various forms of the demonic, and portals to hell.[49] This could be another reason the investigators prefer to interpose technology between themselves and the spirits they try to communicate with.

Sometimes communication is not enough. The climax of each episode of *Ghost Asylum* is the design, creation, and deployment of a unique, yet-to-be-named device that, supposedly, will enable the team to physically capture spirits. Classic tinkerers, the guys put together pseudo-scientific, makeshift gizmos while working out of low-tech settings like an alley or a converted garage. In the "Hayswood Infirmary" episode, for example, the "Limestone Water Pump Trap" combines "a submersible water pump" with a Mason jar holding a piece of limestone (a rock alleged to have spiritual properties). The theory (complete with labeled diagram) is explained by "Brannon, Inventor": "There is an ancient belief that spirits cannot travel along moving water because of the electrical charge produced by kinetic energy in the water's current." The pump, Chasey explains, is "gonna give us a whirlpool for a constant water flow," driving the spirit toward the rock. Team leader Chris asks, "So you're thinking maybe the energy'll be contained in the limestone?" Chasey Ray: "We got water and electricity. What could go wrong?"

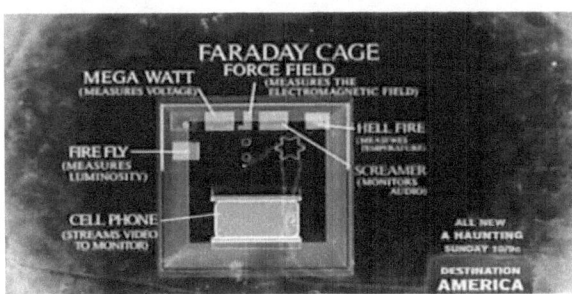

Ghost Asylum

Despite the *Ghost Asylum* team's ingenuity and "can-do" spirit, the devices they create never quite work, a disappointment assuaged by humor. When the energy meters light up to indicate a spirit is present in the water pump trap ("I really think we caught something this time"), they tag their catch "ghost in a bucket." They return to Tennessee where they use a home-made Faraday Cage and a K2 meter to detect "spiritual presence," but when they pour the piece of limestone out of the Mason jar their tests fall flat. Keeping things in perspective, Chris ends the episode by concluding that, in his opinion, "We just talked to a wet rock." Such self-deprecating humor humanizes the team members as they acknowledge their own fallibility and, in the process, reassert their common sense.

Humor plays a complex role in horror, defusing tension as it allows the audience to temporarily disengage and let down their guard. At such moments viewers acknowledge their self-consciousness about participating in a socially dubious practice, though, as Annette Hill points out, sharing a laugh—at the program *and* at themselves—may in itself be a source of pleasure.[50] More provocatively, Steve Connor suggests that engagements with the occult have always rested on this fault line between giggles and screams. "Seeing spiritualism steadily, and seeing it whole means recognizing its entanglement with facticity, fraudulence and farce," he argues, underscoring "its irresistible tendency to collapse into comedy."[51] *Ghost Adventures*, in particular, frequently acknowledges moments of absurdity. Exploring an old mine, the team calls attention to a mysterious metallic knocking. When Aaron reports the alarming news that he has "two eyes looking at me," Zak rushes over "with a thermal imaging camera" only to find that the supernatural beast they had imagined was just a raccoon, its eyes glowing in the night vision photography.

Perhaps the most important function humor performs is distracting the audience from the deeply unsettling suspicion that technology has limits. Even when a seemingly paranormal phenomenon is "captured" on camera or as a sound recording, the proof never holds. While it would seem that one clear recording of a voice or image of the dead would be all that was ever needed, somehow the paranormal evidence the teams gather is never sufficient.[52] A critic who objects to this inability/refusal to provide a definitive answer calls this "the eternal promise of the ultimate sighting, eternally unfulfilled."[53] For those who do find pleasure in the genre, keeping the existence of the paranormal an open question keeps viewers coming back.

If the investigative team's evidence does not conclusively prove the existence of the paranormal, at least no one can categorically disprove it either. As Zak admits in one episode of *Ghost Adventures*, while they cannot prove that the voice they recorded came from another realm, "we cannot argue with this data either."[54] In the logic of television, the hunt for proof of the paranormal *must* fail. If persuasive evidence was ever found, the series would end. Because irrefutable proof is always lacking, the search can be reenacted week after week as the programs return to "almost prove"/"fail to prove" that the paranormal is real and that technology can verify it. In this sense, the paranormal is like masculinity in that it can never be definitively established.

Technical Difficulties

If all the cameras, EVP recorders, EMF detectors, and REM pods fail to positively establish "spirit" phenomena, does that mean technology is inadequate to the task?

Technological failure, a common occurrence in these programs, is easily recuperated as itself proof of the paranormal. Investigators report that suddenly, mysteriously, the batteries in their devices have been drained. The sound cuts out as microphones fail. Cameras "die." Fortunately, there is an explanation. Spirits are said to be made of energy and therefore they use any available energy source (including the physical energy of mediums and investigators) in order to "manifest" (become visible, move objects, or make sounds). Zak implies exactly that when technical problems arise in "Haunted Savannah." "As we keep trying to power on the thermal camera, which has full battery power," he says urgently, "something keeps turning it off whenever we point it back toward the top of the stairs where that purple unexplained anomaly was captured."⁵⁵ As a female medium approaches a locked basement door in the "Black Dahlia House" episode, Zak notes "her microphone experiences strange interference." (On instant replay, a title identifies the sound as "unexplained static.") The implications of this electronic breakdown are stark: "We may have just put ourselves in the crosshairs of this dangerous and malevolent force."⁵⁶

Technological failure has become a key trope in modern horror. The title sequences of all paranormal shows feature "glitches" indicative of technology out of control. Electronic malfunctions disrupt basic television conventions we take for granted. Often, when the equipment stops working, the technical crew out steps out from behind the cameras, interrupting the scene. Routine industrial practice is thus thwarted by the very thing it sought to document. On shows where the crew *is* the cast, their realization that their devices do not work simultaneously obstructs their investigation and confirms the presence of a disrupting force, a staple of horror where the depiction of disruption is the point. At its most frightening, technology turns against the investigators as it falls into the hands of evil entities. In *Haunted Case Files*, amateur ghost hunters are unnerved as stereo speakers begin to blare music from the 1940s even though the receiver is unplugged. A demon appears on a television screen despite the set also being disconnected. Moments later, the telephone rings. It is the demon calling.⁵⁷ The spirits have hijacked every form of electronic media formerly used to contact, track, and expose them.

How does our intrepid team deal with a power so strong it overwhelms technology? Rather than acknowledging that electronic media cannot be trusted, the investigators persevere with that very equipment. This raises the possibility of compulsion: subjects repeatedly doing the same thing for reasons they cannot quite define or ignore, reasons that cannot be examined because to do so would risk questioning the foundation of one's identity.

Regardless of the teams' stated motives for investigating, helping clients is inevitably a pretext for the team's climactic confrontation with the unknown. As technology fails, gaps and fissures in the men's masculine personas are revealed as they flinch, jump, gasp, curse, and try not to scream or run, struggling to maintain control in the face of danger.

Nearly all ghost hunter shows are boys' clubs. On *Ghost Adventures*, *Ghost Asylum*, *Ghost Stalkers*, and *Ghost Brothers*, the on-screen talent is exclusively male, female peers nonexistent, and even references to relationships with women rare. Nick Groff on *Ghost Adventures* occasionally mentions that he is married, making him the show's "grown-up."[58] Everyone else exists in a perpetual adolescence characteristic of fraternities as the individual is subsumed into a team.

Each team adopts a special name, its acronym reproduced on T-shirts, caps, and vehicles, and written on-screen in subtitles. The *Ghost Hunters* are TAPS (the Atlantic Paranormal Society). The *Paranormal State* group call themselves PRS (the Penn State Paranormal Research Society). *Ghost Asylum*'s TWC stands for the humorously gothic "Tennessee Wraith Chasers." These acronyms become part of the show's identity. Like the logo of a sports team, the otherwise obscure initials are easily recognized and understood by fans and team members alike, a shared knowledge that serves as a sign of expertise and belonging. Team members often wear similar clothing or insignia that identify them as members of the group. The Ghost Hunters often have "TAPS" emblazoned somewhere on their clothing, while the men of *Ghost Asylum* adopt military-style camouflage with the heavily bearded look of hunters deep in the woods. These demonstrations of conformity support the idea of average-ness by preventing any one person from standing out from the others due to having special skills like psychic-mediums have.

At the same time, "these hero teams, or hero pairs, are always hierarchical with a distinct leader."[59] Except for *Ghost Stalkers*, where the co-hosts have a roughly equal presence, the opening scenes in paranormal investigation shows inevitably designate one person as the "man in charge." In *Ghost Hunters*, TAPS founder Jason Hawes is the series' fixed point; his partner, on the other hand, is subject to change. Grant Wilson, depicted as TAPS's co-founder and Hawes's sidekick since the show's beginning in 2004, left in 2012 and was replaced by Steve Gonsalves. Zak Bagans in *Ghost Adventures*, Chris Smith on *Ghost Asylum*, Ryan Buell of *Paranormal State*, Jack Osborne on *Haunted Highway*, and John Zaffis on *Haunted Collector* dominate their respective shows. As spokesman, each man provides the voice-over during the title sequence where he gets to define the other members of the team, as when Zak introduces "fellow investigator" Nick Groff and "our equipment tech," Aaron Goodwin.[60] Having been granted the status of narrator, each man's authority carries over into the rest of the episode, his position as team leader reestablished whenever we hear his disembodied voice.

The hyperbolically masculine bodies of "burly men" like Zak Bagans or Chris Smith of *Ghost Asylum* seem to underwrite each man's role as team

Ghost Asylum

leader.⁶¹ Their inflated muscles set them apart visually and reinforce stereotypical images of manliness and heroic comportment. In narrative terms, however, muscular strength is of little use when confronting the paranormal. Bodybuilder physiques also fail to impress other members of the team. At the end of one episode, Chris, wearing his trademark bicep-baring, sleeveless shirt, announces that he is heading for the gym. A heavyset team member retorts, "Why don't you find some sleeves?" The gang laughs, endorsing the kind of lightweight, locker-room putdown that deflates any attempt at self-aggrandizement in order to maintain a team of equals.

The hero-as-individual has no place here. Ghost hunters are plural and rarely alone. Even when one man goes off on his own, he is accompanied by someone with a camera or has someone back at base watching or listening in. Subsumed into a "hero team," the individual's mental and physical abilities are supplemented and magnified by his fellow team members. As John Fiske explains, because the participants' "differences supply each other's lack[,] . . . the hero team can mold individual competencies into something approaching total competence."⁶² At the same time, being a member of a team "hides the insecurity of the individual without threatening his independence."⁶³ Because the desire to merge with other men "is externalized onto a goal, not internalized into a basic need of the male," the shows can sidestep issues that undercut assertions of standard masculinity such as emotional dependence (the "need for male bonding") or potential homosexual attraction.⁶⁴ One way to naturalize the desire to be part of an all-male team is by using familial terms. The *Ghost Asylum* troupe, for example, identify themselves as a "band of brothers." The short-lived *Ghost Lab* (2009) was headed by two men who were literally brothers, Brad and Barry Klinge.

Bound into a team, the men are fearless, rousing themselves with hypermasculine posturing. *Ghost Asylum* announces, "We're kicking down the doors of the most haunted places in America." The same combative attitude appears in the *Ghost Adventures* episode in which Zak compares preparing for "lockdown" to a fighter going into the ring, being pumped up by the crowd.[65] He caps that with a military metaphor, proclaiming, "We're going in [in] super-stealth mode tonight." In another episode, he declares: "Let's grab our gear and arm ourselves for battle."[66] Even comic sidekick Aaron refers to a new kind of camera as if it were a gun: "Let's get the SLS and just shoot the place up."[67] Not surprisingly, threats to masculine identity are defrayed by bravado. When the *Ghost Adventures* team visits the cell of a deceased child molester in an abandoned prison, they vie to show who is less afraid of being locked alone in the cell. Nick brags that if the convict's ghost tried anything with him, the ghost would "get his ass whooped." Each team's reaction to fear, they tell us, is what distinguishes them from other people. As Chris says on *Ghost Asylum*, "When people are scared to go into places, that makes us want to go more. Because the more paranormal claims—the more people who are freaked out goin' in there—the more we want to find out what's causing all the crazy."[68] The only time the men are subdued is in the presence of a masculinity they accept as superior to their own. Both *Ghost Adventures* and *Ghost Asylum* show extreme respect for traditionally male-dominated institutions like the military. In the episode "Battle of Los Angeles," set at Fort MacArthur in California, Zak abandons his usual confrontational stance when addressing a spirit in favor of a deferential, "Can you please manifest yourself, sir?" At the Hayswood Infirmary, where World War I and World War II victims of shell shock were treated, a *Ghost Asylum* team member points out, "We got soldiers possibly in here, so let's be respectful."

Frequently, though, the attitude toward spirits is aggressive if not belligerent. In *Ghost Adventures*, Zak calls out in a loud voice that is alternately commanding ("Manifest yourself!"), provocative ("Hey, tough guy. Talk to us"), or sarcastic ("Tonight's gonna be the night where you show us how strong you are.")[69] On *Ghost Stalkers*, John Tenney addresses a dark energy in an attic. Having heard that "you attack people up here," he states, "C'mon . . . I'm calling you out."[70] There is a strong sense of men showing off, testing themselves.

When people feel the need to endlessly prove themselves (and when identity comes down to self-assertion), credibility is essential. The title sequence of later seasons of *Ghost Adventures* claims defensively, "We have worked years to build our credibility, our reputation."[71] The concept of credibility in these shows leans heavily on gender stereotypes that link scientific rationalism with masculinity and discount intuition/sensitivity as feminine. In a ghost town in "Heritage Junction," the *Ghost Adventures* team prefers accounts from a man from NASA ("talk about credibility," Zak comments) over a female psychic's report about her own paranormal experience in a haunted building. Zak bonds with the man from NASA by asking him if he also thought the woman's account was "bull sh—" (the second syllable is edited out). When we meet the woman (whom we are told does not want to be perceived as being "overdramatic"), Zak becomes protective and authoritative, telling her, "I don't want you near that house. I don't want you inside that house." At other times, the men seem distinctly uneasy when they think that women might encroach on their territory. In the "Lizzie Borden House" episode, Zak grows increasingly uncomfortable as an older woman tries to suggest that Lizzie Borden was motivated to kill her father because of the crimes he had committed against her. (It is implied that Borden was a victim of incest.)[72] Zak cuts the woman off.[73] Overall, female psychic-mediums are welcome as guests on *Ghost Adventures* as long as it is understood that (as Zak insists) their "technique is less scientific than ours."[74] Or, as psychologist and paranormal researcher Williams James asserted in 1885, "'Facts' are what are wanted. . . . What we want is not only truth but evidence."[75]

The use of technology (science in a practical form) differentiates the men from women and shields them from women's unnerving sensitivity. In "Black Dahlia House," a female medium begins to feel overwhelmed by painful emotions as she communicates spiritually with three women whom she says were murdered in the house. In a split-screen, we see her on the right, agitated, staggering, crying, while on the left Zak stands stone-faced, arms crossed, listening to her through headphones. He is separated from the fear and pain by the media he uses and by the way the image is constructed—the split-screen putting him literally on the side of technology.

The men in these shows take pains to distinguish themselves from women by identifying with traditionally all-male institutions like the military, bolstering their sense of masculinity by joining all-male teams, and seeking out opportunities to prove themselves against dark forces. Yet it is hard to be a man. Men are shown to be under a lot of pressure; they are afraid, and they can get hurt.

Male paranormal investigators suffer physical damage. Scratches appear on their skin and they report nausea, headaches, dizziness, and racing heartbeats. Stumbling on stairs, they claim they have been tripped or pushed.[76] On *Ghost Stalkers*, "Whispers Estate," a shaken John declares that he has just been "slammed against a wall." In *Ghost Adventures*, "The Exorcist House," Nick addresses the potential costs of paranormal investigating: "I have a family. I don't want to die from this." The most frightening moments for team members seem to come from simply being touched—a violation of personal space that elicits spontaneous, censored outbursts, and sudden movements. These are privileged moments, highlighted in teasers and repeated so often throughout each episode it suggests that the sight of "men-pushed-past-the-limits-of-masculinity" is part of the genre's attraction.

Basic television broadcast standards are also pushed to the limit when the men express fear by swearing. (Except for Amy Allan on *The Dead Files*, women on paranormal shows rarely do this.)[77] Cursing is presented as a sign of toughness as well as evidence of being under such stress one bursts the bonds of polite society. At one point, Zak is verbally challenging a spirit when he suddenly jumps. "What the f—? Did you hear that?!" On *Ghost Stalkers*, when a home-owner tells John that a figure of a "goat-man" has been seen, Chad puts down his camera and exclaims, "A goat man? What the f— is that?!" While such displays underline the risks the team is willing to take, thus establishing courage, they also make it clear that the men can be afraid—something they openly admit. "Oh my God, this place is so f—ing scary," Zak says, talking to himself while sitting in a dark hallway.[78] Less recuperable are scenes where the men scream or run, examples of fear overpowering their ability to face a challenge.

The 2014 series *Ghost Stalkers* is particularly overt in its depiction of masculinity on the brink. In its first episode, "Whispers Estate," we are introduced to co-hosts Chad Lindberg and John E. L. Tenney. A former actor, Lindberg combines a solid build with a vulnerable manner. (He was once cast as a gay, deaf Patsy Cline impersonator.)[79] Lindberg appears very fearful, his voice quavery. Before he goes in to spend the night alone, he is physically sick. Preparing for lockdown, he begs John to be extra-vigilant when monitoring him. "Do *not* stop listening for a second, I swear to God." Inside the haunted mansion, he begins his interaction with the spirits who might be present by disowning his earlier posturing. "I know I talked a big game," he says, but the truth is that he is scared. In the basement where there might be a portal to hell, Chad keeps up a constant patter about his fearfulness. "I'm feeling very uneasy." He screams suddenly and jumps when he thinks someone has touched him. Later, a spirit (captured on EVP) speaks to him. At first, Chad does not understand what sounds like a loud sigh. When he plays it back a third time, subtitles spell out "Chad ... be a man ..." He gets the message. Pumping his fist, he yells out triumphantly, "Be a man! Okay! Alright, alright! I will! [Bleep!]" It seems that even spirits support traditional definitions of heteromasculinity.

In Chad, so-called "male stoicism" is shattered by emotional volatility. Instead of establishing a tough facade, Chad's bleeped expletives demonstrate his failure to control his emotions, especially his fear. Partner John is older and more fatherly, wearing a shirt and tie compared to Chad's baseball shirt, knit cap, and beads. He has a deeper voice than Chad and a calmer demeanor, but even John can be rattled. In "Holmesburg Prison," John has a crisis when all the energy drains from his camera, causing him to lose contact with the outside world. Fearing he is having a heart attack, he calls for Chad who runs to help him (POV of running with handheld camera).[80] The next day, Chad lays out his understanding of their roles. The fact that John needed Chad's help was "like a complete role-reversal," Chad insists, and it is something he does not want "ever to happen again." "You are the strong one," he tells John. That is the way things should be. Men know that the dominant male must never be exposed as vulnerable.

Sensitivity (in the paranormal sense) threatens masculinity because it exposes men's vulnerability. As with the female psychic mediums, ghost-hunting men often locate their first encounters with the paranormal in childhood—something that came to them unbidden when they were young and unprepared. This is stated outright in the title sequences of several shows. Ryan Buell of *Paranormal State* says, "When I was a kid my experiences with the supernatural terrified me and I have been searching for answers ever since." In the first years of *Ghost Adventures*, Zak states: "I never believed in ghosts—until I came face to face with one." The title sequence of *Ghost Stalkers* features each of the co-hosts testifying to a near-death experience which has led him to look for "portals" that allow passage to and from "the other side." For these men, personal experience explains their interest, serves as guarantee of their sincerity, and accounts for the creation of both the show and the team. On *Ghost Hunters*, Jason Hawes announces that he founded his paranormal team TAPS "in 1990 after a personal experience." On the one hand, these stories are presented as brave declarations, as if it takes courage to admit having had a paranormal experience. These stories are rarely expanded upon, however, as if the subject was too painful, a kind of deep, almost shameful secret. It might be necessary to mention it in order to establish one's personal connection to the paranormal, but as with most traumas, the men would rather not talk about it. Unlike mediums whose childhood discovery of psychic abilities led them to pursue a career dealing with the paranormal, these men are embarrassed, upset, and driven to explain paranormal phenomenon and prove it exists.

Occasionally, male investigators abandon technology, temporarily aligning themselves with traits exhibited by female mediums such as intuition, emotion, and physical sensitivity. In one episode, when Aaron begins to feel uneasy, Zak tells us in voice-over, "An intense feeling of discomfort can be just as valid as any visual or audio evidence."[81] Nick adds, "The three of us know when we feel something. Y'know?"[82] But they seldom hold this position for long because the fear of feminization outweighs its benefits.

In nineteenth-century Spiritualism, "feminine" described a condition of being helpless, physically permeable, and susceptible to being transformed into an unconscious device. Falling into a trance and channeling voices from the beyond, women *became* the technology—literally "the medium" through which others communicated. The "instinctual" receptivity of women, combined with their "nervous energy," was said to make them ideal transmitters.[83] In 1924's *Thirty Years among the Dead*, author Carl Wickland reports that the spirits themselves described his wife in technological terms: "She is the live wire," they said. "She is the battery."[84] Speaking through Mrs. Wickland was said to be "like talking through a telephone."[85] If you do not establish yourself as the master of technology, you risk becoming the technology. In "King's Tavern," Nick is drained of energy just like Zak's camera earlier in the episode. It is the first sign that he is being possessed. Recounting another moment of possession, Nick says with memorable disgust, "It was using me."

Externalizing communication through the use of electronic devices is essential for male investigators because when they (and their bodies) betray sensitivities—particularly those they cannot control—they approach a condition of femininity that threatens to erase identity altogether. Of all the dangers men face in dealing with the paranormal, being possessed is the worst. Moodiness is the first sign that one's mind is being influenced, if not taken over, by a spirit or a demon. In *Ghost Adventures*, "King's Tavern," Nick undergoes a "possible attachment" (or possession) by "spirit energy." "It's having an effect on me, man," he announces during lockdown. "I really feel, like, messed up." Standing alone in a room (as seen through a static camera), he states urgently, "I can feel it all around me. I can feel the spirit inside me now." The investigators announce that their emotions are out of their control as they find themselves "inexplicably" overcome by anger or sadness. "I wasn't myself," Nick recounts later, "emotions just fluctuated." Zak, watching on the monitors, testifies to the extraordinary change in Nick: "I don't think I've ever seen him like this." "It's bad," Nick confides to the camera in a close-up, his eyes made strange by the night-vision lighting. Technical advisor Billy is also affected when he enters the house: "I was scared. . . . I felt like there was nothing I could do to stop it 'cause I . . . felt like I was being possessed."[86] Desperate to establish communication—to connect—the men are simultaneously terrified of being overwhelmed. In the episode's dramatic last line, Nick says, "We're skating on thin ice. What is the breaking point where one of us just snaps?"[87]

In an episode of *Ghost Asylum*, the team is forced to call on all its resources when the youngest and most vulnerable member of the group is overpowered by a malevolent entity.[88] Walking through the halls of the abandoned Cannon Memorial Hospital, Brannon begins to call out the hostile spirit using uncharacteristically bold language. "I dare you [to show yourself]. If you don't, you're pathetic and you're a coward." His voice nearly breaks when he screams, "Do [bleeping] something!" In any other show, this would be a typical act of bravado, but Brannon's fellow team members grow quiet, looking at each other uncomfortably. A voice-over explains their uneasiness: "He's never done that. Ever, dude. He's never cursed. Something's not right."

In *Ghost Asylum*'s first episode, Brannon is identified as Chris's younger brother, someone who, it is casually mentioned, is mildly autistic. Brannon is incorporated as a full member of the team in every episode. Respected as an inventor of unique ghost-trapping devices, his presence is taken for granted. In other words, he is treated like family—a status which gives all the men permission to express emotion. Seeing Brannon targeted, presumably possessed by negative spirits, they are deeply moved. "Dude, I'm gonna [bleep]-ing cry," one man says. "This ain't right."

The investigation comes to a halt as the team members focus all their attention on Brannon's emotional state. Taking him outside, they express concern ("You sure you're alright?") and urge him to "break out of this." As

Brannon becomes combative, the others try to deescalate the situation by responding quietly, "What's wrong with you? You're scaring me. This ain't you." Surrounding him supportively, they reassure him: "We love you. We're here for you, okay?" As we saw in the first-person accounts, team leader and older brother Chris blames the building: "This place already seems like it might could drive you crazy.... I'm done with this place." In tears, he cancels the investigation altogether and holds his brother in a prolonged embrace. Back at headquarters some time later, Brannon has fully recovered and the others are simply glad to have escaped "hell in between brick walls."

What would be standard behavior on *Ghost Adventures*—taunting spirits, cursing, preparing to fight—is presented as such an obvious violation of Brannon's true personality that it must be the result of attempted demonic possession. While gender studies have suggested that "society teaches males to find their identity in goals and achievements and females to find theirs in relationships," here the men abandon their ostensible objective (they say they cannot remember a case where they did not complete the investigation) in order to focus on the emotional well-being of one of their teammates.[89] By trying to restore Brannon to himself, they defend his customarily non-aggressive way of being. In the process, they show acceptance of a softer kind of masculinity, not only for Brannon but for themselves as they openly express deep affection for each other.

At the end of this episode, it is clear that *Ghost Asylum*'s stated purpose of "trapping" spirits is not its ultimate goal. What matters is the well-being of the team, that band of brothers—the Tennessee Wraith Chasers. In ghost-hunting shows, technology might fail to capture proof of the paranormal, but each investigation reestablishes the importance of the team. Just as mediums forge a bond with survivors by creating a new relationship built on a shared connection to/recognition of the dead, programs about paranormal investigators show what membership in a team can offer. When the harsh demands of masculinity are tempered by the love of one's teammates, that might be enough to face down all the evils in this world or any other.

Afterlife

Sooner or later, every long-running series is faced with change as cast members leave and costs spiral. Syfy executive Mark Stern acknowledged that on "shows that last multiple seasons, and particularly a show like *Ghost Hunters* [that was] such a huge hit, everyone gets a raise. Rightly so." While it is widely believed that reality TV is much less expensive to produce than scripted/fiction programs, Stern disagrees. "Certainly our shows were not cheap." But as costs rise, "the economics just get more difficult." "If I'm paying $700,000 for an hour of a reality show and for another half million or so I can get a scripted show," that is the better choice. "I can schedule it more. I can bring it back," whereas "a lot of reality shows are one and done." Also, as the market "became flooded" with a "glut" of paranormal shows, Syfy found that the paranormal reality genre "was not getting the audience.... At the same time, all of cable's ratings started to decline." Although *Ghost Hunters* itself would continue for another five years, by 2011 Syfy had decided that it was time to move on.

Cast members were also opting out. "You're always concerned when you have a successful show and then you start to have cast changes," Stern states. The producers of *Ghost Hunters* were concerned when cast member Brian Harnois left after three years, but the "scariest moment was when Grant left" in 2012. They wondered, "Can this franchise really survive?" In Stern's formulation, "Brian was the comic relief/son who was always getting into trouble," while "Grant and Jason were the dads," "the pillars" of the program. Because their familial status was metaphorical rather than literal, there is a noticeable fluidity to the roles Jason and Grant played. "Grant was such a balance to Jason," Stern muses. "In terms of their energies, Grant was the mother figure, the nurturer, and Jason was the gruff disciplinarian Dad. So suddenly Mom's gone and how's that gonna work?" For Stern, the key issue with cast changes is that "you're never totally sure what's making the chemistry work." One way to ease the adjustment to new cast members was to promote from within. Steve Gonsalves, who had been with the series since its beginning, eventually stepped in to replace Grant as the more approachable parental figure. Likewise, when Nick Groff left *Ghost Adventures* after 139 episodes, Billy Tolley and Jay Wasley (members of the crew who had made occasional appearances) became regular members of the cast.

Some cast changes are signs of growth, a means of extending the franchise. Supporting characters are developed into leads. "Tech Manager" Dave Tango and Steve Gonsalves continued to support Jason and Grant on *Ghost Hunters* while helming one of its spin-offs, *Ghost Hunters Academy* (2009). That series made cast changes the subject of the show, staging a *Survivor*–like competition where would-be paranormal investigators vied for roles on *Ghost Hunters* and its other spin-off, *Ghost Hunters International* (2008).[90] *Ghost Asylum*'s team features three competitors from earlier shows: Chris Smith (*Ghost Hunters Academy*), and Scott Porter and Steven "Doogie" McDougal, who appeared on the Zak Bagans-hosted *Paranormal Challenge* (2011). At other times, cast members strike out to create new programs as when Amy Bruni and Adam Berry (a *Ghost Hunters Academy* winner) left *Ghost Hunters* to start their own series *Kindred Spirits* (2016, TLC) or *Ghost Adventures*' Nick Groff put together a new team for *Ghosts of Shepherdstown* (2016, Destination America).

When cast members disappear, the pressures of television production become visible to viewers, revealing what it costs "ordinary" people when they are transformed into television celebrities. The producers of *Ghost Hunters* insist that spending over a decade on a hit reality television series has not changed Jason and Grant: "They're kinda like regular blue-collar guys," they argue. "They don't live large." For example, "Jason to this day will go out on a plumbing call."[91] But on one occasion, a former paranormal investigation team member chose to speak for himself.

After leaving *Ghost Asylum*, Chasey Ray McKnight moved from the producer-dependent medium of television to the do-it-yourself internet, posting a video on YouTube explaining his decision to quit the show. "I'm just a typical person like everybody else," trying to hold down a "forty-to-fifty-hour-a-week day job," he explains. Having a wife and children ("three kids and another on the way"), it was "hard to be gone six months out of the year, filming on location." After plugging the Tennessee Wraith Chasers' new series—one that does not include him—he expresses his gratitude to his former teammates and to the fans.[92] "I've had a good run and I've enjoyed every bit of it. But I'm right where I need to be in life right now. I'm with my family and I'm doin' for me and mine."[93] Using direct address, McKnight testifies to the truth of his own experience. But the most eloquent expression of authenticity, of ghost hunters as ordinary guys living in a recognizably workaday world, is the image before us: an overweight, middle-aged man in a T-shirt, addressing the camera on his computer while seated in the corner of what might be an auto-parts warehouse, under fluorescent light. The real world.

Series about paranormal investigators allow only as much reality as is necessary to maintain a flavoring of authenticity. In this imaginary world people with esoteric expertise are at the same time ordinary, just like us. Technology

Chasey Ray McKnight, *Ghost Asylum*

is not intimidating but available to any bunch of guys out to answer the big questions about life and death over the course of a weekend. Average Joes find all the validation they need from their buddies. They become TV stars by simply being who they always were (and staying that way).

Paranormal reality series focused on psychic mediums have a different vision of the world to promote and a more challenging set of issues to negotiate. In many ways the antithesis of ghost-hunting shows, these series replace scenes of competitive risk-taking and displays of courage with examples of emotional comfort and consolation. Unsettling public sites such as ghost towns, run-down theaters, empty hotels, and old restaurants are exchanged for reassuring domestic spaces. Hard bodies and the "hard" evidence science and technology are thought to provide are jettisoned in favor of "soft," traditionally feminine traits like intuition and sensitivity. If ghost-hunting shows are defined by the contest—men subjecting themselves to a trial, eager for the chance to prove themselves—the shows built around psychics chart the step-by-step creation of a relationship between medium and client as, through their shared emotional investment in a co-authored narrative, they figuratively bring a loved one "back to life."[94] Perhaps most important, in place of a team, these shows depend entirely on the appeal of a single, uniquely skilled individual. In other words, on someone special. Very special.

3

My Favorite Medium
Women's Work

"Tis a beautiful idea, that our departed friends are around us and with us," to "guard" and "soothe."[1]
—Trance medium Achsa Sprague, 1850

In the days before EMF detectors, night-vision cameras, EVPs, and ghost-hunting teams, the most common way to communicate with the dead was through a medium. When the Fox sisters began to hold séances in their home in Hydesville, New York, in 1848, they not only sparked a movement known as American Spiritualism, they invented the modern psychic, an otherwise ordinary person whose special abilities enabled them to convey messages from "the other side." Although these communications were limited to rapping sounds along the lines of "once for yes, twice for no," the very concept of spirit communication held such appeal that "mediums" became a fixture in the popular imagination and have remained so ever since.

Paranormal reality television emphasizes people who claim to hear from and speak for the dead (referred to interchangeably as "psychics," "mediums," or "psychic mediums").[2] The term "psychic" itself covers a diverse range of abilities. These can include clairvoyance (seeing the future), clairsentience (feeling the future), claircognizance (knowing information by spiritual means), channeling (letting spirits and energies communicate through you),

Theresa Caputo, *Long Island Medium*

reading auras (spiritual energy surrounding people), or reading minds (ESP). Practitioners in these and similar fields may be called empaths, intuitives, sensitives, fortune tellers, Reiki masters, or psychic healers (those who use spiritual rather than medical means to address physical ailments). Whatever abilities psychics claim, their powers cannot be verified. This is not, however, the only reason they were and remain controversial.

Psychics of all stripes and in all periods have evoked intense hostility. Because their unorthodox methods undermined religious authorities, Leviticus decreed that "a man or a woman who is a medium or a spiritist must surely be put to death" (20:27).[3] In the post-Enlightenment era, the very idea of mediumship was seen as an affront to reason. At the beginning of the twentieth century, one opponent declared that "Spiritism is the ruck and muck of modern culture, the common enemy of true science and true religion, and to drain its dismal and miasmatic marshes is the great work of modern culture."[4] Contemporary sources can be equally irate. In 2019, the *New York Times* compared psychics to prostitutes by referring to mediumship as "one of the planet's oldest professions."[5] That same year, one television series launched an all-out assault.

In the February 25, 2019, episode "Psychics" on HBO's *Last Week Tonight with John Oliver*, the show's seriocomic host dismisses out of hand the idea that authentic psychic ability is possible. Declaring that it is "easy to dismiss psychics as a joke. Really easy. Fun, too," he argues, "I'm not going to be litigating whether psychics are real. . . . For one thing, they're not." Their seemingly preternatural knowledge is merely an old carnival trick. When, miraculously, they know that your father died and what he died of, it is either the result of a "cold reading" made up of "high probability guesses"—"laughably sure bets" based on "your responses and nonverbal cues"—or a "hot reading," where the psychic and his or her confederates have done "prior research."

What makes Oliver particularly incensed is the role television plays in promoting what he considers professional con artists.[6] "They are everywhere on TV," he declares. He admits that scenes where psychics "bring people to tears" by seeming to make contact with their deceased loved ones "make for compelling TV." It is precisely that emotional power that makes such shows "one of the most insidious parts" of "the psychic industry." The celebrity that can result from national television exposure "emboldens a vast underworld of unscrupulous vultures," members of a "predatory industry [that] relies on popular culture to lend it credence and validity." Oliver reserves his greatest vitriol (understandably so) for a case where a kidnapped girl saw her mother on a daytime talk show consulting a psychic.[7] When the psychic said the woman's daughter was dead, the girl (who later escaped) felt crushed, thinking that her mother would stop looking for her. Oliver lashes out at the alleged psychic, condemning her as "an attention-seeking parasite who feeds off personal tragedy." Television, however, is equally responsible. "Daytime shows are still holding hands with this shit," he insists. Inviting trolls to attack at will, Oliver concludes that "the only responsible way to put a psychic on television" is by "humiliating them." Ridicule their claims. Show them failing. Expose their methods.

What is obvious but unacknowledged is that the unrelenting antagonism toward psychics has in no way diminished their popularity. Inevitably, every medium on paranormal reality television has been denounced as a fraud while their series have been renewed for a fourth, sixth or fourteenth season (*Hollywood Medium with Tyler Henry*, *The Haunting of . . .*, and *Long Island Medium*, respectively.) As historian Simone Natale describes in her book *Supernatural Entertainments*, from the beginning, "doubts about the authenticity of [psychics'] spectacular feats only added to their appeal."[8] As participants in an early phase of celebrity culture, nineteenth-century psychics found that controversy enabled them "to grab the attention of the press and pique the public's curiosity about spiritualism."[9] Whether channeling spirits in the front parlor or performing before an audience of hundreds, the Fox sisters and their successors revealed the affinity between mediumship and show business. "Séances offered not just a confirmation of religious beliefs about the afterlife but also a brilliant form of amusement."[10] Audiences participated willingly, enjoying the "ambiguity between rational explanation and extraordinary experience."[11] Audience members could believe "that they were witnessing real phenomena of spirit agency" and "at the same time" admit they were simply "having fun."[12] The mediums themselves "welcomed manifestations of delight, amusement, and even laughter."[13] The pleasure to be found—for performer and audience—in balancing belief and play is evident in the depiction of television psychics.

Between 1997 and 2003, a series of commercials and infomercials airing on US cable television channels featured a woman named "Miss Cleo." Reading tarot cards and doling out advice while seated on an elaborately carved chair set against a hokey "cosmic" background, Miss Cleo assured customers, "You have questions. I have the answers." Promising (among other things) direct personal interaction between viewers and the woman on their TV screen, Miss Cleo urged customers to call a "psychic hotline" where they would receive fortune-telling services while paying $3.99 per minute for the call. Although the calls were answered by others, it was Miss Cleo who became the face of low-budget, late-night cable television solicitations. In this period cable stations embraced the new format of the thirty-minute "infomercial" as a way to gain revenue by filling late-night schedules with advertising disguised as programming. Twenty-four-hour phone banks created a sense of interactivity between viewers and telephone psychics ("operators are standing by"). Miss Cleo's employer, the Psychic Readers Network, was soon under investigation for running a phone scam, perpetuating the long-established association of psychics with fraud. Critics also questioned whether any aspect of "Miss Cleo"—her cheerful exuberance, Jamaican accent, or turban-like hair wraps—was authentic.

As the indelible image of a woman bestowing golden toast on a benign universe suggests, Miss Cleo's appeal depended as much on her outrageous camp persona as it did on the intersection of changing telecommunications technology, deregulation, and the expansion of cable. Simultaneously comic and serious, high priestess and cheap huckster, Miss Cleo personifies excess and flagrant artifice. Whether claiming actual powers of second sight or as an actress playing a seer, Miss Cleo (whose full name was Youree Dell Harris) occupied a position similar to that of nineteenth-century psychics. Blithely indifferent to "distinctions between authenticity and forgery," Miss Cleo exemplifies the double-reading required to fully enjoy the complex figure of the psychic.[14]

Miss Cleo

Miss Cleo's bold claims to extraordinary powers could also be seen as (entertainingly) transgressive. Since the 1840s, members of marginalized populations (especially women and members of the working class) have used demonstrations of psychic ability to triumph over social exclusion, achieving fame, influence, commercial success, and the social status that comes with them.[15] Facing down alarms like those of the 1920s that linked "subversive mediums" to "the 'modern girl,' masculine degeneration, working-class rebellion, and racial assimilation," Miss Cleo's ubiquity proved that a woman, a person of color, and an immigrant (or someone pretending to be one) could succeed despite opposition from the hegemony of science, church, and state.[16]

The programs developed around psychic mediums between 2004 and 2019 explicitly reject the stylistic extravagance and questionable legality of Miss Cleo and her Psychic Friends. All psychics, however, claim to have special skills that set them apart from the average viewer. Such claims give rise to hostility as the psychics' motives, ethics, credibility, and authenticity come into question. As series about psychic mediums navigate these issues, they seek to minimize controversy by minimizing difference. The first priority, then, is to make mediums seem as ordinary as possible.

Normalization

Writing in the 1960s, paranormal luminary Hans Holzer stressed the importance of de-exoticizing the figure of the medium.[17] Canny mid-century Americans, it was assumed, would no longer fall for the fairground bunkum of "gypsy" fortune tellers reading crystal balls, mind-readers wearing turbans, or mediums going into trances in dark rooms while channeling the voices of the dead.[18] In fact, Holzer advised, people professing the ability to communicate psychically with "spirits" should take care to seem extra-normal. "Please forget your visions of mediums along Gian Carlo Menotti lines," Holzer urged readers (referring to the 1946 American opera *The Medium*). "My mediums are all normal, everyday people who, by the very fact that they are mediumistic, need to be a bit more 'normal' than you or me."[19] (Some of these mediums can be seen in old 16mm footage and heard on reel-to-reel tape recordings in the 2019 Travel Channel series *The Holzer Files*.)

In keeping with Holzer's advice, *Crossing Over with John Edward* (1999–2004) pioneered the normalization of psychic readings on television. Not only was the psychic-medium presented as an average, all-American guy, but the process of communicating with the dead was no longer frightening. Discarding decades of conventions, *Crossing Over* took the scary out, setting the stage for the shows that followed. Stylistically, the series eschewed horror motifs as it attempted to merge the paranormal with a realist aesthetic. Airing on the Sci-Fi Channel weekday afternoons, *Crossing Over* was modeled on 1990s-era daytime talk shows. Like those hosted by Oprah Winfrey and Phil Donahue, it was recorded before a live—and visible—studio audience.[20] The set favored pastels and neutral tones and was brightly lit, dispelling any hint of eerie shadows or dark corners. Edward himself was presented as an unpretentious, middle-class man, born and raised on Long Island—with an accent to prove it. He was young, married, and (the title sequence informed us) he and his wife enjoyed ballroom dancing.

A typical episode from the first season has Edward, dressed casually in jeans and an open-necked shirt, stepping onstage to a round of applause. As with his talk show predecessors, Edward has a primarily female audience, the bright, even lighting creating a sense of shared space as the host engages with members of the audience in a quasi-egalitarian give and take. Explaining how he receives mental impressions in symbolic form ("When I see yellow roses, it means . . ."), Edward declares that he feels "drawn" to a particular section of the audience. He announces the presence of a certain category of spirit ("There's a father energy coming through") and waits for an audience member to confirm the loss of a father. Provided with a microphone, the audience member engages in a dialogue with Edward. He makes a suggestion ("Somebody had congestive heart failure. They had problems

John Edward, *Crossing Over*

in the chest area—") and the family member confirms the details ("He had cardiac arrest while putting a shunt in").[21]

Each episode re-enacts the same confrontation again and again. Edward says he is receiving information from the dead, but it is partial and obscure. He needs an audience member to verify the source and complete the message. Like a séance, this is a shared, communal event but the ritualized aspects of the séance have been removed. What was formerly a private ceremony in a room shrouded in darkness now takes place in a well-lit, public space. Every aspect of *Crossing Over* is designed to give the impression that the process has been brought out into the open. Unlike earlier mediums, Edward does not go into a trance or let spirits "from the other side" ventriloquize through him. He keeps his eyes open, arguing and joking with audience members in his usual tone of voice, keeping the pace brisk, and acting as if communicating with the dead is something that happens every day. On *Crossing Over* it does—five days a week, in broad daylight.

To escape the repetition inherent in its format, *Crossing Over* varied its content in later seasons by adding scenes of private readings with celebrities or by going on location to visit former guests in their homes. Despite these changes, the basic premise stayed the same: the suspenseful moment as Edward waits for someone to affirm the details he has offered, the first steps as Edward and the guest move through doubt, confusion, and disagreement, then the emotional climax when the guests realize they are communicating with someone who has died. While the details of each reading change, the messages conveyed are always the same: your loved ones are always with you, and the medium's psychic abilities are genuine.

The programs that followed *Crossing Over with John Edward* abandoned the talk-show format in favor of a documentary approach. Their main characters, however, hewed so closely to that earlier series' depiction of a psychic, one could have the impression that all mediums are from Long Island. In *Long Island Medium* (2011), *The Haunting of . . .* (2012), *Angels Among Us* (2014), and *Mama Medium* (2018), mediums Theresa Caputo, Kim Russo, Rosie Cepero, and Jennie Marie Cancelmi are all Italian Americans with pronounced New York accents. All four are in their thirties-to-forties, with big hair and figures that evoke the maternal. Although being in New York situates them near a major center of media production (and within hailing distance of the historic home of American Spiritualism), this geographical specificity also distinguishes them from the "otherness" of earlier psychics who were identified with the ancient practices of astrology, numerology, Kabbalah, or Eastern mysticism. Caputo's "ordinariness" is proclaimed by her big hair, fake fingernails, chunky jewelry, and short, tight skirts, while Russo wears short leather jackets and pants. When these women communicate with "the other side" or deliver "messages from spirit," like John Edward they maintain their personas, foregoing trance states or speaking with unfamiliar voices. For example, Caputo demonstrates her flamboyance during readings through large gestures, raucous laughter, and exclamations of surprise at her own abilities—aspects of her personality that we see in scenes of her daily, non-psychic life. Visiting Niagara Falls, for example, she stops and introduces herself to a stranger named Angela. Asked whether she has lost a father figure, Angela indicates a bridge in the background and responds, "My grandfather built that bridge." Caputo's jaw drops. "That's why—are you kidding me?! I'm like, 'Who's the father figure?' and I'm staring at the freaking bridge!" When not demonstrating her psychic powers, Theresa Caputo is an average if apprehensive tourist, worried primarily about the effect of the humidity on her hair. "My hair's gonna get all misty," she complains when invited to tour the falls.

The breakout star of one of the longest-running psychic medium shows, Caputo is an example of what Ouellette identifies as reality programming's "quest for interesting and unusual people."[22] Characteristic of the sudden expansion of reality-style programming after 2000, Ouellette argues that this trend "accentuated . . . voyeuristic and sensational elements, especially when

Long Island Medium

real people cast as outside the mainstream of society [were] involved."²³ No matter how unusual those specializing in the paranormal may seem, however, like other reality television personalities, they are called upon to perform "the ordinariness of their own extraordinary subjectivity."²⁴ *Long Island Medium* and *Angels Among Us*, for example, use observational-style footage to situate the women in middle-class homes—one in a suburban neighborhood, the other in a log-cabin-style home in the country. Cepero does psychic readings while cuddling pillows on her front porch or on the sofa in her living room; Caputo's readings take place at her dining room table or in the homes of clients. Readings also erupt spontaneously as the mediums go about their daily lives—grocery shopping, visiting a hair salon, having lunch at a diner. The women drive their own cars (usually SUVs) as they head out to meet clients or attend to family (Caputo drops her daughter off at college, Cepero helps her son move into his first apartment).²⁵

Like Cancelmi and Cepero, Caputo is defined by her position within a family and shown surrounded by family members. In the show's first seasons, she introduces herself with this line: "I like to think of myself as a typical Long Island mom." She even lives next door to her parents. TLC, the channel that produces *Long Island Medium*, specializes in shows that focus on unusual families including members of ethnic enclaves (*Breaking Amish*, *My Big Fat Gypsy Wedding*), families with many children (*Jon and Kate Plus Eight*, *Nineteen Kids and Counting*), or families with special challenges (*Little People Big World*, *The Little Couple*).[26] When the series began in 2011, the title sequence of *Long Island Medium* was filled with connotations of "spookiness" (canted close-ups of funerary monuments, figures glimpsed in a cemetery) as Caputo declared, "I speak to dead people"—paraphrasing the famous tag line from the film *The Sixth Sense*.[27] This unsettling tone, however, was not sustained by the body of the show with its aggressively mundane scenes of everyday life such as Theresa and her husband, Larry, standing in their kitchen discussing daughter Victoria's driving lessons or deciding whether to take the dog to the vet. As with classic reality shows, these observational scenes are interspersed with footage of each member of the family speaking directly to the camera, giving his or her take on this week's issue of contention—usually something family-centered that viewers can identify with, such as Theresa and Larry trying to lose weight.

The psychic-medium's professional work (scheduled appointments with clients) is also de-mystified by being situated in middle-class domestic spaces. Montages of quotidian detail emphasize the mundane quality of the world in which the women operate: the medium or the client driving up to a middle-class house, knocking on the front door, being welcomed into well-lit rooms. (It is usually daytime.) The readings themselves are presented with few trappings and little or no technology. Caputo jots notes in a spiral binder and uses an old cassette recorder to make recordings of each session for her client. (On several occasions, she calls attention to the tape player's outdatedness.) Cepero, Cancelmi, and Russo do without technology altogether. Rosie and Jennie Marie seem to have dropped by for a chat as they snuggle into sofas and gaze at their clients; Russo's clients lead her through their haunted homes as she describes what she senses. Other than Caputo occasionally preparing for a reading by lighting a few candles or "cleansing" the space by spreading sage smoke, anything that might be construed as exotic or esoteric is kept to a minimum.[28]

Women's Work

Not all psychics depicted on paranormal reality TV are women, but all mediums are celebrated for things women are celebrated for: namely, empathy, compassion, sensitivity, willingness to express emotion, and to extend emotional support to others. Because women—whether "sensitive" or not—navigate the same waters mediums do, ambivalence about mediums can resonate with the women who make up a sizable percentage of the television audience. Mediums, for example, are assailed for the things women are assailed for: being ambitious, laying claim to power in terms of financial success or cultural status, or challenging established forms of authority (i.e., male-dominated institutions) and their ideological underpinnings. Reactions are especially negative if they succeed.

The psychic-medium's professional success can be considerable. Unlike the first-person witnesses whose television exposure lasts for a single episode at most, "stars" of their own television series like Caputo, Russo, and the others have found ways to capitalize on fame—i.e., the "free self-promotion" that comes from being featured "on a wide broadcasting platform."[29] Caputo, for instance, has written best-selling books, does personal appearances, appears as a celebrity guest on talk shows, and—like Russo, Cancelmi, and Cepero—has her own television show.[30] Professionalism, however, raises a series of issues that must be carefully negotiated in order to maintain the medium's "ordinary" status, particularly when the medium is a woman.

The professionalism of female psychics is downplayed in these series by having the readings take place in settings traditionally associated with "women's work." None of the psychics is shown as having any accoutrements of professionalism (dedicated office space, paid staff, a desk, etc.) Instead, each woman makes do by adapting what is already defined as "her" space (the kitchen, the dining room) to serve her psychic work.[31] Consequently, the female medium does not require any visible outlay of capital solely for her use. (In an early episode, Caputo hires an assistant to help her with scheduling, but the assistant is not particularly helpful and does not become a regularly featured member of the cast.)[32] Because it does not require special funding, space, or assistance, women's work can be depicted as an extension of domestic life rather than an interruption. When Caputo works outside the home for a large gathering, it is shown to be as much a social occasion as a professional one. In these scenes, the medium is invited (like a guest) to join a group of friends or family members who have already assembled at a restaurant or in someone's home. Both the guest of honor and the entertainment, the medium contributes to the festive atmosphere as if this was a kind of psychic Tupperware party.

When working outside the home, the female medium confronts another problem, one widely assumed to be endemic for women—the guilt of the working mother. An episode of *Life Among the Dead*, a British program shown in the US in 2007, begins with scenes of psychic Lisa Williams playing with her son while her stay-at-home husband rushes her off to work. She says in voice-over, "As a mum, as ever it's always difficult to leave your child in the morning but, y'know, I have to work." Williams's show and its American counterparts present female psychics as subject to the same pressures presumably shared by all working women. With her heavy West Midlands accent and pink hair, Williams stands out from her American counterparts which may account for her show failing to develop a following in the US comparable to the one it had in Britain.

On *Long Island Medium*, the demands of Caputo's psychic work are shown as constantly directing her away from her domestic role. Running through nearly every episode in the show's early seasons is a low simmering dissatisfaction from members of the family when Caputo's performance of her role as wife and mother is interrupted by the demands connected to her psychic abilities. Each family member expresses frustration at Theresa's tendency to turn the most mundane public occasion into an intense spiritual encounter. (The omnipresence of a film crew goes unmentioned.) Whether eating at a chain restaurant or holidaying at Niagara Falls, Theresa disrupts family time by turning her attention to a stranger in order to convey a message from "spirit." For example, Theresa and husband Larry stop to sample some Buffalo wings at a diner. When the waitress comes by, Theresa begins frowning and biting her lip (a sign, she tells us in other episodes, that "spirit" wants her attention). She eventually asks the waitress if she knows a young man who has died. Told it was the brother of her sister's husband, Theresa says quickly, "Call your sister. This is gonna be crazy. Call her." Larry sits silent as Theresa has a moving encounter with the young family when they arrive a short while later. Caputo's teenage children (Victoria and Larry Jr.) are more demonstrative, rolling their eyes and sighing when Mom's focus is pulled away from them by "spirit." While alternately embarrassed and antsy during these spontaneous readings, Caputo's family members nevertheless admit in retrospect (speaking to the camera when they are alone) that her compulsion to communicate is an essential part of her personality, involuntary and therefore uncontrollable. What is left unsaid is that it is also her profession.

Reiterating traditional gender expectations normalizes the figure of the female psychic in politically conservative terms—terms that are challenged by her manifest professional success. It becomes imperative then for the female psychic to redefine her personal success as a form of service to the family. Caputo's financial contribution to her family often takes the form of home improvement as when she has a bathroom remodeled or a pool added to the backyard. At the same time, Theresa is not allowed to dominate. In the series' first eleven seasons, Theresa defers to Larry, consulting him and awaiting his consent before making any major expenditures. Despite the fact that she is presumably the family's main source of financial support (Larry's work is not specified), the show takes steps to uphold a balance of power between husband and wife. Because they respect the contribution each makes to the family's well-being, many spouses pool the money they earn, actively obscuring any disproportion in their respective incomes. The money Theresa makes thus becomes "their" money, just as special episodes set at popular American vacation spots—all made possible by Caputo's job as a television personality—blur the line between Theresa at work and the couple on holiday.

Displays of wealth or conspicuous consumption are carefully controlled so that nothing Theresa and Larry buy changes how they are read in terms of class. They do *not* buy a larger house or move out of their neighborhood, represented in white-picket-fence caricature form in the early seasons' opening titles. When the Caputos travel as part of the show, it is to American destinations such as Las Vegas or Niagara Falls (not Europe) and to popular amusements (not museums). This urge to maintain class identity regardless of economic means holds true for consumer goods. For instance, when Theresa complains in one episode about her father's beat-up old truck parked out on the street, it could be read initially as a class-conscious statement. Instead of hiding it or replacing it with a more expensive model, Theresa and Larry have the truck reconditioned.[33] It is still the same pickup truck, but shinier. When Caputo has the bathroom done, she insists on having black marble everywhere. Designers at the remodeling center demur, suggesting that such a choice is passé (too '80s). Even Larry has doubts. But Caputo insists that she wants what she wants. This is not presented as a claim of cultural authority, but rather as a working-class person's resistance to attempts by others to assert the superiority of their knowledge and/or taste.

The attention paid to the material details of domestic life supports the illusion that the audience has entrée to the character's private life. As a consequence, shows about mediums rarely call attention to the presence of television equipment or crew members. Unlike series about ghost hunters where characters set up cameras and are seen playing an active role in producing each episode's sounds and images, series about psychics only break the fourth wall for the purpose of bolstering the psychic's claims. For instance, on some occasions the medium receives a message from a spirit that is, surprisingly, meant for a camera operator or gaffer instead of the on-screen guest or client.[34] By stepping forward, the crew member risks breaking the illusion of intimacy between viewer and star and, in narrative terms, between medium and client. Doing so, however, confirms both the medium and her message. At other times, the technical demands of television production emerge in response to (and as a sign of) crisis. When Theresa and Larry separate in season twelve, the fact that they are on a television show becomes the overt subject of several episodes. In one, Theresa has an on-camera discussion with the show's producer about the effect the television series might have had on her marriage. "Y'know we discussed it," Caputo explains, "There was a point that I even said to Larry, 'Do you wanna stop doin' the show?'" Ultimately, she absolves television while reaffirming her status as a professional. "It wasn't about my work," she declares. "It was about me. It was about us." Leaving the show, she emphasizes, was "not gonna solve anything."

Ambivalence about Caputo's media work is a persistent theme. In later seasons a number of episodes present Theresa as physically and emotionally vulnerable: enduring a cancer scare, brain scans, and the emotional trauma of divorce.[35] An episode from the thirteenth season, "An Accident on Tour," draws a direct connection between Caputo's work as a TV star/psychic and being subject to physical harm. Stardom and the labor required to sustain it prove dangerous when Theresa hurts her leg stepping off her tour bus. She is only truly safe when she is restored to the status of a dependent. (Responding to the emergency, her mother and father accompany her to the hospital.) Bringing in Caputo's parents after her two children have left home and she and Larry have separated reestablishes her as a member of a family. It was not easy. Caputo points out that it has taken eight years for her mother to agree to appear on the show, joking that it took major surgery to get her there. But even time-honored mother-daughter tensions can be used to reassure viewers that Caputo's life is similar to theirs (even if having one's own tour bus is not).

The fear that female psychics might be seen as being too independent, having too much authority or too much financial success suggests a degree of continuing social anxiety regarding depictions of women with power. *Long Island Medium*, for example, leans on comedy built around hyperfeminine excess: Caputo's oversized hair, fingernails, and jewelry, and (it is implied) oversized personality. We are also made aware of the limits imposed upon her. The entire trip to Niagara Falls is arranged and financed by the producers who have set up a series of surprise readings for people outside Long Island. Caputo is required to do things she is not comfortable with (including ride in a helicopter over the falls)—scenes that make her look comically overwrought.[36] In some ways, Caputo's limitations invite audience identification and sympathy. She is presented as someone who has overcome adversity. (She refers at times to a crippling anxiety disorder that took years to resolve.) In this way, she is comparable to other female TV celebrities, such as Paula Deen (*Paula's Home Cooking*), who overcame agoraphobia before becoming a celebrity chef.[37] The psychological pressures oppressing both had to do with being overwhelmed by gender expectations—being too fearful, delicate, dependent (Caputo), or too much in the home (Deen). Their triumph over psychological adversity, though, is circumscribed by the traditionally feminine arenas in which they are shown to excel, i.e., consoling others (Caputo) and home cooking (Deen).

Like financial power, issues of authority are inflected by gender as well as class. Historically, when women gained political and financial power as mediums, it was offset by attempts to reposition them as passive "channels."[38] In *The Sympathetic Medium*, Jill Galvan argues that nineteenth-century portrayals of female mediums "commonly return to allegedly feminine traits: sensitivity or sympathy," hence the term "a sensitive" for someone said to have psychic abilities.[39] The passivity of historical female psychics was underscored by their entering trances in order to communicate, a "reversion to automatism, or a state of unconsciousness" that removed the woman "intellectually from the path of communication."[40] Even though the modern mediums do not lose consciousness during readings, contemporary women psychics on television also displace themselves from positions of authority by presenting their psychic abilities as something they have no control over. Lisa Williams, for example, announces, "I just say what I hear and see—and I see a lot"—a statement that reveals the double-sided value of her "gift" (i.e., people might resent it when she blurts out things that are socially uncomfortable or inconvenient, but it is not her fault). She is not expressing an opinion; she is "just" describing what is there.

It's a Gift

The term "gift" serves multiple functions in programs dealing with psychic mediums, all of them designed to mitigate criticisms surrounding psychic practitioners. One way it is deployed is to obscure or erase the financial benefits related to those who perform psychic readings. Paranormal reality programs deflect accusations that psychics exploit the grief-stricken for profit by eliminating any discussion of fees being charged for the psychic's time.[41] Although some nineteenth-century mediums "openly mentioned the amounts of money they were being paid for holding séances" in order to indicate how prominent and successful they were, in paranormal reality television there is no discussion of payment. Caputo may declare that she has been hired to do a group reading at a party or on a cruise, but we never see money changing hands.[42]

The assumption that psychics are motivated by financial gain is mitigated repeatedly by scenes showing spontaneous readings (Caputo at the dry cleaner, Cepero at the fire department). Because these events are presented as free, being offered as a gift by the medium who is operating from her own desire and/or compulsion to pass on messages from "the other side," they demonstrate that the psychic has nothing to gain (except for footage of her spontaneous generosity). Situating spontaneous readings as part of a gift economy helps disguise or sideline financial motives.

The message itself is a gift. Hugging a woman she surprised with a reading at Niagara Falls, Caputo closes the session with a familiar line: "You have received a beautiful gift today." The passive construction ("you have received") directs attention away from Caputo as the gift's source. When a woman, interviewed after a reading, thanks "Theresa" and her producers for giving her the chance to be on the show ("I know how many people want to have this opportunity . . . I am so grateful"), Caputo modestly refuses to accept credit, pointing instead to the spirits who came through. "Don't thank me. Thank them."[43] This use of the term "gift" reconfigures the medium as a passive channel, minimizing her agency.

Depicting mediums as instruments of the spirits helps to off-set the psychic's potentially unnerving power. The sudden exposure of someone's private life must be managed so as not to seem intrusive or threatening. It must not come across as a kind of surveillance, where private thoughts cannot be hidden from authority figures. *Long Island Medium* softens the potentially

The psychic as child: *The Haunting of . . . with Kim Russo*

disconcerting nature of her interactions with the public by positioning Caputo in ways that are anti-intellectual and anti-elitist. She is a messenger (a simple go-between) and an equal (a fellow Long Islander, tourist, or customer). It is important to her that this person receives this message from "spirit" but that she has no investment in its contents. The message often does not make sense to her and must be explained by the recipient. What Caputo "knows," therefore, does not make her superior or intimidating. Such self-effacement diminishes the female mediums' potential presumptuousness.

Each time a female psychic positions her work as a service or a gift, she resituates herself in a less-threatening, classically maternal role in which her primary aim is to put the needs of others first, to nurture, and to console. In the opening of *Psychic Intervention*, Kim Russo says, "When people are in trouble and have nowhere left to turn, I help."[44] In *Long Island Medium*'s title sequence, Caputo reports that she "feels compelled to help others." Even when she appears on stage before hundreds of screaming fans, Caputo figures it as a form of service: gathering everyone into one space is the only way she can accommodate all the people who have spent years on her waiting list.[45] In her personal life, the female psychic is (momentarily) justified in turning her attention away from her family by becoming a mother figure for everyone with whom she interacts. In scenes like these, psychic work, like motherhood, becomes another unpaid job done by women presumably out of love. Psychics are also figured as recipients of a "gift"—that of psychic ability. In the title sequences for *Long Island Medium* and *The Haunting of . . .*, the women announce that their abilities have been with them since childhood.

In a voice-over illustrated with vintage photographs, we hear Russo say, "When I was nine, I was visited by the first of many dead people who wanted to communicate with the living through me," as we see old snapshots of an "ordinary" middle-class girlhood: Russo as a child at the zoo or at the beach.[46]

The inception of these abilities in childhood is presented as proof that such abilities are natural, i.e., real (if rare). In this formulation, because it is innate, psychic ability cannot be claimed as an accomplishment, being neither the product of study/practice/application nor the result of active desire on the part of the medium. The female medium did not decide to be psychic, "it just happened," "a child could do it." This lack of agency is reiterated in the title sequence of *Lisa Williams: Life Among the Dead*, where the host tells us (again in voice-over during the title sequence), "When I was a little girl I discovered I had a gift, communicating with those who are no longer with us." Russo, Caputo, and Williams downplay their own conscious, willful pursuit of authority/financial power, while asserting that that authority is beyond question, fundamental *because* it is not willful. Like their nineteenth-century counterparts, they "did not consciously choose to be psychics"—"the spirits chose them."[47] Because their psychic abilities were not consciously adopted, willfully pursued, or developed intentionally, the mediums cannot be gainsaid on those terms. They were never "going after" any of the rewards that have come to them as a consequence of being psychic.

Male mediums also uniformly claim that they became aware of a preexisting psychic ability at a young age. During the title sequence of *Crossing Over with John Edward*, a narrator informs us that "from an early age John Edward displayed remarkable psychic ability." But while Edward's psychic's ability is located in childhood as the women's were, his trajectory is different. "At age fifteen, a reading by a psychic changed his life," we are told, at which point Edward is described as consciously deciding to "develop" his abilities and pursue a career as a psychic. Edward's mediumship is characterized not as a passively received gift but as the product of active pursuit and hard work. In this aspect, Edward is unique.

Some programs bypass references to the onset of psychic "gifts" in childhood in favor of featuring mediums who are quite young. In 2016, two shows debuted that were built around millennials: *Monica the Medium* (Freeform) and *Hollywood Medium with Tyler Henry* (E! Entertainment Television). The first inserts the paranormal into a coming-of-age reality series about a twenty-something who has recently moved away from home. Monica

Ken-Tae is trying to start her career as a professional psychic, meeting clients in their homes and doing spontaneous readings for strangers.[48] Like Monica (though even younger), Tyler Henry is also a resident of sunny Southern California, though, as befits E!, all of his clients are Hollywood celebrities. Also like Monica, Tyler's youthfulness is an essential element of his persona. While Caputo and Cepero drive themselves to see clients, Tyler sits in the passenger seat. We are told that he is nineteen years old, but he is presented as either not old enough to drive or unwilling to learn. Although we never see him at home, his mother frequently drives him to appointments, giving him the opportunity to enact "adolescent behavior" by rolling his eyes to indicate that his mom makes him crazy. At other times, he is escorted by a young woman named Charlie. Older than Tyler but younger than his mother, Charlie also plays a familial role as a kind of big sister/babysitter, again emphasizing Tyler's youth.

Tyler Henry's demeanor is distinctly childlike, a quality that serves Tyler-the-psychic by making him seem disarming and non-threatening. In one episode, he explicitly addresses his resemblance to a famous child actor. With his mop of blond hair and choir-boy looks, he says, "People ask me to do the Macaulay Culkin face all the time." Framing his face with his hands, he opens his mouth and does the wide-eyed stare from the movie *Home Alone* (1990). When he mentions that he has been working as a psychic since he was sixteen, it draws another parallel between him and child actors such as Culkin. Situated in the entertainment industry (based in Los Angeles and accompanied by a woman identified as his manager's assistant), Tyler Henry is installed within an economic network where children may be both rich and famous yet be exploited by adults (including family members) who depend on the children for their own livelihood. In both *Monica the Medium* and *Hollywood Medium with Tyler Henry*, the mediums' authority is offset by their youth. Their attempts to establish a mature identity independent of their parents coincides with their ability to succeed as paranormal professionals.

Ignorance

Given the universal skepticism regarding psychic-mediums, when a psychic "knows" something deeply personal about a client's family history, it raises the suspicion that the psychic's team has done prior research (a so-called

Hollywood Medium with Tyler Henry

"hot" reading). The psychic medium's trustworthiness, therefore, is founded on ignorance. According to Hans Holzer, "there are strict methods and conditions, and when you work in a field that is still on the fringes of recognized science, the more stringent your conditions are, the better."[49] His first rule, he states, is *never* to tell his "sensitive-collaborators" where he is taking them or why. Dozens of times he insists "his" medium "knew nothing at all about the case; she didn't even know the address where we were going"; "I had carefully kept her in the dark about our purpose and destination"; she "was, of course, totally unaware of the story or purpose of our visit."[50] (All the mediums Holzer worked with were women.) Such statements attempt to establish that the information the medium "receives" is due exclusively to a paranormal source. These claims of ignorance have their own spin when made about female psychics.

Like a Victorian bride, the psychic's value depends on her being kept in a state of ignorance. She is often "protected" from contaminating foreknowledge by a male superior (an employer, manager, or her husband)—a model recreated in paranormal shows. For instance, on *Ghosts in My House* (2015), an authoritative, off-screen male voice situates medium Nadine Mercey in relation to a house she is about to visit by telling us she is "going in blind with no previous knowledge of the residents or ghostly incidents."[51] In other programs, a woman (paradoxically) affirms her own ignorance. In multiple episodes of *Long Island Medium*, Caputo declares her lack of prior knowledge regarding clients, stating, "I don't know anything but first name and address." Psychic Lorie Johnson (*Ghosts of Shepherdstown*) declares, "I don't like to know any information ahead of time. Don't tell me anything. That's a no-no to me." Ignorance is redefined as a virtuous act of will.

It is harder to assert that they have "no way of knowing" personal details of the subject's life when the mediums meet guests with previously established public profiles. *The Haunting of . . . with Kim Russo* and *Hollywood Medium with Tyler Henry* are particularly instructive as Russo and Henry's mediumship is constructed exclusively through their readings of entertainment-industry figures in Los Angeles. In Henry's case, while the producers know who he is going to be meeting with (there are scenes shot in the celebrity's home before Tyler arrives), Henry swears he knows nothing in advance. "I insist that I know nothing about my clients beforehand. When I get a celebrity client, they don't book a reading through me. They go through my manager, Ron. Ron will send a text to whoever's driving me and we both go. Neither of us have *any* idea who I'm reading."[52]

Despite the previously shot vignettes of the celebrities introducing themselves, Henry often claims not to have recognized them even after meeting them. For example, Carmen Electra ventures that he might know her from *Baywatch*, though he would have been three years old when the show ceased production in 1999. The episode cuts to Henry admitting, "I know the *name* Carmen Electra. I know she was a model. And that's the extent of what I knew about her," he concludes with a shrug. As a millennial, he is depicted as being blithely out of touch with the previous generation's icons, and he does not care who knows it. Tyler's limited knowledge of his celebrity clients serves to establish that he is not in thrall to celebrities. This places him on a par with them—or as their superior. It is Tyler Henry, after all, who is the star of this show. *Hollywood Medium* has three or four clients per episode which makes Henry the show's connecting thread, just as the constantly renewed challenge to his competence is the repeated source of narrative suspense and pleasure.

Scenes of non-recognition expose the tenuousness of celebrity itself when a person's alleged fame is revealed to be transitory, insubstantial, or even the result of self-delusion. Tyler Henry's guileless demeanor when he claims not to know who someone is allays any sense that he is being flippant or intentionally insulting—an attitude that could drive away future celebrity guests. One of the tensest moments in the first season comes when a distinctly resistant Boy George confronts Tyler directly, asking bluntly, "Do you know who I am?" When a startled Tyler admits that he does not, George surprises him (and the audience) by saying that he is happy not to be recognized.

Instead of an assertion of entitlement, his question was designed to weed out any hint of prior knowledge—to ascertain whether Tyler had prepared for the reading by doing research on someone whose life has been covered extensively by the tabloids.[53] The psychic's ignorance thus reassures not only the audience but the person receiving the reading.

Ghost Therapy

Kim Russo also specializes in celebrity readings, but unlike Henry and Caputo, who communicate with spirits who are loving and supportive (as are the psychics themselves), Russo leads clients along a more tortured path. *The Haunting of . . .* puts a greater emphasis on frightening the audience as Russo and her guest venture into a paranormal world that is literally dark. Unlike many other psychic-based programs, there is a possibility of encountering sinister forces. "Negative energies" are banished from Theresa Caputo's world. "I don't deal with negative Spirit," she states. "If they're around, I barely acknowledge them."[54] Caputo, John Edward, Jennie Marie Cancelmi, Rosie Cepero, Monica Ken-Tae, and Tyler Henry depict the "other side" as a world of family, love, and light; Russo, on the other hand, reintroduces the element of danger. A spin-off of *Celebrity Ghost Stories*, *The Haunting of . . .* deals exclusively with celebrities who describe their encounters with the paranormal as traumatic. Selecting a celebrity guest from the earlier program, *The Haunting of . . .* expands the original 15–20-minute segment to an hour. Each episode validates the guest's account—as well as their fear—until Russo leads them, step by step, toward what could be characterized as "psychic healing." Figuring the medium as both therapist and teacher, *The Haunting of . . .* meets anxiety with empathy and compassion which prove superior to (meta)physical turbulence every time.

The undermining of gendered assumptions that ally sensitivity with women and action with men stands out particularly well in an episode featuring an imposing, muscular young man identified as a mixed martial arts champion. In *The Haunting of Tito Ortiz* (the title completed each week by the name of the episode's guest), the athlete and professional fighter is frightened at the idea of going back to a house where he used to live. "I'm a little scared," he tells the camera while riding in the car. "Actually, a lot scared." Much of *The Haunting of . . .* is made up of reenactments of frightening encounters and

Kim Russo, *The Haunting of... with Kim Russo*

violent deaths. Distorting lenses, smoke, and filters turn actors into apparitions who menace the viewer with harsh words we cannot quite grasp and faces we cannot quite see.

Though horror film tropes make fear a central part of *The Haunting of...*, audience and guest are led past that fear as Russo begins to humanize the ghost. First, she reintroduces the positive side of the paranormal. Talking to Ortiz soon after they have met, she tells him that she sees a spirit accompanying him: "The fellow that came with you, I think he's your other grandfather. He's one of your guides. He watches over you."[55] By focusing on family, she rewrites the spirit world as a place where one can find safety and support. As Russo learns more about how the source of the haunting died (the details of which are verified by title cards and newspaper stories), Ortiz begins to see the ghost as a victim rather than a threat. In the process, the guest releases his or her own feeling of having been victimized. The spirit is redefined as someone who needs our understanding. "He didn't do that to scare you," she explains. "He never got the right closure." It is the spirit who needs Ortiz's help to pass on. "He's stuck," Russo insists. "We need to put him to rest." In the end, the tables have turned. Under Russo's guidance, Ortiz realizes that, rather than being the victim of evil forces, he is uniquely empowered to bring peace to a troubled spirit. Together Russo and Ortiz help the spirit "move to a higher plane" as they set about securing "him a house in the sky." Like most episodes of *The Haunting of...*, this one ends with Russo and the guest testifying that the location feels lighter and happier. Kim congratulates Ortiz on the "good deed that you did" in helping a troubled spirit "go to his loving home." The altruism of Ortiz's act is underscored by the fact that he is, in effect, helping a stranger. (The "scary" ghosts are usually attached to the location and not personally connected to the guests.) Through her guidance, the celebrity-victims are taught a new way of interpreting the past, healing themselves by joining the psychic in an act of healing.

Although a classic ghost story complete with haunted houses, each episode of *The Haunting of . . .* depends on the assumption that fear, like grief, is the result of a misunderstanding. Death is not a permanent severing from loved ones, nor should it be a source of fear. As an expert who has been brought in (presumably by the show's producers) in order to help a celebrity, Russo's psychic work is depicted as professional, therapeutic, and altruistic—an act of compassion for the living and the dead.[56]

As it does with ghost-hunting shows, paranormal reality television takes subjects that could be deeply unsettling and finds a way to make them safe. Under the psychic's guidance, what had been terrifying no longer seems so bad. Persuaded that the dead are always with us—a permanent spiritual presence—the grief-stricken become reconciled. It is not, however, the repudiation of death-as-absolute that forms the foundation of the television psychic's appeal. That rests on something obvious for which the paranormal is merely a pretext.

Every episode of every series centered on a psychic outlines the development of a relationship, the formation of a bond that enables people to come to grips with trauma. Accomplishing the therapeutic work of grief counseling, the psychic succeeds when s/he makes the grief-stricken client feel better (something enacted multiple times per episode). As the loss is assuaged, the psychics persuade the grievers that they have permission to move on. For viewers, repeatedly seeing suffering people released from grief (if only momentarily) allows those who believe in the paranormal to be reassured; skeptics wary of exploitation may be disarmed by the knowledge that placebos do no harm and, through the recipient's belief, may be beneficial. The encounter between medium and client, no matter how brief, is declared to have lasting value.[57] Tina, for example, who has lost her daughter, knows that her experience meeting Theresa Caputo is going to "stay with me for a very long time." "It's a sense of relief, y'know," another man says, "like it's given me peace of mind." A friend confirms it: "I definitely think this was life-changing." Little wonder that these sessions often end with tears and a hug.

Whether motherly (Caputo, Cepero, Cancelmi, Russo) or youthful and childlike (Monica Ken-Tae, Tyler Henry), the psychics of paranormal television make themselves available to those in pain. They are good listeners, hearing what others cannot, as they attend to clients who feel that their pain has not been recognized or adequately addressed. As the clients validate the psychic's powers ("that's my grandfather!"), she validates them, their feelings, and, more important, the people they have lost. An appearance on *Long Island Medium* is an opportunity to create a lasting, nationally broadcast testimonial, transforming private grief into a public tribute. Photographs and videos of people who have died are provided as survivors relate how special their loved ones were and the lasting impact their lives will have (evidenced by everything from memorial tattoos to children).

If the question of the "ordinariness" and "authenticity" of the psychic cannot be fully laid to rest, the same cannot be said for the people she encounters. Mediums are shown to "spontaneously" reach out to people whose humanity is routinely overlooked—another aspect of these series' appeal that is only tangentially connected to the paranormal. The people Caputo surprises, for example, are usually people who interact with the public for a living. Working behind a counter, in a hair salon, or waitressing, they are used to being spoken to on a superficial level without really being seen. Caputo interrupts the transactional nature of otherwise everyday encounters by rewriting the "waitress" or "repairman" as a complex individual with a personal history, someone who has had close relationships and deep emotional bonds.[58]

At the same time, it must be noted that although people in service jobs are established as individuals having psychological depth, such qualities are granted them by virtue of their having been selected by Theresa-the-TV-personality. Dignity is conferred *on* them, not asserted *by* them. Their individuality is allowed to the extent that it fulfills the purposes of the show— primarily, reiterating that the star of the series is "extraordinary," a celebrity, and a representative of the power of television. Such encounters mirror the imaginary one between television celebrity and viewer. The idea that you, too, could meet a celebrity who would quickly show an intense interest in your personal life became explicit in *Long Island Medium*'s "Knock and Shock" episodes. (Viewers register for the chance of a reading with Theresa who surprises the winner by arriving at their front door during a special "live" episode.) Nevertheless, by inviting the people she encounters to step forward *as* individuals, as more than the jobs they perform, Caputo and her camera crew guarantee that their love, pain, losses, and connections to others will be recognized. The rarity of such acknowledgment is evinced by their surprise when she makes it clear that—at the deepest level—they have been seen.

Psychic Detectives

Just the Facts, Ma'am

Not everyone can be comforted so easily. There are situations when the circumstances of a loved one's death are so disturbing they eclipse even the most positive psychic's ability to console the living or make things right by helping the spirit to "move on." Sudden violent deaths, whether due to accident or murder, are profoundly disturbing for the victim's survivors. By suggesting that existing institutions (religious, medical, judicial) have failed the people who need them, another kind of paranormal reality series presents psychics less as reassuring figures and more as people willing to subvert the status quo.

On *Psychic Detectives*, psychics achieve justice by supplying the empathy and intuition missing from an evidence-based, male-dominated criminal justice system.[59] In production for five seasons (2004–2008), *Psychic Detectives* adheres to a formula established by reality-based crime shows like *Forensic Files* (over 400 episodes since 1996). In both, the police call on experts to assist them after standard investigative techniques have reached a dead end. Although male psychics are consulted occasionally, most of the mediums featured on *Psychic Detectives* are women.[60]

Each episode of *Psychic Detectives* is a kind of fantasy in which the scope and value of a woman's knowledge is (finally) acknowledged. The story begins with men failing. Bitterly aware of their own inadequacy, these hard-bitten, practical men turn to psychics in desperation. (Female members of the police force rarely appear.) Intensely skeptical, the men come to realize that what the women have to offer is exactly what was missing from their scientific approach. This leaves them amazed and indebted. The women, meanwhile, are modest but forthright, confident of their own powers. Like Agatha Christie's

Miss Marple or television's Jessica Fletcher (*Murder, She Wrote*), these female amateurs effortlessly outshine the empirically oriented male professionals.

The women in this series bring something to television that is rarer than psychic ability: like their fictional forbears, they are all visibly middle-aged or older.[61] As such, they belong to an historically maligned group. Denigrated as hags or crones, older women throughout the centuries could find themselves defined as outcasts. Sometimes widowed and no longer raising children, older women could be construed as a potentially destabilizing force within societies that had no role for single women, especially women who had a degree of independence, having outlived traditional family obligations. This led, in Europe and America, to periodic witch-hunts in which the disproportionate number of those accused and executed were women over the age of forty.[62] In contemporary culture, women this age are more frequently simply overlooked, ignored, or urged to try extreme methods to sustain a youthful appearance. The women on *Psychic Detectives*, on the other hand, proudly sport wrinkled skin or gray hair and use minimal or no make-up. Some even wear glasses. They demonstrate a liberating disregard for fashion, their clothes, and hair, emphasizing ease-of-maintenance. Those who do sport more elaborate coiffures maintain an unapologetic loyalty to outmoded styles. Their bodies, rounder and heavier than those featured in most television programs, are draped in serviceable but "nice" department-store separates, i.e., what a middle-class grandmother might wear to church.

Unlike the domestic setting where much of *Long Island Medium* takes place, the psychic detective's home is at most a backdrop for her current-day testimony. Just enough is shown of these studiedly nondescript spaces to establish them as ordinary, middle-class, "lived-in," and explicitly bare of anything that might signify the paranormal or occult-related paraphernalia (zodiac charts, Ouija boards, crystal balls, etc.). More important, we do not see the psychic's husband or children. The female psychic detective claims her home, status, experience, and wisdom solely on her own authority. An episode featuring psychic Carol Pate illustrates this pattern.

Beginning with a 911 call, "While You Were Sleeping" recounts what happened when the police discovered the body of a man who had been shot in the head. As the investigation proceeds, various members of the department explain police procedure, using technical terminology to establish their expertise. For example, when they find a cartridge, they know on sight that it held "a 158 grain, round-nose lead bullet, thirty-eight caliber." But,

Carol Pate, *Psychic Detectives*

the ubiquitous male narrator explains, there is only so much the police can do. "With no clues, no motives, and no suspects, the investigation grinds to a halt." "Desperate for answers," the detectives contact psychic Carol Pate.

An experienced psychic consultant, Pate has a firm sense of her own ability. Addressing the camera, she tells us she was recommended by another detective who "knew that I was very good at what I do." Sgt. T. J. Farley, however, needs proof. Bemused, Pate recalls their first meeting. "T. J. decided he was gonna test me which was fine 'cause I was used to that." When she picks the murderer out of a series of six photographs laid face down on a table, Farley is stunned. "I sat there and I said, 'I don't believe this.'"[63] Remembering the moment, Pate magnanimously allows for his surprise. "You don't believe people can do this stuff," she notes. "Nobody does. And then when you do it, it's like their whole paradigm just goes—boom." Taken to the scene of the crime, Pate "sees" more of what happened: "I got more pieces of the puzzle." Her visions revive the investigation, leading the police to new evidence that results in an arrest and a conviction. The episode ends with the obligatory endorsement from former skeptics. "I would recommend her to any agency," Sgt. Farley swears. "Do it. I'd laugh at you if you didn't."

The power of these testimonials depends on our recognizing just how desperate the police would have to be before they would consult a psychic and/or woman. Farley's partner, Sgt. "Buddy" Miles, admits that consulting Pate only happened because "we were pretty well out of directions to go. After you've done about everything you can do and you're sitting there stalemated, anything'll help." In another episode, Detective Kenny Kirkland also uses desperation to justify his change of heart. "I did not believe that a psychic could help us in any way and it was kind of hokey. But anytime that you have a crime and you've exhausted all the evidence, you look to other sources."[64]

Psychic Detectives

As with any information provided by psychics, validation is in the details. At his first meeting with Carol Pate, Kirkland confirms that the details she described were "exactly what witnesses had told us."

Psychic Detectives tries to balance two ways of knowing: the intuitive work of "sensitives" and the practical logic of armed men who represent the state. On one hand, these episodes seek to bolster the women's status by associating them with the police. In "Psychic Warning," we are told that Carol Pate has helped "law enforcement agents find answers to baffling questions." Psychic Noreen Reiner has "worked with police on some four hundred cases. She's even lectured at the FBI academy."[65] Psychic skills seem nebulous by comparison. Trying to describe how she knows what she knows, Renier says, "I'll see a flash of this, a flash of that. It's not like our reality. Sometimes I don't see anything, just words come out."[66] Carol Pate relies on a technical analogy. "I use what's known as psychometry," she explains. "I fine tune my frequency to the frequency that I'm touching."[67] When the police give her the victim's shirt in the episode "While You Were Sleeping," she reiterates that what she feels while holding an object is comparable to "tuning a radio station or a television station. And once I've hit that signature frequency, then I know all about the person."

Because their approach is more empathetic, the psychics identify with the (often female) victims, vicariously experiencing the violence they suffered. In "Prior Engagment," Renier tells Detective Collins, "I'm getting very strong images, very violent images.... Someone or something has hit her. I feel my head snapping back.... My head, my face." The seamless transition from "her" to "I" and "my" shows the fluidity with which the psychic's perspective shifts between her own identity and the other woman's. In another episode, Renier channels the mental disorientation and physical symptoms of a woman who has gone missing. "I'm hurting," she reports, "My chest—I'm hurting. I can't breathe."⁶⁸ In "The Flower Girl," Carol Pate seesaws back and forth, from observing the scene at a distance to reliving the victim's last moments. "He's dragging her through the woods.... She's struggling, fighting for her life." "I was her," Pate insists. "I was seeing what she was seeing."

Sometimes female psychics are shown to be emotionally and even physically overwhelmed by their visions of violence and death. In *Ghosts in My House* (2015), for example, psychic medium Nadine Mercey is called in to validate a family's suspicion that their house is haunted. Distinguished from female psychics like Caputo and Russo by her intense physicality, Mercey's psychic insights are expressed through her body.⁶⁹ As she walks through a haunted house in "Ghostly Vengeance," she reports, "I'm getting shaky." The intensity increases: "OK, now I've got a pain in my stomach." "My heart's really pounding in this room," she says. "I don't feel good in here at all. It's making me sick." Ultimately Mercey realizes that she is psychically reliving what a young woman went through when she was raped and murdered nearby. Mercey calls off the session and flees the location in tears. "I can't take this," she cries. "Get me out of here. I want to go. Oh my God, so much pain." Though her psychic exploration does not lead to identifying the murderer, Mercey validates the victim's suffering and makes vivid the violence done to women and its lingering effects.

Although the narrator tells us that psychics have "help[ed] investigators solve their most baffling mysteries," the mediums at times adopt socially appropriate feminine modesty by minimizing their own contributions. Like the psychics discussed above, their "gifts" came to them unbidden in childhood. As the narrator informs us, "visions of the unknown have been haunting" Carol Pate "since she was a little girl."⁷⁰ Pate depicts her position as one of helplessness. "It was very, very difficult, and there was no one there to explain it to me. No one." Reclaiming control of her life, Pate "learned to put her skills to use." In the process, she has "helped hundreds of families," reaping praise and validation from conservative social institutions like the police. At the same time, Pate downplays her contributions, saying, "I don't have the facilities or the means or ways of solving a case, but I can give the police a way to go, a place to look, an area or an avenue that they did not know exists."⁷¹ Although the narrator in "Prior Engagement" tells us that "Renier's visions were accurate," Renier credits the police with cracking the case." "The police solve crimes," she states. "I'm just an investigative tool like any other tool they would use in their investigations." The families of victims disagree. Taking "matters into their own hands," they "reach out to a psychic."[72] Television plays its part as the daughter of a missing woman contacts Noreen Renier after seeing her on an episode of *Psychic Detectives*.[73] When her mother's body is discovered months later, she knows who to thank. "It's totally to Noreen's credit that they found her." Openly taking sides, she declares her loss of confidence in the social institutions that have let her family down.

Each episode of *Psychic Detectives* constructs a narrative designed to contradict detractors like John Oliver who denounce would-be crime solving psychics as vultures and parasites. The psychics' alternate ways of knowing produce practical results for which the women claim a justifiable pride. Jeanne Borgen remembers the day she heard that a killer she had identified psychically had been arrested: "That was probably one of the greatest days of my life."[74] All modesty aside, Noreen Renier asserts, "I don't need a police report.... My mind is my tool." Where detectives pay tribute in stereotypically manly language (Pate "was dead-on on things she told us," Kirkland reports), Pate sums things up simply. "I knew I needed to come here and wrap it up. And that's what I did."

On paranormal reality television, mediums domesticate metaphysical questions about life after death. They comfort the grieving by releasing them from guilt (over what they might have done or said) and reassure the haunted by calming their fears (persuading them that spirits exist to help us or because they need our help). Above all, mediums acknowledge the centrality of emotional connections. When mediums are women, however, possessing extraordinary abilities poses a challenge to traditional definitions of gender. To counter the potential transgressive power of female mediums, shows like *Long Island Medium* reinforce the psychic's identity as a wife and mother, insisting that her abilities primarily enable her to serve others. Fundamentally conservative, such programs require women to disavow ambition and depict themselves as flighty, childlike, or willfully ignorant. Older women, acting on their own with the wisdom they have earned over time, stand up to male-dominated institutions, exposing the flaws in a results-driven masculine culture that stresses stoicism over expressions of empathy. But, as we will see, even when failed institutions have been abandoned they can continue to haunt.

4

Confronting Evil
A Short Trip to the Dark Side

If there is one area where "sensitive" psychic-mediums and technology-wielding teams agree, it is on the paranormal's potential destructive power.[1] In paranormal programs it is relatively easy for participants to adapt themselves to the idea of ghosts. Ghosts are recognizably people (who were) like us, with faces, bodies, names, and histories. They can be welcomed (the loved ones who send messages through Theresa Caputo or Tyler Henry) or demystified and then sent into the light (à la Kim Russo). Occasionally, though, mediums and ghost hunters encounter things they can barely describe. Subsumed into the overarching category of "evil," "negative entities" cannot be explained by the familiar psychology applied to ghosts such as the desire to communicate a trauma (e.g., that they were murdered) or a lasting attachment to a person or a place. Existing solely to torment and destroy, the diverse array of "dark forces" pose specific challenges on paranormal reality programs. Addressing evil allows a series to ratchet up the intensity, increasing the stakes of the drama by going beyond matters of life and death into the realm of possession, the satanic, and hell itself. But encounters with evil also threaten to reveal the inadequacy of television's paranormal professionals as they are forced to step aside, ceding control momentarily to specialists. Facing down a nemesis that can never be conclusively defeated, everyone on paranormal reality TV agrees on one thing: confronting evil is not for amateurs.

Exorcising a demon, Cathedral of Orvieto, circa 1357–1363

Don't Try This at Home

"What happens when the untrained dabble with the other world? Do they unleash forces they can't control?" Host Lawrence Chau poses these suggestive questions at the beginning of "Play with the Occult, Pay the Price," a 2011 episode of *Ghostly Encounters* that makes explicit the perils of amateur attempts to contact spirits.[2] A middle-aged woman named Sharon Hayward explains how evil entered her life when she dabbled with the paranormal—in her case, by "playing" with a Ouija board. At first, she recounts, the sessions seemed harmless. "We thought it was fun, y'know? It was a game." It also made her feel powerful "right from the beginning." Now she realizes that it actually revealed a fatal weakness in her character. "Like a narcissist, it just made me the center of attention and I think that was the lure really, is what it was." What is worse, Sharon has unwittingly unleashed evil on her family. Finding a paranormal tempest in her child's room one day (drawers opening and closing, the crib shaking), she realized "there was something evil going on" and vowed to stop toying with the supernatural. "I never should've gotten involved in all this stuff." With the Ouija board as her emblem of evil, Sharon situates the paranormal within an explicitly religious context: "I didn't want that kind of life. I wanted to be a good Christian." She calls in her pastor who has her collect everything in her house connected to the occult and burn it in the front yard. Now she states, "I won't go in a house that has a Ouija board in it."

Professional psychic Theresa Caputo agrees. "You couldn't pay me to touch a Ouija board," she writes.[3] "With these devices, you can call in whatever Spirit and energy is out there and available, and there's a good chance you'll channel an energy that will be sneaky and not benefit you in any way. You do not want these souls in your life."[4] Like most paranormal TV psychics, Caputo is a "positive" medium who refuses to engage with "dark entities," though she acknowledges their existence. "I don't see negative Spirit," she insists, and tries "to avoid them at all costs." Blocking out anything potentially disturbing, she explains, "I never even get negative information during readings. Only good things, that's all I want."[5] In case she has not been clear, Caputo reiterates, "If I've said it once, I'll say it a million more times: *no Ouija boards*."[6]

Caputo is not alone in her blanket rejection of the do-it-yourself, pseudo-séance device. Designed, patented and trademarked in Baltimore in 1891, the Ouija board has long been the subject of controversy, especially as its popularity began to soar in the 1920s. In his 1924 book about working with mediums, Carl Wickland, MD, declares that he is personally familiar with numerous examples of the "disastrous results which followed the use of the supposedly innocent Ouija board."[7] In his exposé of fraudulent Spiritualists the same year, Harry Houdini (for whom the terms "fraud" and "Spiritualist" were synonymous) lists case after case. "In March, 1920, it was reported in the papers that the craze for Ouija boards . . . had reached such a pitch in the little village of Carrito, across San Francisco Bay, that five people had been driven mad."[8] While such stories smack of newspaper sensationalism, Houdini backs them up with reports by high-powered medical professionals like "Dr. Curry, Medical Director of the State Insane Asylum of New Jersey," who "issued a warning concerning the "Ouija-board" in which he said: 'The 'Ouija-board' is especially serious because it is adopted mainly by persons of high-strung neurotic tendency who become victims of actual illusions of sight, hearing and touch at Spiritualistic séances.'" Houdini predicted that "the insane asylums would be flooded with patients if popular taste did not swing to more wholesome diversions."[9]

One hundred years later, twenty-first-century paranormal reality television programs present similar cautionary tales. Multiple episodes from first-person programs feature young people who come to regret playing with the spirit world as if it were a board game. In *Paranormal Witness*, "From H.E.L.L."(2016), "life turns hellish for three young girls" who "break the rules when playing with a Ouija board." On *A Haunting*, "Dangerous Games," three siblings play with a spirit board and let good and bad spirits into their home.[10] On *Paranormal Survivor*, "Beasts from the Beyond" (2013), a teenage session with a Ouija board exposes a woman to years of paranormal persecution as an adult. As host Jonette Bekovic warns on the religious program *Women of Grace*, "so many people do not realize the danger that there is in occult activity. . . . They develop a type of insatiable curiosity about it, maybe a morbid curiosity, and it can lead us into terrible things."[11]

Employing the board for occult purposes is not the only thing that exposes the user to evil: the board itself can be hazardous. In an episode of *Haunted Collector*, team members find a broken Ouija board in an attic. They call leader John Zaffis who orders them not to touch it. If a board has an entity attached to it, he explains, when the board is broken it could "release a lot of energy." (His instructions come too late; the team members have already picked up the pieces and examined them.) Emphasizing the dangers that could result from an untutored person's interaction with occult paraphernalia contributes to a fear-filled atmosphere (central to horror as a genre). It also gives paranormal professionals an opportunity to promote their own expertise. Not only are they more informed about the proper care and handling of such items, but, as experienced professionals, they know who to call. After consulting with a woman who specializes in Ouija board arcana, John removes the damaged artifact to his museum of haunted objects and encloses it in glass, "nullifying its energy with sea salt."[12]

Caputo is equally adept at handling the dangers of a Ouija board, though her display of professionalism is balanced against her show's taste for comic excess. When Theresa's daughter Victoria brings her a Ouija board as a gag gift, Theresa cries out, "Ew! What are you *doin'* with that?! . . . What is wrong with you?!" Without touching it, she pushes the board off the counter and onto the floor. Dousing Victoria with spirit-cleansing sage smoke, Caputo announces, "I'm gonna be saging for days over this. . . . You can never have too much sage." Once the board is taken outside and burned, Theresa gives Victoria a "clear quartz crystal" for protection, explaining that it "absorbs all negative energy, negative emotion," and any other sinister things the board might have stirred up. Distinctly unimpressed by either the danger or the efficacy of spirit-infused objects, Victoria later confides to the camera, "What the hell am I gonna do with a rock?"

While Zaffis and Caputo neutralize the Ouija board's menacing properties with objects of positive spiritual value (crystals, sage, spirit-nullifying salt), a special *Women of Grace* series on the occult titled "Things that Go Bump in the Night" recommends nothing less than a complete purge.[13] It turns out that protecting yourself from evil spirits is simply a matter of cleaning house. First, remove anything connected to the "occult, witchcraft, or a medium." Symbolic jewelry should be jettisoned immediately, as well as anything bearing the signs of the zodiac or associated with divination such as tarot cards.[14] If evil *has* gotten into your house, it is probably your fault. Co-host Sue Brinkmann explains that if a house is cursed or infested with a demonic presence, "eight times out of ten . . . somebody inside that house was doing something involved in the occult. They're doing séances in the house. They're playing games that have some sort of a satanic theme to them, like Ouija boards."

Ghost-hunting teams can be just as explicit when exhorting viewers about the perils of trying to contact spirits on their own. In the *Ghost Adventures* episode "Zozo Demon" (2014), Zak Bagans states: "Ladies and gentlemen, I want to use this investigation to show you that conjuring up demons on a Ouija board is something we would never suggest."[15] (For most of the episode, the team uses generic terms such as "spirit board" in place of "Ouija board," presumably because of copyright issues.) The case in point deals with a man who "used a spirit talking board." "What came through this board has tormented his life." Step by step, we learn the consequences of his rash act. The demon he contacted is called "Zozo" because it makes the Ouija board's planchette zigzag violently from Z to O. Wherever the "Zozo demon" appears, people are said to be persecuted by dark thoughts.[16] The man who "unleashed" the Zozo demon by contacting it "through a spirit board" felt afterward that he was being "raped repeatedly." Having heard about the "severe physical and psychological damage" the demon can inflict, the team members begin to experience negative effects themselves. Zak reports the next day that he has had awful nightmares. Dreaming that he was possessed by a brutal entity, he "can't even say what I was doing to people." Later, teammate Nick Groff begins to sense a sexual menace while taking part in a session on the spirit board. Afraid of being violated, he calls out, "Zak! I feel like something just—basically, just entered my body." (This is Groff's last episode on *Ghost Adventures*.)[17] Shaken and unable to handle the demonic on their own, the team calls in a specialist, a man they identify as "the world's foremost expert on spirit boards." The expert, Robert Murch, downplays the risk of engaging with a Ouija board, suggesting reasonably that when people approach the board with fear they are likely to find fearful things in return. But, as the Zozo demon proves, the greatest danger from Ouija boards is what direct, unsupervised contact/communication with the paranormal might lead to.

Anyone for Demonology?

At the top of the demonic hierarchy is the Devil, the personification of evil. On paranormal television, anything demonic pushes the limits of representation. Often, negative, nonhuman spirits communicating through the Ouija board are left to the imagination. Sometimes classical imagery is used to show the audience what a demon looks like (e.g., seventeenth-century etchings of men with horns, cloven hooves, and tails), though such figures are less impressive when transplanted to a contemporary setting. When Beverly

Devil as a goat-headed man, *Demon House*

Johnson on *Celebrity Ghost Stories* looks in the bathroom mirror and sees "a dark presence," horror conventions require that we see something standing behind her. Unfortunately, the figure we glimpse is clearly just a man in face paint. When a demon crawls onto the ceiling of Susan Flores's room in *Ghostly Encounter*'s "Refuge in Rosaries" ("a dark figure, like a devil"), it is someone in a head-to-toe leotard similar to the ones worn by the acrobatic aliens in Méliès's *A Trip to the Moon* (1902). On *Haunted Case Files*, the Devil is simply a person wearing a goat's head pacing back and forth on a haunted television screen.[18] As in most horror films, the "monster" is disappointing if you see it too clearly.

It is equally difficult to represent demons through sound, especially when they are characterized as literally unspeakable. Saying their names amounts to a summoning (i.e., "speak of the devil.") On a special two-part episode of *Paranormal State*, Ryan Buell tells a medium that a certain name has been stuck in his head for weeks ("The Name" and "The Devil in Syracuse," 2007). She writes down what she senses he is thinking and he nods. Showing the note to another team member, Ryan cautions her, "Don't say it." They meet a client later who says the name repeatedly and Ryan explains to him, "Just for the record, it's not good to say the name you heard out loud." Even though the name is erased from the soundtrack, each time it is aurally absent we see vivid graphics rapidly spelling it out, one large red letter at a time.

A similar technique is used on *Ghost Adventures* when the team visits a former cement plant in Utah that has been turned into a kind of occult-themed amusement park ("Fear Factory" [2014]).[19] Hearing rumors that black masses have taken place at "The Hell Silo," the team is shown an "actual satanic bible" (a book containing satanic rituals) said to have been found at the site. When a young attendant agrees to read aloud from the book, the soundtrack cuts out and large red letters cover the image: "WARNING EXPLICIT CONTENT." Zak tells us in voice-over that even hearing the words is potentially harmful so they will be replaced by a long steady tone for the viewers' sake.

In these narratives, once a demon has been summoned (intentionally or not), the danger quickly escalates. Investigators and interviewees report that something has followed them home or attached itself to them. In the worst cases, they are physically and mentally taken over, "possessed." At this point, there is only one thing left to do: call in an exorcist.

Exorcism (the official term for expelling a demon) crops up across the paranormal reality television spectrum. *Paranormal Witness* alone features exorcisms in episodes such as "The Long Island Terror" (2013), "The Molech" (2014), and "The Fireplace" (2015). *Demon Exorcist* (2011), an hour-long documentary originally produced for Animal Planet, is structured like a pilot for a series. In a by-now-familiar move, the central character "Dwayne Claud, Demonologist" is both a specialist and an ordinary guy. The first half-hour tells the story of how Claud came to be in this line of work ("Case: The Black Shadow, Chester, Virginia"). Unable to help his own family when their home became infested with hostile spirits, he was forced to call in a demonologist. During the year it took to rid the house of its malignant visitors, Claud was able to observe and learn until he felt qualified to go out on his own as a professional exorcist. A conversion story where a skeptic learns the hard way that the paranormal exists, this biographical sketch also reiterates the pattern of the man of the house reduced to helplessness in front of his children; an "average" homeowner confronting overwhelming forces; and the chance to reclaim control by moving from ignorance to expertise. As with mediums or paranormal investigators, exorcist Dwayne Claud straddles a line between amateur and expert, his skills gained informally, outside the purview of accredited institutions connected with either church or state.

The *Paranormal Witness* episode "The Exorcist" (2013) explores the explicitly religious beliefs underpinning exorcisms, featuring a priest who is the official, Vatican-certified exorcist for the Roman Catholic archdiocese of Indianapolis. Simultaneously sensational and prosaic, "The Exorcist" depicts the most extreme cases of demonic possession while normalizing those authorized to cure it. Resembling actor/comedian Bob Newhart with his quiet demeanor, round face, and studiously blank, somewhat mystified expression, Father Vince Lampert remains as bland as his decidedly un-exotic Midwestern home base. He remembers when his bishop first asked him to assume the role of exorcist in 2003. "I could not believe those words came out of his mouth," he recounts. "To be honest, I never realized that exorcists actually even existed." Accepting the job, he is sent to Rome for training by the "Vatican's most learned and experienced exorcist."[20] (Cue piercing choral music as we see the dome of St. Peter's standing stark against a dark sky filled with ominous clouds.)[21] Once Lampert has completed his initiation into the Church's rites and ceremonies for expelling demons, the rest of the episode is made up of the by-now familiar dramatizations of people possessed by the Devil (e.g., violent thrashing, speaking in tongues, growling with voices that have been electronically altered, etc.).

The most extreme example of evil, demonic possession would seem to be the ultimate challenge that paranormal reality programs could offer, with exorcism the greatest victory. Attempts to build entire series around this subject, however, have had limited success. In 2008, the producers of *Ghost Hunters* thought they had a sure winner with a program called *The Real Exorcist*. "When we went into this," production company executive Gretchen Stockdale recounts, "we thought people would come to it in droves."[22] The series lasted three episodes. Other attempts had equally abbreviated runs. Destination America's *The Demon Files* (2015), centered on an ex-New York City-cop-turned-exorcist, ran for three episodes.[23] *I Was Possessed* (Lifetime Movie Network, 2015), promising two exorcisms per episode, lasted six. Asked why *The Real Exorcist* failed, Stockdale offered several possibilities. "I think it was, at the time—still to this day—maybe a little bit too religious. . . . It was scary. Advertisers may have not really liked it." While there might be "a niche audience for that sort of thing" (perhaps "the fundamental religious folks"), such material "gets rejected by the majority." "The idea that there really is a devil that exists is really hard for people to swallow," she ventures. "What are you gonna do with that? . . . It's a very scary thought."

In a bid to increase their appeal to a wider audience, some programs dealing with possession have denied the paranormal altogether, substituting a secular/medical explanation in place of a theological one. An episode of *Paranormal State* expresses doubts about a client's claim of being possessed, suggesting that she might be suffering from a mental illness. In "The Devil in Syracuse" (2007), a young woman, freed from possession in an earlier episode, seems to be courting possession again. When Ryan and his team hear the demonic presence has returned to torment her, they drop everything and go. Noting how socially isolated the young woman is (living with her parents in a rural area), the paranormal experts recognize that, despite the physical suffering it causes her, being possessed allows her to bask in the attention of a wide array of investigators. At the same time, they do not dismiss her need for attention as "merely" that. Rather than pathologizing her claims of spiritual subjugation, *Paranormal State* meets the woman on her own terms and arranges another exorcism. Afterward, they gently point out that her physical suffering has an emotional pay-off and recommend long-term counselling as a defense against future attacks. (Whether that counselor should be a priest or psychologist is left open. The main point is that she will have someone to talk to.) By leaving the matter open to scientific as well as theological interpretation, episodes such as this one invite audiences to insert the disturbing concept of demonic possession into whichever paradigm they are more comfortable with.

Even the most orthodox churchgoers can opt for a medical diagnosis in place of a metaphysical cause. Although the hosts of *Women of Grace* believe that "the devil is a person . . . that truly exists," and that he can "infiltrate everyone's individual psychology" and undermine their "moral balance," when it comes to the issue of demonic possession they are quick to point out that "of course, you have to rule out psychiatric problems with all this."[24] A proper exorcist, they assure us, works from a firm foundation in medical science: "The Church always insists on that."

Despair

Entering its eleventh season, *The Dead Files* has succeeded despite routinely dealing with some of the darkest and most negative spirits on paranormal reality television. Although the show sidesteps the extreme case of "demonic possession," what psychic Amy Allan encounters often cannot be defined: "It's not an animal. It's not human. This is very, very dark."[25] A random sample of such beings includes "a monster that looked like when tar is bubbling," "this black fuzz coming up onto the bed . . . surrounding the person that's closest to the window, engulfing them," a giant, looming female figure with long spiky hands and hair and the face of an alien, as well as "little creature things" that "scurry" across the floor and appear to people in the shape of "a child-sized black mist."[26] Even ghosts can pose a threat; as Amy tells one client, "a lot of the dead are extremely angry."[27] Having encountered demons, shadow figures, spirits summoned by voodoo curses, and other nonhuman "things," Allan often ends the program by advising people to flee their homes. The forces of evil, she explains, are too strong.

While the result may be the same as those depicted in the first-person programs where the paranormal forces people to abandon their dream houses, the effect is different. In those series, the audience is led to identify with families driven out of their homes; on *The Dead Files*, we identify with the experts (Allan and her partner Steve DiSchiavi) who tell people to leave. A woman who has been having unexplained health problems is warned, "It's not really safe for you to be here right now."[28] Amy tells another woman who hopes to turn a former school into a museum, "This cannot become what you want. It's far too dangerous."[29]

To soften the impact of the nonstop bad news that characterized the program's surprisingly bleak first season, later seasons feature Allan (at times reluctantly) telling families that it might be possible for them to stay in their homes if they follow a strict regimen of spiritual cleansing. Often this requires an elaborate process involving several steps and multiple consultants. Some of the experts Allan has recommended to shell-shocked clients are mediums who can guide spirits to the other side (such as "a male medium who is tough" or one who specializes in "counseling" and "healing"); a "Reiki master"; "a chaos magician"; people familiar with different spiritual traditions such as voodoo or Native American religions; and, of course, a priest "to bless the property line" and "do an exorcism of the house."[30] In fact, she tells one client to "get several different types of holy people. That way you're hitting as many religions as possible."[31]

By leaving the solution to paranormal hauntings up to the clients, *The Dead Files* can, in effect, attribute the failure to expunge evil to its victims rather than the experts whose help they requested. Although nearly everyone vows to heed Allan's advice, the actual end of each episode is a title card that informs us whether or not the clients followed through. We are told, for example, that the woman with the unexplained illnesses "failed to follow" Amy's instructions. As a result, her health deteriorated and she is now "seeking a priest" to begin the exorcisms she should have sought out more promptly. Whenever people hesitate, the episode ends with these ominous words: "The activity continues." By making the client responsible for the outcome—as well as passing decisive action to other specialists—the series obscures the implication that Amy and Steve cannot really help at all.

To be fair, *The Dead Files* does not promise (and rarely delivers) a happy ending. This does not seem to have harmed the show's popularity.[32] In fact, the series is so invested in the possibility of bad news, it advertises itself with the tag line, "Is it safe for you to stay? Or time to get out?" In its own way, the pessimism of *The Dead Files* validates the conviction that the adversities Americans face are so entrenched and so massive there is no hope of overcoming them. But if it is no longer the job of paranormal experts to help people bedeviled by unexplained phenomena, and if medical science blames the victim, where are people to turn?

God Help Us

> "Of course, when people have been robbed of everything, like you and me, they seek salvation in other-worldly powers."[33]
> —Mikhail Bulgakov

As we have seen, television's representation of the paranormal can reinforce traditional religious beliefs. There is even an officially sanctioned way for individuals to communicate with otherworldly spirits: prayer. In an episode of *Paranormal State*, Ryan Buell begins a session of "dead time" with a prayer reaffirming the positive attributes of divine aid: "The light of God surrounds us. The love of God enfolds us. The power of God protects us." Prayer is a regular feature on *Ghost Asylum*; in every episode, the men of the Tennessee Wraith Chasers ask for spiritual protection before they begin an investigation. In "Old Cannon Memorial," founder Chris calls the team together, saying, "Let's get a little humble, guys. Fist bump to the Big Man." As they gather in a huddle, voices call out, "Yeah," "Let's do it," and "Let's get Him rollin' in this with us." In "Hayswood Infirmary," Chris begins the prayer by saying, "Before we go try to find some nasties and some spookies, let's talk to the Big Man." He leads the others in prayer: "Holy God. . . . Please go with us through this place. Lead, guide, guard and direct," to which they all answer, "Amen." The overt references to God in this show signify its "southern" identity, proclamations of faith being presented as characteristic of evangelical, "born again" Christian denominations. Praying also has personal meaning for the members of the team. When younger brother Brannon seems to have been momentarily possessed, Chris insists, "I'm calling on the Lord right now." At the end he adds, "Y'know, five burly guys sayin' a prayer. That means something to me."[34]

Although paranormal reality programs present a vernacular hodgepodge of traditional religious beliefs (what Donald Antrim calls "the ad hoc religions of the New Age"), Christianity is by far the dominant theological system underlying series produced in the US.[35] Within the various branches of Christianity, Roman Catholic rites take center stage when dealing with the demonic. When things get really bad on *Paranormal State* (for instance, when Ryan believes he is being taunted in his dreams and pursued by a demon), he recites an official Roman Catholic prayer explicitly designated as an appeal for supernatural aid against the forces of darkness: "St. Michael the Archangel, defend us in battle. . . . By the power of God, thrust into hell Satan and the other evil spirits who prowl about the world for the ruin of souls."[36] Buell also frequently consults with clergy, inviting them to perform official exorcisms complete with holy water, the sign of the cross, crucifixes, and canon-certified rituals.[37] In "Do Bad Things," he threatens a negative entity with something greater than his own prayers. "You want me to bring in a Roman Catholic priest?" he taunts. "I will bring in that priest," Ryan continues, "and when he starts doing his thing, you're gonna feel a lot of pain."

Other programs adopt what could be called a generic Christian style. *Demon Exorcist* Dwayne Claud is careful to state that he does not belong to any specific religious denomination, although everything he does during the dramatizations of exorcisms has explicit Christian roots. Claud says the Lord's Prayer to calm a woman whose parents abused her as part of a satanic cult. Before beginning an investigation, he joins hands with his team as they bow their heads and pray.[38] He blesses a house with holy water while making the sign of the cross. He also speaks openly about his religious beliefs *as* religious beliefs. "I would say a demonologist is a bringer of faith," he announces. It is his mission to teach those harassed by demonic forces how to use "faith as a shield." In confrontations with the Devil, the best defense is usually a religious defense.

Other personalities on paranormal television keep their religious beliefs under wraps. Asked directly, "Are you religious?" Zak Bagans gives a long sigh then says unenthusiastically, "I do my prayers."[39] In her book *There's More to Life Than This*, Theresa Caputo states openly, "I believe that my intuition is a spiritual gift.... I accepted my abilities directly from God—who, in so many words, said that I have it for a reason."[40] She explicitly points out, however, "I don't say this on my TV show."[41] Given the centrality of religion not only in paranormal television but in American culture as a whole, what would account for this reticence?

There is considerable overlap between paranormal beliefs and standard religious tenets. Both deal with the metaphysical. Both acknowledge the existence of spirits, the possibility of interaction with a spiritual realm, and the spirits' potential to manifest in or have an effect on the material world. If organized religion is adamant in its opposition to the paranormal, it may be because religion and the paranormal are too close, engaged in a constant, low-level power struggle over who has the authority to define and interact with (or control the means of interaction with) God and the Devil. But while paranormal reality is comfortable incorporating existing religious beliefs, established religions are not eager to return the favor.

Judeo-Christian doctrine has long prohibited paranormal pursuits, with prohibitions against psychics, mediums, clairvoyants, and any other kind of paranormal practitioner dating back to Leviticus and Deuteronomy. A few millennia later, programs on contemporary religious channels are openly hostile to aspects of the paranormal that are outside accepted dogma. Referring to *Long Island Medium*, Jonette Bekovic on the explicitly Catholic *Women of Grace* advises viewers: "Let's not let ourselves be duped."[42] Not only are gullible people apt to become dependent on so-called psychics, she suggests, but such people could lead you into contact with the Devil. After all, it is well known that demons can pretend to be the ghosts of loved ones.

The suggestion that ghosts are simply an illusion (if one with an underlying metaphysical cause) is raised consistently as a means to call into question one of the most attractive things the paranormal has to offer: the chance to communicate with deceased loved ones. When Nick Groff calls in "religious demonologist" Tony Spera on *Paranormal Lockdown* ("Hinsdale House," 2016), Spera warns him that "a lot of times, [demons] come in the guise of human spirits." "See, that's the key," Spera explains. "You have to know the difference between human and demonic." Even Martin Luther advised his followers that "all ghosts and visions, which cause themselves to be seen and heard . . . are not men's souls, but evidently devils."[43]

The simplest way for modern religious institutions to marginalize the paranormal is by dismissing it as superstition. Paranormal entities such as fairies, goblins, or leprechauns (the nature-spirits of pre-Christian or "pagan" European animism), and practices such as knocking on wood or rubbing a rabbit's foot for luck, are tolerated as essentially harmless. What cannot be incorporated or appropriated from pagan customs (e.g., Christmas trees) is relegated to the category of folklore. Consisting of stories and practices based on oral tradition rather than written history, folklore is the repository for cultural practices that persist within a particular culture without being endorsed by its official institutions. As such, it includes beliefs and practices that precede (and exceed) Western scientific and religious paradigms. As a branch of folklore, the paranormal occupies a space outside the dominant culture. This marginal position can be powerful. Operating in/as a parallel sphere, paranormal beliefs challenge scientific definitions of reality and subvert religious institutions' authority to define and delimit the spiritual realm.

No paranormal television series sets out to dispute or contradict mainstream religious beliefs. But the persistence of belief in the paranormal—despite the hegemonic view that it is nothing but superstitious nonsense—suggests that part of the population is unpersuaded by or resistant to dominant explanatory systems. Part of that resistance may be a reaction against orthodoxy's demand for complete submission. When Sharon Haywood on *Ghostly Encounters* decides to be "a good Christian," she must surrender her curiosity, attack her own character (her "narcissistic" desire to be the center of attention), and submit herself entirely to the authority of her church. Even then, established religious institutions can seem censorious and unyielding. As *Women of Grace* reminds us, "eight times out of ten" victims of the paranormal brought trouble on themselves.[44]

Presenting just enough metaphysical speculation to achieve their entertainment goals (and no more) these television series look to produce thrills, not religious conversion. But perhaps we can now see that when ghost-hunting series repeatedly fail to prove or disprove the paranormal, it is not merely a ploy to attract repeat viewers. I would argue that paranormal reality television's imperative to keep questions open meshes with a cultural proclivity for dissent. In a quintessential example from *Ghost Adventures*, Nick Groff stands alone in a haunted house and shouts into the darkness, "I just want to know that you're here. I want to know what the message is from the other side. I want you to communicate with me and give me an answer to what happens when you die. Can you tell me that?"[45]

The main difference between searching for answers in the paranormal realm and professing religious faith is that in the latter fundamental questions such as "what happens when you die" are assumed to have been answered.[46] The fact that belief in the paranormal persists suggests that some find established religious doctrine unpersuasive and of little comfort. Belief in the paranormal is a declaration of doubt—an assertion that established belief systems of any kind have not, will not, or cannot explain everything. Nagging at orthodoxies of faith and reason, the paranormal becomes the name for the space where doubts will not be silenced and unanswered questions linger.

5

Abandoned Institutions
"It's in the Walls"

In the middle of the twentieth century, the classic haunted house was Victorian in style, two or three stories high, its bleak façade punctuated by elongated windows, elaborately carved architectural detail, stained glass, and the always evocative turret. Run-down and sometimes abandoned, these stately homes exemplified elegance in the process of being consumed by decay. Although the haunted houses featured on modern paranormal television shows bear no resemblance to those depicted on child-friendly sitcoms like *The Munsters* (1964–1965) or *The Addams Family* (1964–1966), half a century later, there *is* an architectural style that exemplifies hauntedness.

Paranormal television returns almost obsessively to abandoned prisons and hospitals. Every episode set in one of these institutions bears a strong resemblance to every other, regardless of the program. *Ghost Adventures* has devoted nearly thirty episodes to abandoned prisons, jails, and hospitals.[1] *Ghost Asylum* was designed to focus exclusively on investigations of former mental hospitals. By its second season, prisons and reformatories were brought in to fill out the menu. In addition to the predictable narrative structure of these programs, it is not uncommon for multiple shows to visit the same sites. *Ghost Hunters*, *Ghost Adventures*, and *Ghost Asylum* have all visited Missouri State Penitentiary (in 2011, 2013, and 2016 respectively). The Trans-Allegheny Lunatic Asylum in West Virginia is the subject of episodes

Eastern State Penitentiary, Philadelphia, Pennsylvania

on *Ghost Hunters*, *Ghost Adventures*, and *Paranormal Lockdown* (2008, 2009, 2016). One of the most popular settings is a former tuberculosis hospital in Louisville, Kentucky, called Waverly Hills Sanatorium, which has been featured on not only *Ghost Hunters* and *Ghost Adventures* (2006, 2010) but also *Most Haunted, Hauntings and Horrors, Paranormal Challenge, Ghost Asylum, Paranormal Lockdown,* and *Kindred Spirits* (2008, 2014, 2011, 2015, 2017, and 2019, respectively). In their first episode at Waverly Hills, *Ghost Hunter*'s Grant Wilson tells us that it is "on every investigator's list of places to go check out."[2] Even on those occasions where the investigators claim to be the very first paranormal team allowed through the chained doors and boarded-up tunnels of some shuttered institution, the similarity in locations, how they are presented visually, and how the episodes are structured, give a sense that we have been here before as show after show obsessively circles the same issues.

What are the producers looking for in these deteriorating hulks? Initially, every show wants the things that make for "good television," which, in this case, would be thrills, suggestions of unearthly powers, scenes of technology (its ability to calibrate and define natural phenomena as well as its ultimate failure to conquer the unknown), and "amateur" ghost hunters pushed to their emotional limits. What they find are hollowed-out monuments to reason, scientific progress, and social control. They find a system recognized from the beginning as an ideal way to create ghosts.

Monumental Façades

Every episode investigating an abandoned institution opens with establishing shots of the central structure. Images of the main façade reveal the institution's immense scale, the scope of the builders' intentions and indicate the size of the financial investment necessary for these massive projects ostensibly designed for the public good. Simple establishing shots, however, are not sufficient to prepare us for a paranormal experience. Instead, montages punctuated by dramatic music give us our first glimpses of the building from multiple angles as dynamic editing fractures any sense of a single, overarching perspective. The shots in each montage combine disorienting aerial points of view with images taken from low angles that make the building loom above us, or canted angles that put the image off-kilter, visually undermining any sense of balance. Wide-angle lenses distort parts of buildings, making them seem unreal or unnatural, visually obtruding beyond the plane of the television screen.

Even without the stylistic license of the images or the dramatic music, the structures in these images declare their status as architectural anachronisms. Some, like the Eastern State Penitentiary, built in 1829, flaunt exuberant details such as the crenelated towers of Gothic Revival popular early in the nineteenth century. Others display the arches and coloring typical of the Richardsonian Romanesque, the first example of which was the 1870 Buffalo State Asylum for the Insane. Alluring and appalling in equal measure, these structures proclaim their roots in a past historically and culturally distinct from our own. As with decaying Victorian mansions, the continued presence of these ruins raises questions. Unmistakably outside their own time, they lead us to wonder "what were they for?" Deserted and forbidding, it is difficult to imagine "who lived there." Historians look for connections to the present, asking, "What does this building have to say to us today?" and "Why is it still here?" Paranormal programs ask one additional question: "Is the building truly empty or is someone or something still inside, trying to tell us something?"

Massive structures designed to house large numbers of involuntary occupants, these buildings offer a jumbled array of idealism and failure. Such sites are places where eighteenth- and nineteenth-century assumptions—about progress, conformity, medicine, the law, and the relation of the individual to power—were codified, put into practice, and made manifest in bricks and

Eastern State Penitentiary, Philadelphia, Pennsylvania

mortar. Externally the buildings were often arranged in compounds, microcosms of society where the relation of building to building and structure to grounds demonstrates the subjection of the individual to a totalizing vision of social order. The interior of each building was scrupulously thought-out so as to conform to its decreed function. These buildings became synonymous with the institutions ("mechanisms of social order") they housed. Despite the idealistic visions that spawned them, these institutions came to be known, in turn, for their dehumanizing conditions, discredited methods, and overarching coercion of helpless members of society. The horror brought to mind by modern contemplation of these buildings and systems is reinforced visually by endless shots of decaying walls, empty corridors, and gaping doorframes, all attesting to failure, abandonment, and discredited ideologies. Sites of large-scale trauma, they are exactly the kinds of places modern paranormal investigators expect to find troubled spirits crying for solace and demanding justice.

The subject of episodes on *Ghost Hunters* (2004), *Ghost Adventures* (2008), and a live episode of Britain's *Most Haunted* (Christmas 2007), Philadelphia's Eastern State Penitentiary (also known as Cherry Hill) was "once the most famous and expensive prison in the world."[3] Reduced to "a haunting world of crumbling cellblocks and empty guard towers," today its "grand architecture" and "vaulted, sky-lit cells" stand in ruins.[4] As the decaying remains of one of the first prisons built on the principles espoused by eighteenth-century penal reformers, Eastern State can serve as a model for the irreconcilable contradictions at the heart of this zealously rational form of architecture.

Institutionalized Penance

"In the later eighteenth century and the first decades of the nineteenth, the alliance between reform and architecture was producing a series of new building types—the hospital, the orphanage, the prison, the lunatic asylum, the workhouse."[5] Monumental, symmetrical, and repetitive, the façades of these structures proclaimed the triumph of an imposed order, a rational system that would be expressed in spatial as well as practical terms. The "patron saint" of this "distinctively institutional" architecture was philosopher Jeremy Bentham (1748–1832).[6] Hoping for a sinecure as a warden (or "governor"), Bentham spent years designing and promoting a new kind of prison.[7] "The Panopticon" was conceived as a circular edifice surrounding a central observation hub that would allow unlimited, continuous surveillance of multiple tiers of cells placed along the outer walls.[8] Although Bentham's Panopticon was never built, it epitomized the fundamental precepts that were to dominate prison and asylum architecture throughout the nineteenth century: the isolation of inmates in individual cells, constant surveillance, and complete supervision and structuring of the inmate's time, speech, dress, and activities. Above all, the building and its systems of operation were designed to function as a machine for producing moral and psychological change in each inmate. As such, the Panopticon became what one historian calls "the most haunting symbol of the disciplinary enthusiasms of the age."[9]

As Michel Foucault explains, in this period the purpose of prisons changed as reformers sought to balance the punitive aspects of imprisonment ("the deprivation of liberty") with a focus on moral reformation.[10] By switching "from punishment of the body to discipline directed at the mind or the soul," the reformers hoped to develop within the prisoners regret for their actions and a resolution to become productive citizens and sin no more.[11] To achieve this aim, buildings and systems were designed to produce penitence as a predictable outcome. Thus, one student of penal reform could declare in 1821 that a prison, as "an apparatus for transforming individuals," "must be of itself, a machine whose convict-workers are both the cogs and the products."[12] In fact, "it must be the most powerful machinery for imposing a new form on the perverted individual."[13] The only question was how.

"The first principle was isolation."[14] The greatest threat to the individual's spiritual transformation was moral contagion. Prisons were "a place where all evil was brought together," giving them "an enormous power to generate corruption."[15] Inevitably, paranormal programs reaffirm this belief, though at Holmesburg Prison, *Ghost Stalkers* attributes that power principally to the architecture. Commenting on the building's radial layout that leads to a central hub nicknamed "the Terror Dome," John Tenney comments that "the prison's construction, with its multiple hallways converging beneath a parabolic dome, created a situation where over a century's worth of negative human energy was collected and trapped beneath the central rotunda."

"Every hallway leads to this location," he explains excitedly. "It's just rushing energy toward this Terror Dome right in the center." If there is a portal to hell somewhere in the building, he suggests, "it took Holmesburg's unique design," coupled with "decades of the worst humanity had to offer, to tear open a gateway to another realm."

The original purpose of the multi-spoked radial design of Eastern State Penitentiary (one of the most influential modifications of the Panopticon) was to replace coercion and physical punishment with "the gentle efficiency of total surveillance."[16] A centralized warder could "maintain [the prisoners] in perfect visibility" at all times.[17] As they move through facilities consecrated to surveillance, characters on paranormal programs inevitably declare, "It feels like we're being watched."[18] In each paranormal investigation, the building's original purpose is revisited, unraveled, or inverted. Doors that kept others closed in and confined, gape open. Spaces that were once off-limits, such as offices, morgues, basements, subterranean tunnels, and body chutes (Waverly Hills), can be explored at will. Despite being allowed to roam about unconstrained, the investigators are not exactly free. Moving through the Trans-Allegheny Asylum on *Paranormal Lockdown*, Katrina Weidman senses the presence of something unseen, she exclaims, "I don't think we're alone right now."

The long halls of the radial plan provided not only "surveillance of the inmates" but "surveillance of the silent space that separated them."[19] Because evil spread "through association and communication," it was imperative to

Eastern State Penitentiary, Philadelphia, Pennsylvania

separate the convicts from each other. If it was impossible to maintain complete seclusion, total silence would do.[20] Silence became the new guarantor that each convict was fully separate and thus safe from moral contagion. It followed that the entire institution must be kept silent so that any attempt at communication between inmates would be detected instantly. Guards at model prisons such as Eastern State in Philadelphia and Pentonville in London wore "thick felt overshoes to mask the sound of their footfalls as they patrolled the galleries."[21] This practice made it possible for guards to "approach unheard as well as unseen," endowing them with uncanny qualities as they moved silently through space like spirits.[22] Prison walls not only guaranteed but came to epitomize silence. "In the Pennsylvanian prison, the only operations of correction were the conscience and the silent architecture that confronted it."[23]

Tap Tapping

> While I nodded, nearly napping,
> suddenly there came a tapping,
> as of someone gently rapping,
> rapping at my chamber door.
> —Edgar Allan Poe, *The Raven*

Because of its ability to travel through walls, sound was a particular challenge to the nineteenth-century prison's panoptic regime. In Britain in 1836, the celebrated scientist Michael Faraday was hired to "build walls" at the Milbank prison, "through which no message could pass."[24] After a series of experiments on acoustic conductivity, Faraday and his associates concluded that trying to stop sound altogether was impractical.[25] What *could* be accomplished was the suppression of "*the meaning* in sounds."[26] They designed a new kind of wall that turned speech "into a muddled blur."[27] Ultimately, the goal was not "to reduce the transmission of noise" but "to eradicate the transmission of information."[28] As one historian describes it, "it was less a question of acoustics, more a question of the scientific destruction of information."[29] In 1839, two French visitors who had toured American prisons reported the "satisfaction of knowing that nothing intelligible could ever be transmitted."[30] The naïve assumption that meaning exists exclusively in words is expressed most chillingly in the assertion that "even the most violent shouting was reduced to a meaningless confusion of sound."[31] (Screaming from an unseen source, especially in the context of a prison or an asylum, is never without meaning.) Eventually even the supervisors of prisons were forced to acknowledge that "intercommunication, though made more and more difficult, was never made impossible" as sound continued to escape "through ducts, pipes, windows, ventilators and doors."[32]

Using audible dots and dashes as a means of communication, Morse code became the foundation of the American telegraph system in 1844. Poe's *The Raven* was published in 1845. Three years later, American Spiritualism began with séances where spirits communicated by rapping on tables and walls. In this period, prisoners in the new-style penitentiaries also learned to communicate by code, tapping on pipes that led from one cell to the next. Authorities called this system "the prisoner's electric telegraph."[33] Prison tapping codes are a message from an unseen source who could be threatening or friendly. The practice is always forbidden. Whether it represented paranormal manifestation, technological marvel, or prohibited association, tapping as such could be heard loud and clear but its meaning was never self-evident. It is as true now as it was then that such sounds require interpretation. They must be decoded.

Not all sounds of paranormal origin are willed attempts at communication. "Residual energy" refers to sounds (and other paranormal phenomena) that linger in the environment but have no precipitating cause.[34] Like an echo, they re-sound regardless of whether anyone is there to hear them. Like echoes, too, they are the product and reflection of their physical environment. As he touches the rough walls outside Missouri's gas chamber, *Ghost Adventures'* Zak Bagans explains, "These rocks were here at every death. . . . And they absorbed the imprints of those moments." As Benjamin D'Harlingue suggests, in his discussion of "haunted prison" tours, "the violence of state-sponsored death produces an eerie affect that sticks to the very materiality of the prison building."[35] In paranormal terms, traumatic events explode energy onto the nearest surface where—like waves of heat, light, or sound—it is absorbed, then radiated back. "Sometimes," Zak adds, the traces of these spiritual events "are so profound that they can manifest within the physical world." In the process, the world becomes a form of technology. Zak compares the rocks to "tape recorders." (On *Paranormal Lockdown*, Nick does the same when he describes a spirit at Shrewsbury prison as being caught in a tape loop as it endlessly repeats its last walk to the gallows.) Because residual energy is a kind of atmospheric force, like thunder or lightning, its effects cannot be interpreted as attempts at communication. The residual can be proof of the paranormal but it does not respond to or interact with the investigator. It is not a conscious entity.

Although an "intelligent" response is a sign that communication is taking place, what is actually being communicated often remains opaque. As Nick says at Shrewsbury: "This spirit voice is trying to tell us something"—but what? Communication is often reduced to nothing more than a tap. In the morgue at Trans-Allegheny asylum, Katrina asks a spirit to confirm its presence. "Maybe you can just bang," she suggests, knocking the metal wall with her knuckles. Silence. Then—two soft metallic clinks and a loud knock. "Ooh!" Katrina responds to the camera, her eyes wide. Heightened by suspenseful moments of intense listening, the significance of the slightest sound is amplified when it does occur.

Tapping can be read as proving several things. As it did in nineteenth-century penitentiaries, tapping proves that there is another intelligence "out there." Another consciousness is trying to get through to us—though whether for its own sake (to get a message out) or for ours (to tell us something) is not clear. Despite formidable obstacles, this other intelligence cannot be suppressed. Prison administrators may have tried to reduce language to "a muddled blur," but they could not stop sound. As such, tapping is a form of communication that evades the sanctions of power.

Trying to decipher what they hear, the investigators pose hypotheses in the form of questions. When Nick Groff (during his time with *Ghost Adventures*) hears moaning in the dungeons at the Missouri prison, Zak Bagans notes, "They say men went insane down here. Is Nick hearing the final words spoken by an inmate before he took his own life?" The proffered explanation is always provisional, along the lines of "could this have been the ghost of so-and-so trying to tell us something?" Rhetorical questions posed to the audience, these preliminary readings are also admissions of an unresolvable ambiguity. In his struggle to understand a sign from the "other side," Zak acknowledges, "It's hard to make out," before conceding that his interpretation (any interpretation) is open to debate. "If an inmate was stabbed . . . and left for dead," he wonders, "this might be his last vocalization before his spirit left his body. What do you think?"[36]

Ultimately, it is the impression of interacting with another consciousness that is more important than any message it might transmit. Even with a variety of technical devices like "word generators" or radio-frequency scanners that pick words out of static, the investigators rarely receive complex—or even complete—answers to their questions. Simple words are garbled as we see in episodes where an EVP is played back two or three times; even with the audio enhanced and subtitled, it remains difficult to hear what the investigators say they hear. What matters, then, is not content but contact, the awareness at a specific moment of interacting, communicating with another being. For that, tapping is enough.

Another factor determining communication is power. The only persons allowed to speak in the plans for nineteenth-century prisons were "the governor, the instructor, the chaplain and other 'charitable persons,'" all conveying accepted moral doctrine.[37] To facilitate the top-down transmission of morally elevating sentiment, Bentham proposed running "conversation tubes" from the warden's office to each cell, "enabling the governor to instruct and admonish each inmate" individually.[38] Such one-way and hierarchical communication was, of necessity, disembodied—a voice without a source. To guarantee that this voice of authority would "not be overthrown by any other influence," unsupervised communication between prisoners had to be thwarted.[39] But those who had been silenced continued to resist.

The Uncanny

No system of repression is ever complete. Something always seeps through, some remnant left unattended. At times, it is the very act of trying to hold

Eastern State Penitentiary, Philadelphia, Pennsylvania

something down that forces it out through unforeseen fissures. In the ruins of Eastern State Penitentiary, for example, there are cells that are occupied by dead trees. Belonging to an "incredibly aggressive" invasive species, the trees took advantage of flaws in the structure, flourishing in the mixture of soil and rubble that fills the hollow walls. Once quite powerful ("they literally have taken down walls"), the trees have been (presumably) rendered harmless.[40] "We killed them all, so they're all dead now," a member of the staff asserts confidently. The museum administration keeps a few examples around for aesthetic purposes. "Paranormal investigators love 'em."

In the Freudian logic of repression, what is disparaged or dismissed is what is most likely to return. In her book on "eighteenth-century culture and the invention of the uncanny," Terry Castle identifies the Enlightenment as the moment when "traditional belief in spirits" became relegated to the status of "vulgar superstition."[41] Western society sought to free itself from "the coils of superstition, mystery, and magic" through an increasingly fierce commitment to science, logic, systematization, and "a yearning for categorical distinctions."[42] The unshakable confidence in reason (or its applied form,

Peeling paint, Eastern State Penitentiary, Philadelphia, Pennsylvania

science) was inseparable from a deep hostility to the supernatural or paranormal. As Adam Smith proclaimed in 1776, "Science is the great antidote to the poison of enthusiasm and superstition."[43] The intensity of this resistance is, in Freudian terms, telling. As Castle points out, the vaunted Age of Reason was "fraught with political, moral, and psychic instabilities."[44] Thus (if we can psychoanalyze an age), the Enlightenment produced and/or "discovered" the uncanny, a "familiar and old-established" aspect of itself that had been disowned, disavowed, but which was suddenly, unexpectedly, brought to light.[45] Like the paranormal, "the Freudian uncanny," Castle writes, "is itself a sort of phantom, looming up out of darkness: an archaic fantasy or fear, long ago exiled to the unconscious, that nonetheless 'returns to view'—intrud[ing] on ordinary life."[46]

On paranormal reality programs, the first views of the interiors of abandoned institutions take us to the heart of the matter. Once inside, the camera travels through empty hallways past walls scarred by graffiti, broken windows, and peeling paint. Given its ubiquity, it is amazing how frightening peeling paint can be. Technically, peeling paint is the result of variations in temperature between the atmosphere and a surface. Asked about the phenomenon, a spokesperson for paint manufacturer Sherwin Williams had a scientific explanation ready (as opposed to a supernatural one).[47] "Peeling paint is due to both age and environmental factors," she pointed out. "Exterior paints are more flexible," moving more easily as an outside wall "shrinks or swells with extreme temperature changes." On the other hand, "if a rigid interior coating [i.e., interior paint] is exposed to several seasonal temperature changes, it will lose adhesion to a substrate."

In other words, it is not the paint that changes but the walls. Unprotected from the elements (lacking window panes or a reliable heat source), the interior walls shrink and swell, leaving the paint broken, cracked, and separated. Paint peels when there is no longer a clear distinction between inside and out. To turn a scientific explanation into a metaphor, we could say that the flaking paint shows what happens when what was meant to be kept out (the uncontrollable phenomena of seasons and extreme fluctuations in temperature) intrudes on spaces designed to be stable and predictable (man-made interiors). Peeling paint reveals the inadequacy of logic when confronted with chaos. Put another way: when one world intrudes on another, breakdowns occur.

Hospitals

One of the most striking things paranormal reality television reveals is the equivalence between abandoned prisons and derelict hospitals. More than simply signifiers of the past, these institutions share a similarity in architectural layout and underlying purpose that becomes clear as each program contextualizes, condenses, and reworks so-called "historical" material, often through the use of voice-over narration. In *Paranormal Lockdown*'s "Trans-Allegheny Lunatic Asylum," the opening montage of establishing shots is accompanied by the voice of an unidentified male narrator.

> The Trans-Allegheny Lunatic Asylum sits on 666 acres of pure hell in Weston, West Virginia. Originally designed to house 240 patients when it opened in 1864, at its peak it held 2400 mentally ill, criminally insane and neurologically damaged souls.... After the asylum was shut down in 1994, its owners allowed a select few paranormal investigators inside.

This description situates the hospital in both historical and paranormal terms. It begins with demonically suggestive references to "666 acres of pure hell." The discovery of hell—a place of mythic importance—within the familiar and prosaic (twenty-three miles south of Clarksburg on the I-79) epitomizes the uncanny as it erupts into the ordinary spaces of daily life. The hospital becomes the site of a cosmic metaphysical struggle when the people it was designed to protect are described as "souls" trapped in hell. At the same time, barriers are erected that make it difficult to identify or sympathize with the inhabitants.

From the start, *Paranormal Lockdown* describes the institution as a means for excluding people from society. Not only is the archaic, pejorative term "lunatic asylum" maintained, but the inhabitants are disparaged through the use of distancing or derogatory terms such as illness, criminal, insane, and damaged. These darker designations help set the tone for horror. One *Hauntings and Horrors* episode opens with a male narrator introducing us to "the ghosts of the ruins of the Waverly Sanatorium where thousands died of tuberculosis. The deserted hulk stands like a decayed fortress, stripped of its power to heal the sick. Its ruins are a magnet for would-be ghost hunters." As the camera pans slowly across the hospital's grim façade, this mélange of the supernatural, architectural obsolescence, high ideals, and poor clinical outcomes establishes an ominous tone and the need for a thorough paranormal inquiry.

Paranormal shows use introductory narration to conjure up a sense of fear and mystery while holding firmly to the "realism" of documentary style. The use of dates and statistics establishes that the team has done its research, giving their project a patina of respectability. On *Ghost Hunters*, we are duly informed that "Waverly Hills Sanatorium was opened in 1926 and was considered the most advanced tuberculosis hospital in the country."[48] As reformist ideals erode and systems begin to fail, complex problems like overcrowding at the Trans-Allegheny asylum are made easy to grasp through simple multiplication: designed for 240 patients, it housed 2,400 at its peak. (Numbers can also be a reminder of simple, old-fashioned superstition as when we are told later that the Trans-Allegheny compound contains "thirteen buildings" overall.) The narrator on *Paranormal Lockdown* tells us both the year the asylum opened (1864) and when it closed (1994). Arranged like dates on a headstone, the numbers imply that an institution, like all things mortal, was born and died: Eastern State Penitentiary (1829–1971), Missouri State Penitentiary (1836–2004), Waverly Hills Sanatorium (1924–1982).

More important than when the institution closed, however, is the fact *that* it closed. When *Ghost Stalkers* co-host John Tenney visits Philadelphia's Holmesburg Prison and tells us that "Holmesburg officially shuttered its doors in 1995," he is situating it and all its yet-to-be-described horrors in the past. By emphasizing the fact that these institutions have been "abandoned," closed, shut down, these episodes *begin* by distancing the audience from the troubling legacies associated with these discredited prisons and hospitals. Before the full extent of those horrors can be laid out, the audience is assured that whatever abuses may have taken place, they have been recognized as such and ended. In other words, "we're past this." This comforting thought, however, is at odds with one of the key functions of paranormal pursuits: to reopen what others deem closed. Paranormal investigators believe, as Faulkner did, that "the past is never dead. It isn't even past."[49] The conviction that we are free of the past is challenged by the inescapable, looming presence of the buildings themselves.

When Nick Groff and Katrina Weidman approach the Trans-Allegheny Lunatic Asylum on *Paranormal Lockdown*, Nick proclaims, "The minute we cross this threshold our investigation begins." "Oh, wow!" Katrina interjects. Being allowed inside a space that is off limits is a primary attraction for investigators as well as viewers. Regarding Waverly Hills (*Ghost Hunters*), Grant gushes, "This is a dream come true. We've always wanted to go in there. We've heard so many stories about it and I'm just excited that we get the chance."[50] Each show stresses how privileged the team is to have been given access, the chance to explore the unknown. When Nick and Katrina visit the Women's Auxiliary Building at Trans-Allegheny, Nick brags that others have investigated the main building but no one else has ever been allowed in here. "Due to its deteriorating condition it has been off-limits," but now the owner "has agreed to allow us *first-time access* into this uncharted territory."[51]

For paranormal investigators, an empty building is an invitation to imagine things. Before the investigation even starts, *Ghost Hunters* tells us that Waverly Hills is "notorious for being haunted."[52] When paranormal teams arrive at these uninviting sites, their initial reactions undercut any sense of stability or safety. Getting a first glimpse of the sanatorium, one team member exclaims, "My God, this place is monstrous, dude!" While the camera rises from a low-angle shot of the building to a high angle looking down on the intimidating central tower, another gasps, "Holy Mother of God. Look at this!" When the *Ghost Asylum* team visits Old Cannon Memorial Hospital for the first time, Doogie states, "The minute I pulled up to Cannon, I had this really sinking feeling in my stomach."

Exaggerated expressions of dread help hype the fear factor that is essential to the horrific aspects of the paranormal. It is not surprising then that superlatives make a regular appearance. In the title sequence for *Ghost Stalkers*, for example, we are told that the co-hosts will "spend forty-eight hours isolated in some of the rawest, grittiest haunted locations in the world." When they visit Holmesburg Prison, Chad says, "This could be the most evil place that John and I have ever set foot in." *Ghost Adventures* goes even further, telling us that "in 1967 *Time* magazine called" the Missouri State Penitentiary "the bloodiest forty-seven acres in America."[53] Seeming to blame the land the prison stands on, Zak announces dramatically, "This is hell—and we're right in the heart of it." It is not clear whether "hell" refers to the prison or whether Missouri, in the exact middle of America, is also in the middle of hell.

The seeds of dis-ease are held in check by the use of graphics, maps, charts, and floorplans which establish a symbolic sense of control. While aerial shots reveal the daunting expanse of each complex—the ominous main building, its position in relation to others on the compound, their place in the landscape—shows like *Ghost Asylum* and *Most Haunted* reduce a massive space to a simple sketch. On *Ghost Asylum*, a drawing of the exterior of Cannon Memorial appears with names and arrows in red indicating which floor the various team members will be exploring. (In later seasons, the buildings are represented as rotating, three-dimensional cubes.) The British series *Most Haunted* makes regular use of basic floorplans that depict an overhead view of the layout of each floor. As the crew splits up to explore dozens of rooms in a stately home, a pulsing light indicates where each person is at a given time. Graphic representations impose a sense of order. Seeing "where" they will be before they even enter the building gives the impression that investigators "know their way around." It also reassures us that the space (and whatever secrets it may hold) is ultimately knowable.

The overview of a floorplan serves as a visual expression of distanced, critical perspective of the kind associated with the practice of history. In addition to exploring the site itself, paranormal shows incorporate other kinds of materials associated with historical research such as documents, old photographs, names of historical figures, and archival footage. Instead of conferring legitimacy on the paranormal project, however, the use of these materials leads to a minefield where, in a moment, socially acceptable historical interest can become rank exploitation.

Many of the former prisons and hospitals visited on these shows are managed by people who confront on a daily basis the challenge of balancing history with entertainment. These large-scale abandoned buildings often need a great deal of restoration and/or maintenance to stay standing, something that requires steady financial support. Those that have not been torn down or converted to condominiums (the former Northern Michigan Asylum for the Insane ([885–1989], for example) are once again opened to the public in the form of museums, paranormal sites, or both.[54] Nearly all the prisons and asylums discussed here stage "Haunted House" events around Halloween, including Eastern State Penitentiary, Waverly Hills Sanatorium, Pennhurst Asylum, and the Trans-Allegheny Asylum. These four also have regular ghost tours, as do the Missouri State Penitentiary and Rolling Hills Asylum. Allowing producers in to film paranormal investigations provides these businesses with publicity for their own events.[55]

Combining a haunted house with a museum produces conflicted feelings for administrators who see their mission as primarily historical. For Sean Kelley, the director of interpretation and public programming at Eastern State Penitentiary, there is a clear line between the "historical" and the "paranormal." "We really try to keep them distinct," he insists. "This building wasn't saved to be a location for paranormal shows." The "haunted house" event, for example, "is somewhat quarantined from everything else." Unlike the more traditionally "historical" daytime tours of the prison, the haunted house is "an evening thing" that is "clearly marked as not an educational experience." For many, though, the prison is primarily "a haunted attraction." During Halloween, up to 5,000 people can come on a single night.[56] Unlike the "enlightened" investigations of nineteenth-century prison tourism, conceived as part of a reformist "social project," twenty-first-century prison tours are "geared toward entertainment," with "the ideology of the prison industry . . . distilled in the form of mass community spectacle."[57] Kelley admits that there are clear financial benefits to indulging the public's pursuit of paranormal entertainment. "We don't live and die by that income," he states, "but it's nice to have it."

As the curators of these institutions recognize, the difference between "history" and the paranormal lies in how various material and sensual phenomena are read. The urge to read crumbling walls in supernatural terms is particularly strong at places like Eastern State, where major renovations

Eastern State Penitentiary, Philadelphia, Pennsylvania

were eschewed in favor of "stabilizing the ruins."[58] Although this decision initially followed an economic imperative ("The first ten or fifteen years," Kelley points out, "we didn't have enough money to do anything"), its continuation is not neutral. The aesthetic consequences of maintaining a certain level of decay may even be historically misleading. With its dark, bared stone walls, Eastern State's "center surveillance hub" is "evocative of a dungeon." But historically, Kelley explains, "no officer or inmate ever saw a stone" because the walls were smoothly plastered and painted when the prison was in operation. Nevertheless, the gloomy attractiveness of the dungeon-esque clearly appeals to the public Eastern State attracts. In "monthly exit surveys" going back to the 1990s, the message has been consistent. "Visitors say 'Don't fix it up too much.'"

People Tell Stories

Since it takes more than moving images of walls to animate stone, witnesses are brought in to revivify uninhabited space with stories. Their reminiscences guide how we read the detritus-filled hallways and scarified walls. At Holmesburg prison, *Ghost Stalkers*' John and Chad introduce "former deputy warden Dave Adams who reluctantly agreed to give us a tour." Standing in his old office, Adams tells them about two officers who had been murdered there. As he describes the stabbing deaths of his predecessors, we see streaks on the ceiling and walls that might be read as spattered blood. Historical violence is transmuted into paranormal experience as Adams remembers one particular night when he was overwhelmed by a feeling so oppressive he had to leave the office and spend the rest of his shift in the hall. Stories like these locate violence in the actions of the prison's inhabitants. When Adams cites a riot in 1970 that left over a hundred guards and prisoners hospitalized, Chad knows which side he is on. "I feel like I'm hearing my dad," he interrupts. "My dad's been a cop for over thirty years." He assures Adams, "I just have nothing but the ultimate respect for you." Perhaps surprisingly, deputy warden Adams feels sympathy for the inmates, an ambivalence he expresses through another anecdote concerning an uncanny experience. When he takes John and Chad to "H-block," he recalls a young prisoner who came up to him, said his name, and died. "I don't even know how he knew my name but he knew me," he muses, "and I was the last person he called on on Earth." He pauses, momentarily choked up. "That kinda got to me for a while," he says quietly.

The effects of these stories ripple outward, moving the listeners as well as the speakers. On *Paranormal Lockdown*, Nick and Katrina talk to Beth, a bubbly woman who worked at the Trans-Allegheny asylum thirty years earlier. Moving cautiously with her walker, she pauses to gaze up at the entrance. "Wow! The grand old dame still stands." She laughs heartily but is soon near tears. "It's gonna be very emotional to do this," she explains and gestures with her hands. "Memories just are flooding." We cut to an interview with Katrina, who puts Beth's testimony in context: "When we talk to somebody that was actually there it brings in a human element that sometimes, as researchers, we lose. It's not just paper and words and dates. It becomes . . . souls." When Beth recounts in vivid detail how two patients were murdered, it is Katrina whose eyes fill with tears when she hears that, the morning they died, the victims ("children as far as their mind capacity was concerned") had "sat coloring" quietly at the feet of a nurse. For Beth, the best way to describe their murderer is in intangible emotional and spiritual terms. "He was *frightening*," she says with emphasis. "He had—and you might laugh at me—but he had blackness, an evilness about him."

Witness testimony serves the same purpose for paranormal investigations that it does for standard historical research. Beth's story provides an occasion for empathy by personalizing tragedies in which people died in numbers too large to imagine. When *Ghost Hunters*' Jason Hawes visits Waverly Sanatorium, he asks, "So how many people actually died here?" He is staggered when their tour guide answers, "Sixty-three thousand."[59] On *Paranormal Lockdown*, Nick explains that any one story should be seen as part of a larger picture when he points out that "Beth's memory represents just one of hundreds of stories of the lives lived and lost here at the asylum." Beth's story also presents us with a clear distinction between good and bad, innocent victims and unremitting evil. In the process, positive feelings are generated for the subjects of the story, the teller, and for the hosts of the program who are shown to care deeply for the victims of the past.

Sometimes, the stories witnesses tell are not about individual murderers but how the system itself is the true source of violence. A nineteenth-century memoir recounts the severe forms of corporal punishment prisoners were subjected to despite the institution of so-called "reforms." Austin Reed, an African American inmate at New York's Auburn Prison in the 1840s and '50s, recalls prisoners being flogged; bent over a barrel and handcuffed in place; chained from the ceiling and left to stand on tip-toe; hung from ropes "spread eagle"; made to wear an iron cap; put through the "showering bath" (a process akin to waterboarding); and weighed down "with a heavy iron yoke and a fourteen weight ball attached at each end of the yoke."[60] At Holmesburg Prison a century and a half later, *Ghost Stalkers* John and Chad are taken to see "the Klondike," a suite of punishment cells where "four unruly prisoners were locked in and roasted to death after the guards set the radiators on high" in 1938. Hearing this, Chad (who elsewhere refers to the inmates as "the worst of the worst") is stunned, his respect for law enforcement deeply shaken. "I'm sort of at a loss for words, to be honest."

Documenting the Dead

Paranormal reality programs visualize the past (and individualize the dead) by using traditional kinds of documentary evidence. Newspaper headlines and black-and-white photos are handy for setting up ironic juxtapositions, as when *Ghost Hunters* presents a photograph of Waverly Hills Sanatorium when it was "the most advanced tuberculosis hospital in the country." The postcard-style view provides a stark contrast with today's "deserted hulk."[61]

This episode also uses photographs to repopulate the building, presenting shots of nurses on a terrace with young patients, wards filled with rows of occupied beds, and staff arranged at the entrance for a group portrait. The people in these pictures are rendered generic; they fulfill expectations by filling the categories of people we would expect to see at such an institution. As "types," they are defined by their clothing—uniforms that signify who is a guard and who a prisoner, a member of the medical staff or a patient. Briefly glimpsed variations, such as different hairstyles or shoes, establish the period rather than the uniqueness of each individual.

Photographs of individuals *as* individuals are more problematic. When photos are coupled with names in these episodes, the individual is identified as a "real person." The question of that person's rights arises immediately. Whether sentenced to prison, executed by the state, or confined to a hospital against their will, these were people robbed of their power to consent. Long dead, they can neither grant nor refuse permission for the use of their image as part of a television series.[62] Some photographs are found posted on the walls of prison museums. At Missouri State's gas chamber, the camera pans across a poster of the "thirty-nine men, one woman" executed there as Zak loudly recites each name. Similar photographic records are exhibited in Shrewsbury Prison's hanging room (*Paranormal Lockdown*, 2016) and at Eastern State Penitentiary (below).

Often, whether for ethical or legal reasons, generic images fill in for photographs of the people whose names are mentioned on the soundtrack. When the *Ghost Asylum* team tells the story of J. W. McCann who died in a fire in his cell at the Pauly Jail in Alabama, we see a mugshot of a white man with the upper part of his face blurred, implying that this is a photo of McCann that has been altered to protect his privacy. Like putting hoods on nineteenth-century convicts, the practice could be seen as an attempt to shield convicts and their families from the embarrassment of being publicly associated with prison. It becomes much more troubling, however, when in the same episode, photographs of African American inmates are shown to illustrate the disproportionate number of Black prisoners held during the segregationist era. In old pictures from the 1920s and '30s, their faces have been blurred, their identities as individuals rubbed out. While the ostensible object of the episode is to tell the stories of victims of injustice, visually the show renders them literally faceless.

B-2850: Kate Hogan was sentenced five times to Eastern State Penitentiary, at least four times for larceny (non-violent theft). More than half of the women sentenced to Eastern State were convicted of this crime.

B-3018: In 1904, Catherine Danz was convicted of murdering her husband with poison. Initially sentenced to death by hanging, her sentence was changed to life imprisonment. Mrs. Danz maintained her innocence, claiming that "she had bought powders...and administered them to her husband for the purpose of curing the drink habit." She received a full pardon and was released from Eastern State in 1911.

B-3094: Sadie Smith (alias Sadie Schowell) was a career shoplifter. She was sentenced to one year and six months at Eastern State for larceny.

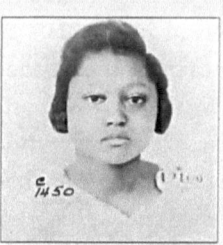

B-2661: Rosa Pilnick and her husband (B-2662) were convicted of "Keeping a Bawdy or Disorderly House" in 1905. The couple was connected with at least ten houses of prostitution. They were previously convicted of "harboring a minor for immoral purposes."

C-1450: Lucy Stewart, her husband George, and another man were tried for the murder of a taxi driver in 1921. During the course of the trial George Stewart took full responsibility for the killing, trying to absolve his wife. His efforts were unsuccessful; Lucy Stewart received 9 to 15 years in prison. Her husband received the death penalty.

B-2731: Sarah Hews and two men were found with $500 in counterfeit currency and "molds and materials for coining bogus money" in 1905. A federal court sentenced her to serve two years at Eastern State Penitentiary.

B-3026 and B-3027: According to their victim, Thomas Zell, Edna Hartz (left) and Mary Davis (right) allowed him to drink beer freely during a carriage ride until he became dizzy. They then "dealt [him] a terrific blow over the head with a beer bottle.... He fell to the ground unconscious," and the women stole $30 from him.
Edna Hartz received one year for "Robbery, Felonious Assault and Battery, and Administering Stupefying Drugs." Mary Davis received two years for robbery.

C-280: Eva Cole, a chamber maid in Dauphin County, was sentenced to one year for felonious assault.

B-2563: Mary Dunn was sentenced to 15 years for murdering her sister-in-law during a street brawl. The sentence was severe: a typical murder sentence for a woman at Eastern State was ten years or fewer.

C-721: Lillian Thomas, sentenced to one year, three months in Dauphin County for receiving stolen goods.

B-2637: Elizabeth Ashmead was convicted in 1905 for performing abortions. She was later sent to Kansas State Penitentiary where she was imprisoned for another five years for "Using the Mails...for the Purpose of Arranging for Illegal Operations."

Eastern State Penitentiary, Philadelphia, Pennsylvania

The use of names, even without connecting them to photographs, can seem ethically questionable. Eastern State's Sean Kelley finds the use of names on paranormal shows to be a matter of particular concern.

> We're very serious to encourage our visitors to remember that there were men and women who lived in this building and they weren't here by choice.... If you want to say that you saw a misty figure at the end of a cellblock, that's just goofy. It doesn't seem like anyone's hurt by that. But if you want to say Norman M—— was an inmate who killed himself in 1967 in this building—his daughter's still alive and she visits. He was a real person with real problems, was beloved by many of the men who served time with him, and it doesn't seem appropriate to turn that into a plotline for a television show.

Even more controversial is the use of archival footage. A staple of historical documentaries, scenes of actual prisoners or patients have a visceral effect beyond that provoked by still photographs or descriptions of violence. Kelley, for example, points to a display at a rival museum/tourist attraction (a former asylum) that "includes video of children with severe developmental disabilities tied to beds."[63] Although historically this footage had a positive effect, leading directly to the closing of the institution, as a modern visitor touring the facility Kelley found it "jarring." "The children are clearly suffering. To see it as the set up for an entertainment experience.... It was really—I did find it offensive." For Kelley, those who use such footage are "shamelessly exploiting the worst aspects" of their institutions' pain-filled histories.[64]

One way producers avoid the ethical questions raised by employing actual historical footage is by using reenactments, though this approach has problems, too. For example, when Nick on *Paranormal Lockdown* describes the Trans-Allegheny Asylum's past, his narration accompanies staged scenes of actors portraying "mental patients." In voice-over, we hear that "medical treatments were primitive and patients were subjected to barbaric practices—lobotomy, isolation and, electric shock." (The last two terms are illustrated with a shot of a woman with disheveled hair standing listlessly behind bars, "and another of a man grasping the fencing of his cage as if the wires carry electric current.) Is this better or worse? Knowing that the gore and suffering are fake distances us from the reality of decades of abuse as the undeniably cheesy scare techniques risk rendering historic suffering ridiculous. At the same time, reenactments do not exploit subjects who cannot consent.

In this case, it may be the best choice when what history leaves us with is worse than what the horror genre can imagine. (At times, it is difficult to determine whether a photograph is genuine or staged. At the Missouri State Prison, following a warning that viewers might not want to see this, *Ghost Adventures* presents what appear to be crime scene photographs of an inmate murdered with a hammer. Although the close-ups of "Walter" covered in blood are undeniably gruesome, it is not possible to tell from watching the episode whether they are authentic or counterfeit.)

Whether archival or staged, the "historical" photographs and moving images are kept stylistically distinct from the rest of the episode. Aesthetically situated firmly in the past, the horrors depicted are denounced then quickly laid to rest, thus affirming the triumph of modern values. Sean Kelley grants that the "idea that it's done and that it's safely in the past is very comforting." People "want to hear, 'That's over and we've moved past that.'" Sometimes though, that assumption cannot be maintained. Members of the *Ghost Adventures* team might spend time inside the former gas chamber at Missouri State Penitentiary trying to imagine the last moments of the men executed there, but three years later, at the Nevada State Prison, they cannot visit the "death house" because it is still in use. People are still being killed there, their deaths carried out by the state. *Where* this happens in this episode is vague; it is implied that it is somewhere close by but the exact location remains inaccessible, hidden.[65]

No matter how much "people want to see history tied up with a bow—and they don't want it to be messy," Kelley insists, some of the past's "mistakes have not been acknowledged." Paranormal investigations do attempt (to some extent) to address the social and political issues that led to the large-scale failure of these abandoned institutions. Episodes that deal with hospitals, for instance, often include historical footage showing forms of treatment that have come to be seen as medically sanctioned forms of abuse (lobotomies, shock treatment, the use of restraints, or using patients in medical experiments without their consent). Recapping the history of one hospital, *Ghost Asylum* takes a surprisingly nuanced stance when contextualizing its history. At Cannon Memorial, we are told, "severe overcrowding and negligence caused the patients to violently fight back against the staff." By depicting the patients as reacting to abusive conditions, the narration implies support for their resistance and condemns the greater evil of institutionalized mistreatment. At Missouri State Penitentiary, the *Ghost Adventures* team similarly find themselves sympathizing with the individual as opposed to the state. "What these people did I'm sure were awful things," Zak Bagans says. "But they were still human beings and they were still killed behind this wall."

By physically occupying spaces the dead occupied, the investigators try to intensify their identification with previous occupants. As Zak says outside the gas chamber at Missouri State Penitentiary, "If you occupy that same space and you touch those same surfaces, it's as if you can still feel" what it was like for those who "died right there." Telling us "the last thing that they saw was this door being shut," he instructs teammate Aaron to sit in the gas chamber and film the door closing from the point of view of the condemned—to see it literally from their perspective. Granted, neither investigator nor audience member can know what enforced confinement was really like, nevertheless, trying to put oneself in another's shoes is a crucial step in the attempt to understand.

Trying to merge emotionally with former inhabitants of prisons and asylums is presented as both laudable and risky. At Trans-Allegheny, Katrina finds Nick sitting alone in a room, staring into space. The walls around him are scarred with peeling paint. When she asks him if he is alright, he responds with an emotional description of someone else's feelings. "Patients—people that were once living here—must have felt scared to be in the darkness—distraught, not understanding what's going on, confused." *Paranormal Lockdown* acknowledges the potential drawbacks of too much empathy. Nick and Katrina remain isolated at a location for seventy-two hours straight, hoping that "mental exhaustion will open our minds to the paranormal world." The danger, however, is that they may find themselves "too weak to resist any physical attachments by the souls who remain here." If you identify too closely with others, you could lose yourself.

Interior, Night: Corridors

As night begins, those in the present are surrounded by fragments of the past that refuse to stay in the past. Our identification with the investigators increases with the sense of imminent danger. At Trans-Allegheny, Katrina declares, "It honestly feels like we're in the middle of a horror movie." Although she is an experienced investigator, she admits, "I'm scared of this place." Bunking down in an empty corridor, Nick remarks, "Honestly, this is one of the creepiest hallways I've ever slept in." Alone in the dark, he feels besieged: "I feel like they're coming at me from all angles."

As the night deepens, the buildings come alive. Sometimes hosts express this figuratively: "The sadness, the violence—it's almost as if this building's alive to me," Zak muses at the Missouri prison. The "as if" drops away as the impression of architectural sentience grows stronger. "It's like it's aware we're here," he states. Loud noises at another prison are figured as "the building laughing at you."[66] After a series of mishaps at Shrewsbury prison, Katrina jokes that the building is trying to kill her. The notion of a malevolent building persists regardless of whether you couch the idea in humor or distance yourself by attributing the sentiment to others. As Chris says during *Ghost Asylum*'s visit to the abandoned Cannon Memorial Hospital, "With reports of mysterious screams and strange whispers coming from inside . . . some even say the building has a mind of its own."

More frightening than the thought of an animate building, perhaps, is the moment when the investigators realize that the massive walls have become permeable, no longer able to maintain the distinction between inside and outside. Mists appear and the temperature drops suddenly. "It's getting cold," Nick says urgently. "Did you guys feel that?"[67] Unable to depend on the solidity of stone, the ground (figuratively) drops out from beneath their feet. The world is not what they thought it was.

Struggling to understand what is taking place, the investigators track every sensation whether physical or emotional. Anxiety or waves of sadness are, potentially, as meaningful as a glimpsed shadow, a creaking floorboard or a sigh. Every detectable phenomenon is reported—either to the camera or to each other—so that it can be validated. Some emotions are simply announced while others produce verifiable visual effects. Stating that a surge of electricity just passed through him, a man shouts, "Look! The hair's standing up on my arm," as the camera operator zooms in for a close-up of his wrist. Katrina, lying on a slab in the morgue at Trans-Allegheny, confides her fear to the camera. "I'm literally shaking," she says, and holds up her hand as proof.

Questions proliferate, simultaneously establishing that the investigator has sensed something and eliciting confirmation: "Did you guys feel that?" "What was that?" "Did you hear that?" If nearby witnesses do not immediately verify that they heard something too, instant replay is available. But despite repetition, the phenomena—whether "captured" on tape or filtered through the investigators' senses—remains stubbornly elusive.

Eastern State Penitentiary, Philadelphia, Pennsylvania

In these episodes, paranormal reality television confirms what observers knew when these institutions were first built. Prominent social commentators of the day such as Fanny Kemble, Harriet Martineau, Gustave de Beaumont, and Alexis de Tocqueville recognized the nightmare these state-of-the-art prisons could be for those literally trapped inside the logic of the system. Even at its inception, Bentham himself saw how the "silent sequestered imprisonment" at the heart of his system would produce a sense of being haunted: "In a state of solitude, infantine superstitions, ghosts, and spectres, recur to the imagination."[68] When the men who operated these new institutions opened them to the public as tourist attractions, Charles Dickens wrote that while he "admired the 'perfect order' of the prison building and recognized the benevolent intentions of the founders," he thought "the inmates seemed . . . like people 'buried alive.'"[69] The "soul-killing" spiritual death produced by isolation was, for Dickens, "immeasurably worse than any torture of the body."[70] "Incarcerated in tiers of tomb-like cells, the deep silence broken only by the muted footsteps of ghostly masked figures," the people who walked these halls became remnants, removed from the world and made unreal to the outside world and to themselves.[71] Later in life, Bentham acknowledged misgivings about the world he had designed. "I do not like . . . to look among the Panopticon papers," he wrote. "It is like opening a drawer where devils are locked up—it is breaking into a haunted house."[72]

In entering these buildings, paranormal investigators reopen a past that seemed to be put to rest. Their questions, colored by the knowledge of the tragic/criminal history of the location, may anticipate a pre-imagined response, but by continuing to ask—and to listen—these researchers assert that there is something more we need to hear, something that still has not been addressed. What the investigators and viewers of these shows risk is an encounter with the uncanny—hearing, discovering, coming face to face with something you already know but do not want to know. For example, how much these institutions continue to resemble society at large, or how flawed the principles are on which these institutions (and society?) are founded.

As Zak says, "The Missouri State Penitentiary is much more than its limestone walls and decaying paint." Whatever "energy remains here *reached out to us*—to be heard, to be felt." It is incumbent on us that we listen. Coming from a site of confinement, any attempt at communication challenges the dominant order, even a simple tap. A sign of something trying to break through, such sounds are a form of resistance, at odds with the silence that maintains the status quo. And despite numerous investigations, the forces of silence are still at work. At Trans-Allegheny, as Nick, Katrina, their cameraman, and two guest experts pass an open door in the deserted asylum, they hear a soft, disembodied "shhh."

6

In America There Is Real Evil
Excluded Americans

Introducing the first episode of a new series, a portentous male voice informs us, "There's a new team of paranormal investigators here to answer two questions about ghost hunting." The first question: "Are ghosts for real?" The second, posed by a young African American man looking directly into the camera: "Why is everybody white?!"

Debuting on Destination America in 2016, *Ghost Brothers* is a late entry in the genre, appearing twelve years after *Ghost Hunters*, the show on which it is modeled. Built around a group of three friends, all African American, *Ghost Brothers* confronts head-on the issue of race in the paranormal genre—particularly the *absence* of people of color as on-camera personalities, whether as investigators, psychics or witnesses.

African Americans are one of two groups who are often referred to in paranormal programs but who rarely appear. Like Native Americans, they are constructed as absent, serving almost exclusively as signifiers of a distant past. Native Americans are equated with death and the land (literally merged with the soil in the trope of "Indian burial grounds") while the figure of the African American evokes slavery, the Civil War, and Jim Crow. Present as an idea but absent as individuals, both groups haunt contemporary popular culture while being denied an actual presence (the chance to speak, the ability to shape events) in the modern world. The *history* of first peoples in

America and of people of African descent, however, is a frequent subject in these series—usually as a story for white people to tell.

A survey of the dozens of series that aired between 2004 and 2019 leads to the unavoidable conclusion that paranormal reality TV is produced by white companies, features white casts, and explores the problems of white people. In all of these shows, "white" as a category is unexamined, taken for granted, and defined primarily by exclusion. This produces a fundamentally unstable condition that leaves white speakers channeling their unease about themselves through the "ghosts" of others. "Who am I? Do I belong here? What does it mean to be an American?" But rather than being "haunted" in the sense of being troubled or guilt-ridden, the people in these programs seem willing, even eager, to accept Native Americans and African Americans as ghosts because it is as spectral figures that they can be commodified.

Episodes about Native American and African American hauntings bring the free publicity of national television coverage to "heritage" sites such as museums or historical societies, small businesses (bars, restaurants, hotels), or guided tours. They also attract audiences to paranormal television programs. Placing the personalities who appear on these shows in relation to the documented life and death struggles of others symbolically raises the stakes of their investigations. Incorporating material defined as "educational" boosts the genre's cultural standing and adds gravitas to the hosts' personas. This, in turn, contributes to the development of a star system which can be used as the foundation for promotional material, special episodes, and spin-offs. As it pursues simple economic gain, however, paranormal reality television finds itself caught in a struggle, simultaneously confronting and evading the bleakest facts of American history.

The most reassuring thing about history as depicted in these programs is its utter disconnectedness from the present. For the hosts of paranormal

TV, "history" is something that happened to someone else. The past is back there—way back. It is only glimpsed now and then when you go ghost hunting, and that begins and ends when you choose. Establishing distance enables producers and audiences to avoid a cultural legacy of guilt: "*I'm* not responsible for what happened. *I* didn't do that." But even if there is a chance that one might be momentarily overcome when faced with the horrors of the past, it is preferable to dealing with the present. Engaging with people whose lived experience in modern America is radically different than yours, allowing potentially controversial subject matter into mainstream, escapist programming, or running the risk that an issue (a place, one's identity, "America" itself) might be defined on someone else's terms are all evidently more frightening than dealing with ghosts.

First Peoples: Geography and American Identity

"In America there is real evil. It lurks in the darkest shadows in our most ordinary towns."
—*A Haunting*

A Haunting is not the only paranormal show to identify the United States as the precise geographic location of evil.[1] America—its peoples, geography, and history—recurs as a subject in countless paranormal investigator and eyewitness programs.[2] A typical episode begins with views of small-town America. Aerial shots, made affordable through the use of drones, sweep across idyllic landscapes. These opening images present a familiar iconography, one redolent of calendar kitsch and Norman Rockwell-style Americana. When such shots appear at the beginning of a horror film, however, they are read differently, as the places usually presented as safe and secure ("home") become suddenly terrifying, threatening, and are ultimately exposed as the locus of evil.

Although paranormal programs are bound by generic and narrative demands to expose the darkness lurking behind a pleasant surface, it is hard to argue that there is any intentional critique implied by situating evil in the geography and history of the US. There is, however, meaning in the way land and history function in these narratives. As John Sears points out in his book *Sacred Places*, "From the beginning Americans had sought their identity in their relationship to the land they had settled. It was inevitable

... that they would turn to the landscape of America as the basis of that culture."[3] One's vision of land, however, is already the product of culture. "Landscapes"—for example, images of geographic space—"are never found in nature but only in our culturally specific ways of seeing."[4] Our understanding of geography, our vision of "the land," is overlaid with history, accounts of the people and human events that took place there. These are often signaled through place names or, as is common in the US, by a series of names layered on top of each other over time: for example, Indian names in a series of different spellings that are then displaced by English, French, or Spanish names, or local road names overlaid with state or federal numbering systems. Past and present coexist, with "what used to be" glimpse-able underneath or nearby. The process by which the past is papered-over by the present is also readily visible. "American" as an identity (an imaginary construction of the self in relation to an idea of nation) was and is built on a series of displacements and exclusions: what or who is foregrounded and what or who is overlooked.[5]

References to Native Americans appear in every kind of paranormal reality program. Mediums like Theresa Caputo or Kim Russo perform psychic cleansings by smudging (spreading sage smoke with a feather). Ghost-hunting teams explore asylums, tourist attractions, and stately homes built on Native lands (*Ghost Adventures*, "Nopeming Sanitarium" [2015], "Dakota's Sanatorium of Death" [2016]; *Ghost Stalkers*, "Wheatlands Estate" [2014]; *Paranormal Lockdown*, "Oliver House" [2016]). First-person accounts relate non-Natives' fear that the woods are haunted (*A Haunting*, "The Shadowman" [2014]); that there is "some sort of primal spirit connected to a space out there" (*Paranormal State*, "Who is the Lurking Man?" [2010]); that the ground is saturated with the blood of Native Americans (*Ghost Adventures*, "Leslie's Family Tree" [2016]); or that, as new inhabitants, contemporary non-Native Americans might inadvertently disturb spirits by digging up ancient burial grounds (*A Haunting*, "The Unleashed" [2006]). Disrespect for sacred sites is always depicted as inadvertent. Afraid they might find themselves paying for America's past, the modern-day residents equate ignorance with innocence, presenting themselves as unaware of evils committed by others decades or centuries earlier, or by themselves the day before yesterday. Nevertheless, even if the land was left "undisturbed," there are traces of the past that still need to be dealt with. Whatever you think was laid to rest resists being buried.

Theresa Caputo using sage, *Long Island Medium*

Wilderness Without and Within

As soon as Europeans arrived in the Americas, they began to tell stories about the peoples they encountered there. These stories served the purposes of the newcomers as they attempted to make sense of their own experience. In constructing "the symbolic landscape" of their new home, Puritan settlers ("predisposed" by their "strong religious tradition") drew a picture of that landscape that was far from neutral.[6] Inevitably, the world they saw reflected their own doubts and deep-seated fears. Characterized as "wilderness," land untempered by Man's designing hand could only be considered evil. "Something about the place seemed to attract the attention and energies of the devil."[7] As early as 1696, Increase Mather wrote that "it is the Judgment of very Learned men, that in the Glorious Times promised to the Church on Earth, America will be Hell."[8]

The Puritans were afraid that the wilderness would change them before they could change it. The evils "out there" might become part of them, an internal condition that could not be expelled.[9] For Puritans, "Man" was already characterized as having a "wilderness within" where the fallen sons of Adam "harbored strange creatures who were only partly human."[10] For example, some Englishmen—the wrong kind, not the Puritan kind—were already considered "nothing but wild beasts and beastlike men."[11] Without constant vigilance, man could become "one flesh with a Beast" and it was the land that was to blame.[12] "Something in America seemed to hold out to unruly men the opportunity to give free rein" to their animal natures, "their repressed wildness," their affinity with evil.[13] The greatest danger was that living in "an alien environment would transform English people into Americans—new creatures more compatible with the wilderness."[14] Having designated "the native peoples as the human face of the American wilderness," a Puritan leader like Cotton Mather could place them firmly on the side of the occult.[15] Their "chief Sagamores," he wrote, "are well known . . . to have been horrid Sorcerers, and hellish Conjurors, and such as Conversed with Daemons."[16] It was up to Puritans like himself to "wrest America out of the Hands of its old Land-Lord, Satan."[17] This meant subduing both the land and its Native peoples.

In the 1890s, after three centuries of nearly ceaseless military campaigns, skirmishes, massacres, and forced relocations by the British and US governments, the figure of the Native American reemerged as a privileged denizen of the supernatural world. In the era of "the vanishing Indian," the formerly terrifying occupant of the wilderness was refashioned by the Spiritualist movement into the benevolent figure of the Indian spirit guide, an imaginary entity who served white Americans by addressing the things they were haunted by. According to historian Kathryn Troy, "During Spiritualism's heyday in the late nineteenth century, more than eighty spirits were identified as deceased Indian chiefs."[18] Psychic mediums would call upon ghosts with names like White Hawk or Black Feather to act as a go-between or guide to the spirit world. (Theresa Caputo identifies one of her spirit guides as a Native American she calls "Chief.")[19] Far from "vanishing," "to nineteenth-century Spiritualists . . . the ghosts of Indian dead walked among them."[20] Redefined as "the noble savage," the Native guide transformed what was fearsome and unknown into a welcoming space for the newcomer. Historical figures like Sacajewea, who had used their superior geographic knowledge to guide Europeans through the challenging terrain of the "New World," became the models for these spectral beings willing to reveal to strangers the secrets of "other" worlds. A benevolent, selfless figure, this version of the vanishing Indian was also conveniently self-erasing. A specter, he appeared when summoned then vanished, becoming literally nonexistent when he was no longer useful.[21]

In twenty-first-century paranormal reality television, the figure of the Native American continues to intersect with the land, the occult, and America's conception of itself as a nation. For "Americans," geography is identity, but it is an identity that is never clear or fixed. In her book on the Hudson River Valley, Judith Richardson writes that "ghosts congregate here because this is a complex, contentious place."[22] Hauntings "emanate from social and historical tensions," and in America, she argues, those tensions are about the land.[23] (As Buse and Stott note: "Where we find ghosts, there are bound to be anxieties about property.")[24] American identity depends on the answer to the unresolvable question of who has rightful claim to the land. For Americans of Native heritage, the history of their relation to the land is a series of disruptions: wars with a shifting series of enemies, displacement from one place and confinement in another, legal contests that make any sense of home precarious and impermanent. Non-Natives, surrounded by names left by people who have been displaced, constantly remember and forget, simultaneously knowing and not wanting to know the histories of earlier occupants. As one paranormal show's website has it, "America has a dark past so it's logical it is haunted or filled with ghosts."[25] What the term "dark past" euphemistically obscures is history, a series of specific policies and actions that could be characterized as unjust, criminal, or even evil. In paranormal terms, when a nation seesaws between the recognition and suppression of uncomfortable truths, haunting is the only possible consequence.

As the Puritans suspected, the unnerving instability of American identity begins in the woods.[26]

The Woods

The camera glides over forests surrounding a stately house in Middleborough, Massachusetts. A voice-over situates the Oliver House amidst "fifty-four acres of untamed New England wilderness."[27] From the first, *Paranormal Lockdown* investigators Nick and Katrina are troubled by the landscape. "There's something definitely ominous about these woods," Nick states. "There's something in this woods [sic] that is lurking." As they are filled in on the history of the house, Nick and Katrina's reading of the landscape becomes more complicated. A guide explains that "there were many Native American villages" in these woods until 1675, when disease "knocked out almost ninety percent of the Native American population." A narrator picks up the story, elaborating some points and blurring others. "After occupying the woods for thousands of years, entire villages of Wampanoag Indians perished from a plague of disease brought on by the first colonists." While the pre-colonial era is reduced to a featureless expanse of undifferentiated time ("thousands of years"), the Native population becomes a distinct tribe ("Wampanoag Indians"). Unfortunately, the moment these original inhabitants enter "history" (when they are recognized and named) is when they are eliminated. If the "plague" that destroyed them is not identified, its source is (the colonists). Nick, however, sidesteps the details, transmuting history into the paranormal with a discursive sleight of hand. When "you have land that has so much history, and so much tragedy," he states, it provides "the perfect recipe for a haunting."

As they pick their way through the forest, Katrina notes that "literally thousands of families died in these woods. I wonder what we're stepping on?" Absorbed into the landscape, Native Americans become literally part of the land, the ground "America" stands on. By implying (erroneously) that the Wampanoag have "tragically" ceased to exist, the episode acknowledges their original right to the land, a concession that costs nothing as long as no one is left to make a legal claim. Any sense of guilt for the mass casualties that made it possible for the colonists and their descendants to gain ownership is sidestepped by imagining that symbolically the Wampanoag never left, i.e., Native Americans cannot have been permanently dispossessed of their land if they are still physically part of it, discursively inseparable from it. Native peoples are thus granted rights to the land on the condition that they are dead.

Being one with the land becomes literal in the trope of Indian burial grounds. Popularized in films in the early 1980s (*The Amityville Horror* [1979], *The Shining* [1980], and *Poltergeist* [1982]), the trope that paranormal forces are unleashed when an "Indian burial ground" is disturbed is both widely parodied and accepted as a symbol of wrongful appropriation and cultural culpability.[28] In *A Haunting*, "The Unleashed" (2006), "a man discovers an Indian burial ground on his property."[29] The narrator sets the scene:

> Standish, Michigan, a rural town near the shores of Lake Huron, was once the hunting grounds of Native American tribes. To this day, many of their descendants believe in the divine power of the spirit realm. With this comes a profound respect for the dead. And a warning. Whoever disturbs sacred burial grounds will unleash the unholy. The year is 1974.

Randy, an aimless young man in his twenties, is helping his father renovate an old house. Digging in the basement, they find human bones. While the son thinks this might be evidence of a murder, the father (illogically) responds that "this house is a hundred years old"—as if the passage of time would alter the cause of death. Putting the bones in a cardboard box, they consult a local doctor who confirms that the bones belong to an earlier era, backdating them to a time before the town existed. The entire area, he tells them, can be considered an "old Indian burial ground." The men conclude that the proper thing would be to put the bones "back where they belong," and they rebury them without ceremony back in the basement. Randy, however, "becomes fascinated by Indian burial grounds and the mysteries that surround them" and begins to read up on "how to summon spirits." Here, however, the story takes a turn as Randy is drawn to a book on witchcraft, which leads him to start casting spells, become possessed by the devil, and so on. Although Randy has indeed "unleashed the unholy," it is meddling with the occult that nearly does him in. Like the bones in the basement, the topic of respect for Native American remains is unceremoniously dropped. Unlike the intangible presences, shadows, and feelings found in the woods in "Oliver House," episodes dealing with Indian burial grounds present tangible evidence of the deaths of individual human beings—whose stories are left untold.

Vanishing

Numerous episodes of paranormal reality television begin with brief glimpses and enigmatic references to Native Americans, suggesting that this time what haunts America will be identified, contended with, and addressed. Teasers or opening montages designed to draw in the audience with promises of frightening moments, dramatic confrontations, and sensational subject matter are often replete with references to Native Americans, but time and again, as the episode unfolds, the subject of Native Americans is abandoned, replaced by unrelated occult matters that are depicted as more pressing. Early in each episode, the hosts of investigative shows are quite eager to connect the paranormal to anything Indian. In "Leslie's Family Tree" (*Ghost Adventures*, 2016), the owner of a café in Utah is talking to host Zak Bagans about her paranormal experiences when she casually mentions, "I did see an Indian one day." Zak leans forward in his chair, and presses her for more. "The Native American Indian that you saw, I wanna know details," he insists, as the soundtrack fills with familiar indicators of things "Indian" (a flute, drums, chanting).[30] The image cuts to a silhouetted figure in a feathered headdress, lit from behind by the red light of dancing flames.

Excited by the potential for more, Zak gathers the crew. "I think that what's lacking here is the history," he announces. "Let's find a library, let's find a museum, let's go there and do some of our research." On the way, teammate

Jay fills us in on the 1850's "Walker War" between Mormons and the Utes. Jay surmises that the café has become the target of "such vicious attacks" because the land it stands on "is literally covered in blood." A red stain spreads across an animated map as Zak states that "both Mormon and Native American blood . . . saturate this territory." The cause of that bloodshed is muddled, however, as we hear two competing official (i.e., white) accounts of what happened. At the library, a historian says that the war began when a white trader shot an Indian and a member of his tribe shot a white sentry in revenge. A short time later, the investigators visit a monument that attributes the "first murder" to "an Indian feigning friendship." The discrepancy is not discussed. For Zak, the critical point is that "a Native American Indian [*sic*] *could* have died here." While the possibility alone seems sufficient to satisfy Zak, the deaths of Native Americans are not pursued as the episode shifts to the deceased members of the café owner's family, then changes once more to deal with the effects of the investigation on members of the team. The "vanishing Indians" vanish again; they are introduced with great fanfare only to find that the story was not about them after all.

Originally, the owners of Leslie's Family Tree called in Amy Allan and Steve DiSchiavi of *The Dead Files* to investigate paranormal phenomena but they were not pleased with the result.[31] As owner Cory tells Zak, Amy "told us we would have to get a person from every religion—have them come here at the same time and bless the building." And they did try. "We've done a few Mormon blessings and we had a few Indians come, and they've shown me a couple of times how to do things to help spirits cross over." Overall, however, she thinks it only "stirred the whole place up."

Watching *The Dead Files* episode, it is clear why the owners of Leslie's Family tree were so dissatisfied with Amy's advice. Arriving at the site, Amy reports right away that there was "something about this place that felt so wrong." "The land's energy was calling out to me like it had a story to tell," she explains. "The ground is cursed," she concludes. "It is holy land." She confides to the cameraman that there is "only one way" to deal with the café's paranormal problems. "They just need to f—ing knock it down, to be perfectly honest, okay?" Preparing to confront the family, Steve acknowledges that owners "Leslie and Bobby definitely weren't ready for what Amy and I had to say." Amy informs them that a Native American "did a ritual and, like, cursed it." As the owner told *Ghost Adventures*, Amy suggested they "bring in possibly different religious leaders" to spiritually cleanse the property. Steve: "How many are we talking?" Amy: "As many as possible." Leslie agrees ("We'll move on to getting it blessed"), but a title card informs us that, "8 Months Later," "despite multiple offers from mediums and shamans, Leslie and Bobby have done nothing." But we know from *Ghost Adventures* that they did consult someone; they "had a few Indians come."

By keeping actual Indians at arm's length, these episodes inevitably privilege white readings of Native cultures. When a young woman on *My Ghost Story: Caught on Camera* is beset by an inhuman entity, her local (non-Indian) paranormal investigator declares that she is "probably dealing with a shapeshifter." He explains that, according to his understanding of Native American beliefs, souls can choose to come back in either human or animal form. Later, he reports that he has talked "to the elders" to get "counseling" on how best to proceed. Rather than accepting their authority directly in this matter, however, he decides to "get three tribes together and take" what he deems "the best from each tribe." This decision not only ignores or trivializes the differences from tribe to tribe, it establishes Native American culture(s) as something the dominant white culture feels free to pick and choose from according to its own needs and values. White mediators (historians, investigators) relay the information they have gathered from (unseen and unheard) Native sources who exist in some unspecified space "out there."

If we accept that these are not Native Americans' stories, but instead stories that use the figure of the Native American, what these examples illustrate is how that process operates and how the figure of the Native American functions in reality television's accounts of the paranormal. Although sidelined in these texts, First Peoples have not vanished or been subsumed into the land as "tragic" figures. Members of many tribes maintain their languages, histories, and beliefs across the American continent(s). When it comes to paranormal television, though, one is tempted to wonder whether any "real" Indians will ever show up. As historian Jill Lepore points out, "White Americans came to define themselves in relation to an imagined Indian past. That definition, however, required that there be no Indians in the present, or at least not anywhere nearby."[32]

"We Had a Few Indians Come"

Now and then actual members of existing tribes appear in paranormal programs though they tend to populate the fringes rather than being the central

"Bonnie Springs Ranch," *Ghost Adventures*

subjects of an episode.[33] On *Paranormal State*, for instance, a woman calls in the PRS team because one night she "woke up to more than ten Native Americans standing around her" ("Who is the Lurking Man?" [2010]). "I really don't want you to think I'm crazy," she says staring at the woods in the backyard, but "there are beings" in the trees "watching you." "If you look hard enough, you can see them," she insists; they're "pretty much everywhere." Asked to describe these beings, she says, "They look like Native American men," noting that the property is close to a reservation. The team calls in "Rick, our Native American consultant." Rick uses a large feather to waft sage smoke toward the house but it is Ryan who tells us this is "a cleansing prayer on the land using sage and songs to reach out to the dead and bring peace." In another episode, Ryan and the crew contact representatives of a local tribe to deal with spirits who are bothering a family ("Shape Shifter" [2008]). "Maybe there's something in the woods," Ryan suggests, "something in the land." Visiting the site, Brent Allaire and Ron Strongheart, identified as members of the Penobscot Nation, explain their sense of connection to the land. "The Native people believe that we came from the trees," Brent tells Ryan. When someone disturbs the land, they disturb spirits. Finding that a mound of stones has been shoved aside, Brent declares "the ground's unhappy." "I think when they built the house, they disturbed" a spirit, he suggests. Ron agrees. "They need to atone. They need to give back whatever they moved." The men smudge the location by burning sage in an abalone shell and spreading the smoke with an eagle feather. Smudging is "our way

Brent Allaire, *Paranormal State*

Smudging, *Paranormal State*

of praying," Ron explains. Ron begins a sentence ("As the smoke rises—") and Brent finishes it ("—that will seal it").³⁴

While the hosts of these shows attempt to pay respect to Native cultures by acknowledging expertise other than their own, sometimes it is the distance between cultures that comes across most clearly, especially when it comes to the paranormal. For instance, after Ryan is explicitly warned not to move some stones ("It's extremely dangerous," Brent tells him), he does it anyway. Chastised, he responds, "We can always place them back"—a cavalier attitude that does not meet with approval from the Penobscot elders. When *Ghost Adventures* investigates an abandoned hospital in Minnesota ("Nopeming sanitarium" [2015]), Zak announces, "This is a place of pure f—ing hell." "So much death" has passed through the site, he muses, its "residue gets stuck here, gets trapped here." Chippewa and "Fond du Lac tribal elder" Bob Danielson has a radically different view. "The spirits came through here," he tells Zak. "They were here today, telling me that everything was okay." Referring to his peoples' belief in the beneficial powers of the land before the hospital was built, he explains, "This is where they would take their sick to heal." For Zak, the hospital is a trap, a place to die abandoned in the midst of the Puritans' threatening wilderness. (Ominously, we are told that the name "Chippewa" means "out in the woods.") For Danielson, the building and its history are incidental; it is the acres of forested land that are the true source of physical and spiritual sustenance.

While investigators present paranormal phenomena as threatening because it violates a rational western understanding of the world, for Danielson a sudden cold spot is no more frightening than a gentle breeze. "The spirits ... learn to travel on the wind," he says. "I feel that cold wind that they travel on." Standing in a spot where investigators had encountered phenomena earlier, Danielson says, matter-of-factly, "They're around us right now." According to Danielson, death is not a negative condition or even a permanent separation. "Our elders the Ojibwe's [sic] have ended here. So this is the place they go out from. This could very well be their portal back when they want to interact with us or they need to be here."[35] Danielson's presentation of the Chippewa view of spirits as "living" beings who travel back and forth from a parallel world is akin to the attitude espoused in shows about psychic mediums. As such, it is incompatible with the potential horror, fear, and danger investigative programs rely on to build suspense. After this introductory interview, the "Chippewa elder" is promptly left behind as the team members set off to prove themselves by confronting the unknown.[36] Clearly, it is not Native Americans who are haunted by Native Americans.

Sometimes an episode presents a nuanced, complex view of the history of Native Americans. In *Ghost Stalkers*, "Wheatlands Estate" (2014), the current owners of the estate are eager to explain the land's connection to Native American traditions. In the basement, there is a large geode that, like the crystal in an old radio, can transmit frequencies that enable communication from unidentified, distant locations. The current owners take no credit for knowing this. "We believe it was very special to the Cherokee, and they always knew it was here. They could feel the vibrations." There is also a cemetery that occupies "a site chosen by ancient Cherokee Indians for its proximity with the spirit world." An early settler had a "covenant with the Cherokee" that he "would keep" the burial ground "sacred," they explain. "Nothing was ever built on it." In the midst of this vision of respectful coexistence between Indian and European, though, is acknowledgment of violence and betrayal. A massacre took place nearby. "Twenty-eight were killed here and they're buried in a mass grave beside the creek." Regardless of their efforts to pay respect to Native American traditions by inviting individuals to participate as guests or consultants, these episodes reenact the displacement of Native peoples by privileging the experiences of the show's main (white) characters. At Wheatlands, the subject of Native Americans is dropped altogether as the episode's second half documents the effect of the geode on John and Chad.

The fate of Native Americans is not the only trauma haunting American history. Stories about Native Americans overlap with and are sometimes superseded by slave narratives. On *Ghost Stalkers*, Wheatlands might feature "a trail used by Native Americans over a forty-thousand-year period," but when the hosts learn that the cemetery was also used as a burial ground for slaves, they react as if they have hit a paranormal jackpot. Combine the paranormal potential of a nearby river, a geode in the basement, a "slave graveyard *and* an Indian burial ground," and you have a location that is "ripe for portal formation." In *A Haunting*, "The Shadowman," the woods near a Florida housing development are said to have been "a refuge for escaped slaves as well as Native Americans fleeing the Seminole wars." In "The Dark One: Abilene TX" (*The Dead Files*, 2014), a local historian describes bloody conflicts that existed well before Europeans arrived. After investigator Steve DiSchiavi learns that the Humanos were driven out by the Apaches who were, in turn, attacked by Comanches, psychic Amy Allan shifts the story away from inter-tribal conflict. "Were there slaves in this area," she asks? The rest of the episode focuses on a man who came from Kentucky to start a plantation and brought enslaved people to work on it. Someone steeped "in the voodoo tradition," Amy explains, must have summoned the spiritual force that now haunts the location because that force is "native to Africa." The source of the client's paranormal problems, she concludes, is not the multiple histories of violence that took place here, but "a single entity" she calls "the Dark One." This creature "wasn't a devil and it wasn't a demon," but its presence makes Amy "extremely, extremely worried." Even though they might not be common in Abilene, Texas, Amy insists that the family bring in "a voodoo priest"—and even that, she fears, might not help.

In episodes dealing with Native American and African American history, paranormal programs encounter a darkness that is more historic than supernatural. When Nick and Katrina find that the Oliver House where the Wampanoags were nearly annihilated by disease was also connected to slavery, Katrina describes herself as feeling "a little overwhelmed with the density of the history." Exploring the basement where, purportedly, people who had escaped slavery hid from their pursuers, she is momentarily overcome. "It really just brings it home just how desperate they were. It was horrible." Nick's response is, not surprisingly, inadequate. "Yep. Well, that was slavery."

On rare occasions, African Americans are shown taking an active part in American history beyond the context of slavery, though this is not always an improvement. A white man visiting New Mexico purchases the antique uniform of a Black Buffalo Soldier.[37] Its original owner is identified by name, a nineteenth-century photograph, and documents from the National Archives. Having tried on the coat, the new owner is attacked that night by the bloodthirsty spirits of "two Apache warriors." According to the story's perverse logic, this is all a misunderstanding. The white man is an innocent bystander unwittingly caught between "historic" enemies. "This area is just absolutely filled with the history of the violence that took place between the Buffalo Soldiers and the Apache warriors." The extent of the Black man's guilt, we are told, can only be guessed at: "Who knows how many Native Americans he killed?" Made to bear the full weight of US policy, the soldier "died in a government hospital for the insane," presumably driven mad by Apache spirits.

The combination of Native American history and the exploitation of African American slave labor increases the number of sensational stories available for use in paranormal programs. It also reinforces popular culture's concept of history-as-trauma and the paranormal as a reaction to trauma. In struggling to confront the traumas of American history, paranormal reality TV falls back on the spectral to express the indescribable and unspeakable. But, like the "Dark One" of paranormal lore, some horrors are too profound to name.

Abuses of History

If Native Americans are made to disappear by being equated with the land, African Americans are transformed into signifiers of "History"—something kept at arm's length and securely fixed in a distant past. Figures in other people's stories, they become imaginary/imagined characters conjured up by white narrators seeking to spice up a narrative by presenting graphic and disturbing stories about suffering, exploitation, and death.

Appropriating slave stories requires some finesse. An episode of *Ghost Hunters* illustrates how difficult it is to even find the words. In "Angel of Death" (2016), a (white) client who owns a haunted restaurant in Brandenburg, Kentucky, tells the investigators, Dustin and KJ, about a woman who was hanged there back in the days when the building was the town jail. "Lucy was a slave who, um, was said to have killed, uh, her owner. And she pled not guilty to it, but they, uh, they held her here. And then they took her life, outside here, as well." From the outset, the teller of this tale stumbles. The first time he hesitates is in his characterization of Lucy and what she did. The speaker clearly does not want to say simply that she killed someone. He also does not want to use the term "her owner" when it comes to describing who she (may or may not have) killed. The reasons for his hesitation are manifold. To use the term "owner" risks making him seem complicit with slavery by reproducing/endorsing the nomenclature of a system wherein people were legally "owned." Saying that she killed someone also puts him on the side of those who accused her unjustly. Therefore, he opts for the formulation "was said to have killed" (said by others, not him), and immediately points out that the claim was disputed ("she pled not guilty"). The tale of her hanging narrows the injustice to which "Lucy" was subjected to the single event of her death and not the lifelong injustice of being enslaved. It also limits the character of "Lucy" to that of a victim. If the speaker were to say "she killed," he would risk implying that she was guilty in legal terms and thus deserved hanging. But the fact that Lucy is identified as a slave—someone imprisoned within an unjust, morally indefensible system—could lead the audience to conclude that killing her captor was not simply self-defense (a legal justification for homicide) but a bold act of resistance to the social, legal, and political conditions in which she was forced to live. Rhetorically, by refusing to say "she killed," the speaker constructs Lucy as "innocent" (i.e., sympathetic) at the cost of taking away her power to fight back.

The third time the speaker cuts himself off is when he catches himself obscuring the identity of the people responsible for imposing (multiple) injustices on Lucy. "They, uh, they held her here." This sentence directs attention away from the speaker toward others ("they") while bringing it back to the very spot he is standing on ("here"). He adds oddly, "And then they took her life, outside here, as well." As well as what? Judicial murder—whether judicial or extra-judicial—is framed as supplemental, just one more in a series of violations. Hanging or lynching a woman (who may or may not have killed her "owner"), he adds, was done "as kind of a warning to other slaves not to do the same thing."

Without hesitation, KJ chimes in: "That's right. That's where the slavemasters basically came for miles with their slaves to show them exactly what would happen to them." While KJ eagerly displays his understanding of how slavery functioned, Dustin establishes their distance from it—"Yeah. Horrible stuff"—before adding a few more painful details to make the story juicier. Addressing Lucy, supposedly present in the air around them, he says, "They say that you gave birth to a child and then, shortly after, they took you outside and took your life." Answered by silence, Dustin confesses some doubt regarding his ability to truly understand the character and scenario he has helped create. "I can't imagine how difficult that would be," he says. KJ dismisses the entire exercise, noting, "Well, neither one of us knows what it's like to be a slave . . . so it's hard to imagine what it would be like." These disclaimers acknowledge the limited value of reducing history to a series of "horror" stories while at the same time establishing a safe distance between the teller and the tale. Not only are the speakers not responsible for what was done back then, they cannot even imagine it. The need to disavow their relation to this American legacy (a connection they refuse to imagine) is demonstrated by the way the segment concludes. In one sentence, the ghost hunters deliver a ritualized expression of sympathy that minimizes Lucy's slavery, imprisonment, and execution. "We're very sorry to hear your fate, but you're in a much better place now."

Assuming that hauntings are motivated by injustices that have gone unrecognized, these shows suggest that psychics and investigators can symbolically rectify past wrongs. Routinely able to tell an individual spirit's story and help him or her "move into the light," they can now assuage injustice on a much larger scale. Unfortunately, rather than fully engaging with the long-hidden (or suppressed) truth, paranormal shows often end up papering it over. Like *Ghost Hunters*, "Angel of Death," paranormal programs often opt for sentimental complacency. Regardless of how bad things *were*, everything is better now.

The urge to declare an end to a haunting is at odds with the need to generate terror. Presenting history as a showcase of horrors feeds the genre's predilection for sensationalism. *Ghost Adventures*, "Haunted Savannah" (2014), for example, focuses on the violent deaths of two women.[38] Exploring an antebellum mansion, Zak asks the tour guide for all the salacious details. "We heard that Mr. Sorrel was having sex with a slave" named Molly and "his wife walked in on them," he blurts out. The white female tour guide picks up the story. "Documentation found in the form of family letters" confirms that, shortly after learning of her husband's actions, Sorrel's wife, Mathilda, threw herself off the balcony. Then, "two weeks after Mathilda committed suicide, Molly was found hanging in the very room [where] Mathilda had discovered her husband with her. It's believed that she might've been murdered to cover up the scandal." This sensational tale of sex, suicide, and murder is underscored by a reenactment of Molly's death by hanging. There is a pause as we contemplate a woman's bare feet swaying above the ground.

As the episode proceeds, the details of this lurid story are subject to multiple interpretations. Molly's death is clearly presented as murder as a noose is placed around the neck of a crying, frightened young woman by the hands of an unidentified white man. The question of Molly's death is reopened, however, when Zak and Aaron use "the SB7 Spirit Box" to channel the voices of spirits. A woman's voice comes through, saying "rape." "This might be the motive behind Molly's death," Zak declares excitedly. "Could an event that traumatic have driven Molly to take her own life?" Instead of one suicide, there might have been two, both due to sexual predations by "the master." Then again, both women could have been murdered. If Mr. Sorrel was capable of killing Molly to prevent a scandal, why not his wife as well?

The word "rape" (repeated nine times in a twenty-second span) rewrites the original scene describing a wife discovering her husband with another woman, a situation Zak initially called a "love affair." Two more messages broadcast through the spirit box alter our reading of the scene once more. An anxious woman with an American accent says sharply, "Get him!" to which an older woman with a British accent responds resignedly, "I can't." This snippet featuring "two female spirits" talking to each other foregrounds the relationship between the women, with wife Mathilda helpless to protect Molly from her husband's criminal acts.

Molly—enslaved, probably raped, and possibly murdered—is not the only African American woman to be subjected to violence in "Haunted Savannah." A parallel story at a second location features a reenactment where a middle-aged black woman is being strangled by an unseen force. Zak asks another white female tour guide, "Do African Americans have a hard time investigating" the corner of the building he refers to as "the old slave quarters?" Yes, she agrees, but "it's usually young African American women [who] feel hands around their throats." The murdered bodies of women litter the site which is the reason the team say they were attracted to it in the first place. Three white women were "butchered" there at the turn of the century in a notorious ax-murder (reenacted with numerous close-ups of a dripping ax and women's blood-soaked torsos). Race and patriarchal violence intersect in that case, too. We are told that the police rounded up over a hundred African American men only to find that the killer was the estranged (white) husband of one of the women.

Telling the stories of the dead is a fundamental part of history and does not automatically equate to appropriation, sensationalism or rank exploitation. Now and then, paranormal investigators step up and face the ethical issues involved in "paranormal-izing" history. This happens most memorably in the *Paranormal State* episode "Spirits of the Slave Dungeon" (2010), in which Ryan and his friends are "schooled" on the ethics of using historical suffering to sell tickets to a show. Invited to Charleston, South Carolina, to investigate the "Old Charleston City Jail," the team members soon realize that they are complicit in promoting a for-profit, carnival-style "haunted house" tour. Their tour guide (or "ghost host") rushes through his well-rehearsed patter enthusing that "approximately 13,000 people died in this building"—many of whom, as psychic Michelle Belanger points out, "were probably African American slaves." Tourists are invited to stand where slaves once stood: on a box, their arms placed in ropes above them, waiting to be whipped. (The lash would "strip the flesh right off," the guide says, almost licking his lips. Step right up, folks.) The next day Michelle is sent to consult with Dr. Powers, a professor of history and an African American, who tells her how central the jail was in keeping slavery operating smoothly. Her eyes suddenly open, Michelle tells the rest of the team that they should not believe what they have been told on the tour. "History has been whitewashed."

Suddenly, the investigation is interrupted by an unannounced visitor. Michelle tells Ryan someone wants to see them.

> Michelle: "He's a Yoruba priest—African-based religion."
> Ryan: "How did he know we were here?"
> Michelle: "He woke up. He says the spirits told him to be here."

Although he introduces himself as both a cultural anthropologist and "a priest in the Yoruba tradition," Dr. O. is far from exoticized. Wearing a simple polo shirt and white cap, he positions himself quietly and forcefully as a spokesman. "The spirits of the jail brought me here." He needed to intervene, he says, because Ryan and his friends are potentially harmful, their motives dubious. "I wanted to come to see in what way you were disturbing" the

"Spirits of the Slave Dungeon," *Paranormal State*

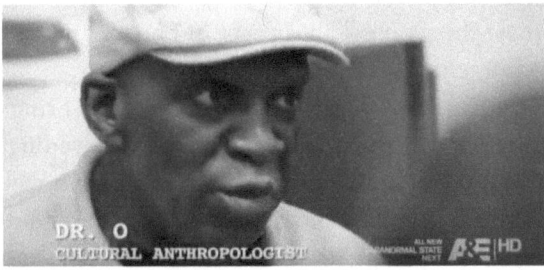

"Spirits of the Slave Dungeon," *Paranormal State*

spirits, he tells them. Balancing his claim of religious authority with western credentials, Dr. O. explains, "I went to graduate school—spent ten years to get a PhD in anthropology so that I can better . . . contextualize what goes on here and to stand up to people who are insensitive." The investigators' attempts to differentiate themselves from the hucksters peddling cheap scares are dismissed out of hand. "What I observed," Dr. O. informs them, "you came to *get*." From the spirits' point of view, "You came to get something from them. You say that your intention is more noble than that, but to them you look like everybody else who come—they come with cameras, they come with inquiries. No one comes *asking*." It is arrogant and presumptuous to demand that spirits make a sign or show themselves, he tells them. "We can't assume that they are gonna appear just because we want them to." He tells them there is a more appropriate, culturally sensitive method. "In the Yoruba tradition, we commune with the ancestors. We believe that they are alive. So I would make offerings to those ancestors. We offer flowers. We offer candles. We offer fruit." Knocked off balance, the paranormal group tries to grasp the extent of their culpability. In the next scene Ryan "answers" Dr. O.'s speech, trying to see things from the point of view of the jail's former inmates.

> Imagine you're imprisoned because your skin is a different color. You are not fed well. You are worked to death here as punishment and then you die here. For whatever reason, you are still bound to this place. And now, here comes a bunch of people with fanny packs, smiling, looking to be scared.

While Ryan accepts the chastisement ("I'm really ashamed of myself ... for not even thinking of the implications"), teammate Sergey tries to deflect blame. "It also lies with the tour guides," he suggests. "There is a sort of sadness to it," Ryan muses, but Michelle dismisses such sentimentality and takes a position that could undermine the entire paranormal reality genre. "If you really believe these things exist," she insists, "they're not just something there for your entertainment."

Following Dr. O.'s advice, that night the investigators bring an offering of fruit and candles to the "torture room" at the jail. The evening begins with a violent thunderstorm that shakes the jail (Ryan describes it melodramatically as sounding like slaves shaking their chains), but we are told that after the team made the ritual offerings, "the storm subsided." Ryan apologizes to the spirits for the previous night's investigation, then thanks them loudly as the team files out, heads bowed.

For the newly enlightened team, however, their work is not done. Ryan calls John, the tour's owner, and arranges a meeting between him and Dr. O. Earlier, Ryan had raised doubts about the ghost-tour project, asking, "Have you ever thought about ethical or moral dilemmas?" John's response was telling: "I'm not a very sensitive person when it comes to the spirit world." Dr. O. uses the meeting as an opportunity to educate the self-proclaimed insensitive white Southerner on the importance of respecting cultural difference.

> African people and their descendants, you know, their appreciation of the paranormal is not at all like the European appreciation of the paranormal. The deceased are not really deceased. We believe that they're ancestral spirits. It's hurtful, you know, to see voyeurs and spectators. It's disrespectful to go to sacred grounds for amusement.

Dr. O. concludes, somewhat surprisingly, that he is "not prepared to discourage what you're doing." He understands that it is not the businessman's "intention to be offensive." It is even possible to imagine a positive kind of tour, he suggests, one that could be "enhanced" with historical and culturally sensitive detail. "It could be illuminating."

Despite ending on a shameless note of self-congratulation (we see a round of smiling close-ups as Dr. O. thanks Ryan and *Paranormal State* for arranging "a meeting that may have never occurred"), "Spirits of the Slave Dungeon" serves as a corrective to the unexamined assumptions that underlie most representations of the slave-era in paranormal reality TV. The team members accept criticism without being defensive. They not only consult with but defer to people who have deeper historical expertise or more pronounced cultural ties than they have and they change their practice accordingly. Granted, this is a single episode in a crowded field and, as such, its impact is limited. But when addressing members of populations that have been socially or historically disenfranchised (or worse), this episode shows how vital it is for paranormal investigators to examine their own positions.

When they don't, the result is an episode like "Pauly Jail."

Clueless

When *Ghost Asylum*'s Tennessee Wraith Chasers head to Alabama and the Pauly Jail to explore lynchings in the early twentieth century, only two African Americans are consulted in the hour-long episode. They are both interviewed early on by off-camera producers rather than appearing on-screen with team members. Ella, a middle-aged woman, and Raymond, the sheriff, see nothing intriguing about the jail. She thinks the town should "tear it down." He avoids it whenever possible. Team leader Chris describes the jail as a "crucible of death" where prisoners (predominantly Black) "were packed in deplorable conditions and lived in mortal fear of spontaneous hangings." It is little wonder the town's African American citizens harbor no fondness for this local attraction.

Much of the episode focuses on the story of Aberdeen Johnson, "the victim of a brutal lynching by an angry mob." In 1911, the twenty-year-old was accused of "violating" a white woman. Dragging him out of the jail, a mob "castrated him and pulled him over the tree limb and they shot him over 150 times." (That last detail is mentioned repeatedly throughout the episode.) Afterwards, his body was hung him from a tree until "his neck was almost in two." These horrific details are related to Porter by a genteel, older white lady who is identified as a local historian. Not all lynchings were so public, she adds. An unknown number of men and women may have been killed inside the jail, though these were not "official" executions. "What's recorded and what has actually happened," she explains, "sometimes is not always the same."

"In the hopes of drawing Aberdeen out," the team arranges a slide show, projecting what they identify as "graphic, racially charged images." Waiting for the spirits to react, the modern white Southerners find themselves unexpectedly affected by the deluge of violent images (a noose, rioting, policemen turning firehoses on crowds). "These images are pretty crazy," a subdued Chris comments. "A whole lotta bad stuff going on back then," he notes as we see a picture of a hooded man in prison garb on his knees, his back against a post. Chasey Ray expresses sympathy for the former inmates. "Some of y'all that was in here wasn't in here because y'all had done anything." He recognizes the likely injustice of many incarcerations: "Y'all were unjustly imprisoned in here and some of y'all was probably even killed." When it comes to identifying systemic racism as the cause, however, the team comes up short.[39]

One member of the team offers the murdered and desecrated Johnson the opportunity to set the story straight, but first the ghost/victim must listen once again to a litany of grim details. "Aberdeen? They did God knows what else to you before they hung you up and they shot you a hundred and fifty times. You wanna tell the world your story? You wanna tell them what actually happened?" Trying to look at things from Aberdeen Johnson's perspective, another man questions the effectiveness of this brutal recital. "Maybe hearing his own tragic story is upsetting him." But instead of toning it down, Porter introduces *the* archetypal racist myth. He suggests (possibly as an intentional provocation) that perhaps the Black man attacked the white woman after all. "Maybe you did do it," he says, and offers the murdered man the chance to confess and "get it off your conscience." Any hope of a non-exploitative account of Americans who were tortured and murdered as a result of racism ends with a literal thud as the *Ghost Asylum* team uses a heavy sandbag to reenact one of the "unofficial," "spontaneous" hangings carried out inside the jail.

Ghost Brothers

Having people of color anchor a paranormal reality show may not guarantee a more informed or subtle discussion of American history, but it is a

Juwan Mass, Marcus Harvey, and Dalen Spratt, *Ghost Brothers*

change. *Ghost Brothers* (premiering on Destination America in 2016) can be seen as what one scholar calls a "mirror show," a series based on a familiar format with "the only significant change" being "the race/ethnicity of the characters."[40] Reproducing the formula of numerous other ghost-hunting programs, the all-male *Ghost Brothers* team is made up of "three best friends who all had paranormal experiences as kids." Each cast member is easily identifiable as a type: Dalen Spratt, the team leader, is enthusiastic, providing most of each episode's explanatory material and voice-overs; Juwan Mass is the serious one, a former Eagle Scout, tall, quiet, and athletic; and Marcus Harvey provides comic relief.[41]

Canny about the genre, the trio know the terrain in which they operate and all its clichés. They frequently describe their experiences through the lens of media. When Juwan and Marcus enter an empty cabin late at night, the door opens with a prolonged creak straight out of a 1930s horror classic. "Oh, hell no," swears Juwan. Marcus declares, "This feels like a freakin' horror movie." Pushing his way through heavy woods alone at night, Juwan walks face-first into a spider web. Over a night-vision close-up of a large, scary spider, he says, "Either this is a bad horror movie start, or I'm about to become a superhero." Sharp on pop-culture references, the first episode alone mentions *Barbershop* ("When I'm not hunting ghosts, my day job just so happens to be a barber," Marcus tells us), *The Mummy Returns* (they are on their way to see historical artifacts that might be cursed), TV's *Dr. Phil* (they debate the expertise implied by the title "doctor"), and the male-stripper film *Magic Mike* (Juwan takes his shirt off).

As with the exaggerated "southern-ness" of *Ghost Asylum* (with its Tennessee Wraith Chasers, characters named Doogie and Chasey Ray, heavy accents, and countrified sayings), the Ghost Brothers are called upon to perform ethnicity. Reality television scholar Laurie Ouellette points out that on reality television in general—and in "look-alike" shows in particular—it is important to "ask how identity and difference are performed on the shows, and for what purposes."[42] If producers "search not only for people with certain demographics, but specifically for people who embody the *assumed traits of those demographics*," the result can be the reiteration of long-standing racist tropes.[43] Enlisting African American performers to express comically exaggerated fearfulness, for example, perpetuates a racist stereotype that can be traced back to Buckwheat (*Our Gang*), Willie Best, and Stepin Fetchit.[44] On *Ghost Brothers*, the characters demonstrate how a knowledge of media history can be used to question such stereotypes while maintaining the show's distinctive comic-provocative tone. After Dalen calls out the entire genre at the start of the first episode ("Why is everybody white?"), Marcus separates himself from the genre: "I can see why they say Black folks don't do this stuff." Later, frightened at being left alone, Marcus confides to the camera, "You know what happens in every horror movie when a brother's by himself." More pointedly, throughout the episode Marcus wears a T-shirt that says in all caps, "Never Sold Dope." Fraternity brothers who met in college, they anticipate the racist lens through which others see young Black men.[45]

Like all investigator shows, *Ghost Brothers* is firmly situated within a capitalist enterprise, promoting its stars as TV personalities while providing publicity for "heritage industry" tours with highly negotiated relationships to the past. The subject of the first episode, the Magnolia Plantation in Louisiana, has served repeatedly as the locus for other paranormal reality series including *Ghost Adventures* in 2009 and *Ghost Hunters* in 2012.[46] A comparison of the *Ghost Brothers* episode with one of its predecessors, however, makes clear the effect of seeing these historic sites from a different perspective.

Ghost Adventures, "Magnolia Lane Plantation," focuses on the death of a white overseer said to have been killed by Union soldiers. Period drawings and reenactments fill out the story of "Mr. Miller" and his brave efforts to save the owner's mansion from being burned. The team calls out to his spirit by name several times during "lockdown," expressing regret for the circumstances of his passing. On *Ghost Brothers*, the same historic events are depicted differently. The team never uses the name "Miller," referring to him exclusively as "the overseer." "By all accounts," Dalen tells the camera, "dude was a dick" [the last word is visible but bleeped]. "So it was a bit of karmic justice," he adds, "that he also died a violent death."[47]

In acknowledging racism, *Ghost Brothers* is careful to distinguish the present from the past. Enthusiastic about meeting Joe (an older, white, paranormal enthusiast who saw an apparition in the window of the overseer's house on a previous visit), Juwan invites him along for that night's investigation: "We would be honored if you would join us." The partnership of the two men becomes the segment's focus as Joe points out how much times have changed for the better. Juwan agrees, pointing out that in the old days "we wouldn't be working together." "Absolutely," Joe adds. Relegating racism's worst manifestations to the past, the men use their genial collaboration as a "trigger object." They surmise that seeing a Black man and a white man working together could provoke the overseer who is assumed to have been a dyed-in-the-wool racist. "He may be a little upset," Joe suggests. "There's gotta be a lot of tension," Juwan agrees. Joe addresses the spirit through a digital voice recorder, "Are you okay with us working together?" he asks. "As *equals*?" Juwan adds pointedly. A close-up of the digital device shows an electronic flare. "When you said 'as equals,'" Joe explains, "something happened": the "emotion just went up in the room." Juwan is clearly pleased to have gotten under the overseer's skin, as it were. "It appears we can actually rile the overseer, so now we're gonna take it to the next level," he says. As Joe goes outside to take EVP readings, Juwan calls to him gleefully from the living room. "Hey Joe! I don't think the overseer's gonna be too happy with me just chillin' in his home, man." Although the mood is upbeat, Juwan admits there is a residue of menace. "The energy is not welcoming at all." Later, in front of the "big house," Juwan confides, "I don't even know how to approach the plantation home. I'm sure *I'm* not welcome."

In trying to imagine themselves as African Americans who lived under slavery, the white team on *Ghost Adventures* indulges in a short-term exercise, spending part of the night in shackles in the plantation house basement. "Can you imagine the dark energy of these slaves being captive" here, Zak asks. "We're trying to recreate this energy right now." The Ghost Brothers are less audacious, acknowledging the distance between themselves and people they call their ancestors. Having trudged across the expansive plantation grounds, an exhausted Marcus stops to rest.

Dalen: "You tired? You got your asthma pump?"
Marcus: "Man, I hate doin' this on a plantation . . ."
Dalen: "You do realize your ancestors worked a little bit harder than that."

> Marcus: "Oh no, I *know*. I felt, like, disrespectful by spraying my inhaler. Like I shoulda toughed it out."

A momentary discomfort cannot be compared to forced labor or a lifetime in chains.

On both programs, the teams meet with Dr. Ken Brown, the archeologist who excavated objects related to voodoo from one of the former slave cabins. *Ghost Adventures* emphasizes the exotic nature of voodoo, especially the secretiveness surrounding it. Pointing to black X's painted on cabin walls, Zak complains, "They're calling it historical graffiti," but he knows better. "It's almost like these park rangers . . . don't want to tell you everything they know." A quick internet search proves his suspicions correct. X's are "used as a symbol for conjuration" in voodoo ceremonies that are explicitly connected with evil, i.e., "calling the demons for help." At the start of their trip, the Ghost Brothers momentarily play with the popular image of voodoo as inherently sinister. "Like voodoo dolls and stuff?" Marcus asks. Dalen nods, "Voodoo, bro." But once on site, they describe the figure of "the voodoo conjuror" as someone who "made medicines and charms and buried them for protection." "The slaves," they explain, "were practicing voodoo to, like, protect themselves from the white master." On *Ghost Adventures*, it is the white master who needs protection. The enslaved Africans, Zak explains, would "take this voodooism and cast these secret curses."

Both episodes use the same antique photograph of a woman called "Aunt Agnes." (The teams differ even when it comes to pronunciation: on *Ghost Adventures*, "aunt" rhymes with "ant," while the Ghost Brothers pronounce it "ahnt" and frequently use the more familial term "auntie.") Entering "Auntie" Agnes's cabin, Dalen introduces himself in Louisiana French. "We should speak to them in their dialect," he explains, "as a sign of respect." (Juwan addresses the spirit as "Tante Agnes.") Before entering the cabin, Dalen announces "[We] come from an angle of, like, love and reverence and deference." Inside, Marcus and Dalen are formal and polite. "Thank you for having us in your home," Marcus says. "We appreciate the hospitality," Dalen adds. The attitude on *Ghost Adventures* could not be more different. Sitting in Aunt Agnes's cabin (identified as "Cabin One" instead), Zak yells, "Is that you, Aunt Agnes?" and starts ordering her around. "Do some voodoo magic on us!" When he commands her to "go in there and touch Aaron!" Aaron rebels.

Aaron: "Dude. Rule Number One. One thing the guy said is you don't taunt voodoo."

Zak: "Am I taunting?"
Aaron: "You're taunting the crap out of it."

Zak relents—a bit—and addresses Aunt Agnes in a more subdued tone. "Alright. I'm not taunting you. I'm just, I'm just yelling . . . I'm just talking loudly."[48]

Needless to say, the Ghost Brothers show respect for Aunt Agnes as soon as they arrive at the plantation. When their camera lights malfunction at the first mention of voodoo, Dalen explains the virtues of diplomacy. "Man, the last thing we wanna do is piss off a voodoo conjuror before we even start our investigation. So we're gonna respect that, give her some space, and just try again tonight." Receiving no response from Aunt Agnes later that night, Dalen and Marcus again reject provocation, positing silence as the spirit's right. "You ain't gotta talk to us. We get it."

The Ghost Brothers' respectful stance comes from thinking about the spirits as if they were family and treating them as such. Left alone in the cabin, Dalen becomes increasingly agitated and starts talking about why he is bothered. "Why I don't wanna be in here by myself?" he asks. "Because if something happens, I'm in here by my *damn* self." He apologizes instantly and corrects himself. "My bad, Auntie Agnes. I didn't mean to cuss in your house." He was raised to know better. "My auntie . . . [she'd] pop me in the mouth for cussing in her house."

By the end of his time in the cabin, Dalen has learned a lesson. Although he cannot see when or how it happened, he realizes that he has lost his lucky ring. It means a lot to him, he explains. He wears it "to every location that we go to." After searching frantically, he realizes, "What really hit me at the last minute before I walked out was, Agnes lost things that she buried in this house." Addressing her spirit, he asks, "Is that how you feel when Dr. Brown dug your stuff up? And misplaced the things that you had?" As we cut back to him speaking directly to the camera, he concludes, "So, I just kinda left it for Agnes. Kinda like an apology." Compare this with the disclaimer familiar from other paranormal shows. On *Ghost Adventures*, for example, Aaron tells Aunt Agnes, "Times are different now. There is no slavery now. I'm sorry you had to go through that." Dalen's apology is personal: from Dalen to Agnes, his hand to hers. He recognizes that people took things from Agnes, after emancipation, even after death, and he accepts that he has a personal responsibility to make reparation by sacrificing something he values.

The ability to consider spirits as analogous to family (as opposed to mere stories) has other consequences. When Dalen first mentions Aunt Agnes's artifacts, Marcus and Juwan think about how their own aunts would feel in a similar situation. "I'm believing that Aunt Agnes couldn't be happy with somebody just, like, digging up the stuff that she set to protect everybody with," Marcus opines. "*My* auntie wouldn't be happy," Juwan agrees. Understanding the paranormal through the lens of family can also serve as a source of humor. When he and Dalen fail to get a response from Auntie Agnes while visiting her cabin that night, Marcus has an idea. "You know what it could be, though? . . . Aunties do go to bed early." Picturing the scene together, they go off on an extended riff about aunts preparing for bed.

> Dalen: "Her hair wrapped and everything."
> Marcus: "Her hair wrapped. She done took her bra off. She got her muumuu on, she got a cigarette. [changing to falsetto] 'Man, didn't I tell yo ass get in that bed?'"[49]

As one series, it is too much to ask *Ghost Brothers* to single-handedly redress the oversights of over a decade of paranormal shows. Not every *Ghost Brothers* episode is as (relatively) progressive as the first. For example, in its second season the show visits the "Old City Jail," where the *Paranormal State* team learned a lesson about showing respect for the thousands of African Americans who were abused and died there. When *Ghost Brothers* arrives, their investigation centers on a white couple who supposedly poisoned hotel guests in the nineteenth century.[50] (The wife is trumpeted as being possibly "the first female serial killer!") The history of slavery and institutionalized racism comes up only once. Driving into town, Marcus identifies Charleston, South Carolina as "one of the first stops when they used to bring the slaves over." Dalen, in the front seat, changes the subject, drawing attention to the beautiful architecture. Around the same time, an attempt to construct a multiracial ghost-hunting team fell flat. On 2016's *Ghosts in the Hood* (WE), a semi-comic group identified as the O.P.O. (Official Paranormal Operations) includes three African American men slotted into the usual roles: "founder" Defecia, "technical expert" Dave, and "comedian" Matty (also identified as the "resident scaredy-cat"). An African American woman (Jasmine) is the team's "verified medium," and an Asian woman, Maunda Oyin, its "chief researcher." Based in Los Angeles, the spooky areas where this team dares to venture are identified as "bad" neighborhoods (i.e., those with majority non-white populations).[51] Places they investigate include a drive-thru funeral home in Compton and a "spirit-plagued piñata shop."[52] Its sixth episode was its last.

The Stories They Tell

Despite radically different (if occasionally overlapping) histories, Native Americans and African Americans occupy a similar position in paranormal reality television's depiction of modern-day America. Both communities are relegated to the past and subjected to the dominant culture's impulse to transform them into figures in someone else's story, someone else's idea of history. When a Native American speaks in the paranormal reality genre, it is usually as a guest on someone else's show. Granted a limited amount of screen time, they are invited to answer the white investigator's questions or asked to clean up someone else's problem with sage and feathers. It is difficult in these circumstances to establish Native culture as a full, living tradition. The pattern of appropriation can be disrupted or at least modified when programs built on first-person testimony offer Native Americans the chance to "speak for themselves"—as subjects reporting on their own experiences from their own perspective and expressing truths about their lives that are not expressed on other paranormal programs. Addressing the viewer directly as they stare through the camera's lens, speakers seem to commandeer television technology, a stance that imbues their words with authority and their images with a powerful sense of presence. Perhaps the most important point conveyed in such moments—and one that needs to be constantly reasserted—is simply, "We are here."

One series, in particular, takes advantage of the first-person witness model to feature actors, musicians, comedians, athletes, and media personalities from a variety of ethnic and racial backgrounds. *Celebrity Ghost Stories* (discussed in chapter 1) routinely presents a more diverse image of America, breaking decisively with paranormal television's standard representation of the population as exclusively white. By its very structure, offering three to five segments per episode, *Celebrity Ghost Stories* has more opportunities for inclusiveness. People of color appear in nearly every episode, including Latino performers (Carlos Mencia, Erik Estrada, Maria Conchita Alonso, Tony Plana), Asian Americans (Ming Na, Margaret Cho), and African Americans (Billy Dee Williams, Chaka Khan, Chi McBride, Giancarlo Esposito, and Sugar Ray Leonard).

Many of the issues discussed above come together in a group of stories culled from this series in which African Americans and Hispanic celebrities recall their experiences with the paranormal. The way they tell their stories reveals once again how recourse to the paranormal—as either an expression of faith or a conceptual metaphor—enables the teller to express insights about identity, culture, and history which the dominant society has overlooked or dismissed. The use of paranormal terms signals a willingness to stand apart and to gain strength from exclusion by openly rejecting ways of understanding the world that fail to recognize what are deeply meaningful relationships and events.

In every case, family is presented as the central unit through which meaning is formed. A site of conflict in shows such as *Paranormal State* or *Psychic Kids: Children of the Paranormal* (chapter 6), family here becomes a haven, the place where identity is formed, and the root of a broader, sustaining community. There is also more at stake in these stories. The fault lines revealed by the 2008 housing crisis, severe though they might have been, were short-lived compared to the generations of segregation, red-lining, and structural economic inequities that dictated housing options for people of color. Where *Psychic Kids* teaches children how to survive their parents, on *Celebrity Ghost Story* a man learns how not to be destroyed by history.

For Academy Award-winning actor Louis Gossett Jr., family is the embodiment of history, the living connection between past and present. Gossett, who was seventy-eight when he appeared on *Celebrity Ghost Stories* in 2014, begins his story by invoking his great-grandmother, "the matriarch in my family." "I was fortunate enough to be in the life of a woman over 110 years old," he says. Although he tries to minimize or constrain the devastation of slavery, allowing only that his great-grandmother "apparently was a slave," what Gossett chooses to make vivid is the moment of emancipation. "She remembers," he says, when they "got on those buckboards" and "left that plantation after the slaves were freed." Family history is thus inseparable from the nation's history. Family is also where one learns about the paranormal. "There was always a discussion of ghosts, growing up." For Gossett, the past lives on, through those fortunate to have a long life and through those present in paranormal form as spirits or ghosts.

Gossett credits his great-grandmother with saving his life twice. The first time, she used a special herbal recipe when he had a severe asthma attack as a boy. The successful application of folk remedies demonstrates the value to be found in traditional kinds of knowledge that are gained outside of formal education. Here, sustaining contact with different cultural traditions is the difference between life and death.

The second time Gossett's great-grandmother saves him involves spiritual warfare. Shooting a film in Louisiana in the 1980s, Gossett finds himself "next door to the old sugar plantations." "I'd never been in that Deep South," he points out, but he knows it is riddled with ghosts. "They're all over the place," he states, "strong, very strong ghost territory." One night in his hotel, he wakes to find the spirit of a large Black man trying to pull him from his bed. "All of a sudden" he smells the scent of vanilla and cinnamon (something he associates with his great-grandmother) and hears "Great-grandmama" tell the dark spirit, "He's not going nowhere." The evil entity instantly disappears. "She was very authoritative," Gossett explains. "My great-grandmother, she saved my life."

In Gossett's story, the "Deep South"—the land as well as its agricultural and economic legacy as the home of sugar plantations and some of the most onerous conditions for enslaved people—embodies a dark force that threatens to pull him under. The potentially fatal weight of that history is something his great-grandmother already defeated once in her life and she does so again easily after death. "A very strong but a very soft-spoken leader," Gossett's great-grandmother is undaunted by death. Consistent across place and time—with the same sensory evidence (scent), the same actions (saving him), the same motive (love for her grandchild)—Great-grandmama establishes family as an unbroken chain, a positive force stronger than history, demons or death itself.

Like Louis Gossett, Della Reese explains in season four how she owes her life to supernatural maternal intervention.[53] One in a line of strong women, Reese's life mirrors her mother's. When Reese was raising her daughter, she says, "it was just the two of us. . . . We were happiest when we were together. Just like my mother and I." One evening after swimming, Reese is running to get a towel when she falls through a glass door. Severely cut, she sends her daughter for a doctor and waits to die. "I was praying, . . . 'Father, I need help.

Send me some help.'" Suddenly, "an arm ... comes around my head like this and it straightened me up.... I somehow ended up in a chair but there was nobody there. I was overwhelmed. I cannot explain it to you, what happened," but "it's the thing that saved my life." Like Gossett, the maternal figure's presence is identified by the intimate sense of smell. The scent of "cold cream and vanilla flavoring overtook me," Reese continues. "I recognized what it was. It was the smell of my mother." As she waited for help, she recounts, "I felt someone touching my hands and I hear the voice of my mother.... She comforted me. She told me that it was gonna be okay." At the hospital, doctors provide emergency medical care ("I had a thousand stitches. I lost seven pints of blood—I only had nine"), but Reese believes "beyond a shadow of a doubt that what saved me was my mother." The fact that her mother had been dead for ten years is both irrelevant to Reese and risks obscuring what is most important. That her mother was, and is, with her. "She's watching over me."

Reese integrates the spiritual and the physical as her story collapses past and present. As with Gossett, what might be dismissed as merely spiritual consolation has a physically unmistakable, multi-sensory presence—through touch, hearing, and smell. For Reese, faith coexists with modern medicine—she still needed stitches and a blood transfusion—but faith is more sustaining. Best known for her role in the scripted series *Touched by an Angel* (1994–2003) and its assertive promotion of Christian values, Reese makes it clear that the appearance of a ghost or spirit is not the result of any subversive occult practice but of a piece with her religious faith.[54] Her mother's presence is the direct result of her prayer to the "Father" to send someone. More to the point, "family" is God's instrument. In place of a generic celestial figure (e.g., Cathy Sheets praying to St. Michael the Archangel in chapter 1), Reese is saved by the member of her family with whom she is most intimately familiar. Nor is Reese disturbed by intra-Christian debates speculating that ghosts are demonic impostors (chapters 3, 4). Unlike other first-person witnesses discussed above, Gossett and Reese never doubt their own judgement. Neither frightened nor confused, they do not seek validation. What Reese and Gossett convey as they tell their stories is conviction in their own judgment, perception, experience, and authority. When they look into the camera and tell you what happened, they're not asking you to believe them. They're telling you.

The depiction of families is not entirely nostalgic. As with Gossett and Reese, a multigenerational line of women (living and dead) sustain and comfort actress/choreographer Debbie Allen. Distraught over her parents' divorce, a nine-year-old Debbie wakes to find an unearthly figure standing at her bedside.[55] "I was so frightened," she says, but then "I realized that it was my grandmother." Though her grandmother died before Allen was born, "I knew that it was her." "It's like she was glowing. . . . Just emanating her own light. She calmed me down." "It was amazing." The next morning, Allen tells her mother. Not only did she seem "happy about the visitation," even better, "Mom believed me." Unlike the young people who struggle to convince their parents of their psychic visions on *Paranormal State* or *Psychic Kids: Children of the Paranormal*, Allen finds unquestioning support.

Actress Pam Grier tells a similar story of a family beset by internal strife. One day her grandfather ("We called him Daddy Ray") takes her to visit his late mother's farm in Wyoming.[56] Left alone for a moment, Grier is approached by a man who seems to appear from out of nowhere. "He cracks this soft smile. And he says, 'I'm Uncle Joe. I live here. It's my home.'" "This is our land," he insists. "This is sacred. You tell Daddy Ray not to sell this house." She persuades her grandfather that the message from beyond is genuine, but the rest of the family scoff and sell the house anyway. "It was very sad," she remembers. Grier, however, returns as an adult and buys "a piece of land that no one else wanted," turning it "into this little oasis" for the living *and* the dead—"a place that Daddy Ray and Big Mama and Uncle Joe would be proud of."

Set within a large, multigenerational family, Grier's story takes us beyond the figure of the valiant single mother or matriarch. Grier's idyllic childhood is peopled by strong, supportive male figures, grandfathers, and uncles who provide a reassuring physical and spiritual presence. Overcoming interfamily conflict, Greer grows up, succeeds financially, and finds a way to retrieve what was lost. Wyoming's western landscape offers Grier and her family a dramatically different relationship to land than the one outlined by Gossett. In place of a visit to the "Deep South," Greir's family in Wyoming is rooted in a western ranching tradition untainted by the antebellum history of slavery. Even the loss of her grandmother's farm is neither tragic nor permanent. If the original land was sold, the memory of it—and the vision of family it represents—may be reclaimed. This moment from her childhood gives Grier a template for the future, a way to come full circle and restore generational and spatial continuity. The segment ends with the younger Grier gazing out over the landscape as three ghostly figures appear behind her, smiling. Agreeing with Reese, Allen, and Gossett before her, Grier says, "I know my family is with me."

In these episodes, staged shots with actors visualize family unity. Debbie Allen's story ends with a similar shot where mother and daughter embrace in the kitchen as the spirit of a benevolent grandmother looks on. Such dramatizations are one of the most controversial aspects of paranormal reality television. When asked if they considered including reenactments in their paranormal-themed reality programs, all three of the producers of *Ghost Hunters* recoiled in unison: "No!"[57] Nevertheless, dramatic reenactments of past events are central to first-person series like *Celebrity Ghost Stories*, enabling television to express visually what witnesses relate in words while shaping stories around moments that can be acted out for maximum dramatic effect. But, as the producers fear, the transparent falsity of having actors pose as the well-known speaker we see before us has the potential to strain the audience's trust that what they see is "real." This is not necessarily fatal to the reception of the speaker's testimony, however. Capitalizing on the image's capacity to condense desire into a single image, these shots are presented as unabashed fabrications, re-creating the speaker's vision of the family as reconstituted and restored. We also cannot forget that every dramatization in a first-person program is authorized by the speaker. When Allen or Grier tell us what happened "when I was a child," they smooth and legitimize the transition to scenes featuring actors playing them. These visual trips into the past can broaden the celebrity's appeal by giving us, literally, another way to see her: as a child, the "ordinary" person she was before she became famous. The use of actors can even expand the potential for identification by depicting the speaker as possessing a multiple-subjectivity. When a celebrity is shown to have lived different lives at different times (and not just the one for which s/he is publicly known), it gives audiences more opportunities to find common ground with the celebrity and the stories s/he tells. While not everyone had the nurturing, supportive, multigenerational families described above, the transformation of these ideals into images makes it easier to imagine oneself there. Presenting/creating images of African American families as models of "family" shifts them to a place central in the popular imagination, momentarily rectifying the pattern of exclusion we see in other paranormal reality programs.

With all its consolations, family can still be shown to harbor or even produce conflicts that, in the most extreme circumstances, erupt into violence.

As a young teen, Puerto Rican singer Lisa Lisa Velez has a happy life with her mother in Hell's Kitchen.[58] She babysits for twin girls who live down the hall, though their "macho" father frightens her. One night, after learning from the TV news that the father and the twins are missing, Lisa dreams she is being murdered. "I couldn't breathe. . . . It feels like somebody's holding—they're choking me." A few days later, one of the girls is found dead. Hearing about the dream, Lisa's mother consults a friend who confirms that Lisa has a psychic gift. "You gotta teach her . . . how to control it," the friend urges, "'cuz it's gonna scare her. It's gonna freak her out."

As we have seen in series about mediums, psychics describe the empathy they feel for the victims as being experienced through their own bodies. ("I couldn't breathe," "they're choking me.") Subjected to visions as children, the mediums discussed above must learn to accept and manage their "sensitivity" so that they are not afraid or overwhelmed by it. Lisa and her mother, however, do not need professional psychics to help them. They have friends they can call on, neighbors; they are part of a community. Because of the support the older women give her, Lisa becomes a source of comfort in return. After the police find the body of one of the girls, the other appears to Lisa in a dream. "I think she wanted me to know that she was okay," Lisa remembers. Instead of reliving the violence or feeling fear, Lisa remembers the encounter in a positive light. "I was so happy to see her." As in other segments of *Celebrity Ghost Stories*, we end with a domestic scene, a makeshift family of two women at a kitchen table reassuring a young girl.

One last story demonstrates how the paranormal can provide symbolic consolation in the face of horrific violence, with family at the heart of both. Professional wrestler and actor David Otunga and his fiancée, actress and singer Jennifer Hudson, rent a new house. "As soon as we stepped into this home, little things would happen that were kind of out of the ordinary," he relates.[59] Kitchen cabinets open by themselves; a painting crashes off a wall. Hearing glass break one night, Otunga thinks someone has broken in. "I got in my SWAT team stance," he says, but soon realizes that paramilitary tactics, martial arts training, or any of the male posturing familiar from ghost-hunting shows is sure to be ineffective, even comic. Instead, Otunga, narratively, steps aside, positioning himself as a witness to the power of others (i.e., spirits) fighting on his and his wife's behalf. Venturing into the kitchen, the couple find chaos. All the cabinets are open and they see "a shadow walking towards us." Then, suddenly, "there's this light and we both felt these spirits. . . . We just stared in awe." With the dark entity driven away by the light, the couple pack quickly and leave. Their realtor tells them they are not the first people to have experienced this; the last tenant stayed barely two weeks. The house is haunted because someone was murdered there.

Confronted with such information, most people in paranormal reality shows simply move. A precondition for a horror story, murder is someone else's problem, something that happens to strangers. Otunga and Hudson know murder and its consequences firsthand. Hudson's mother, brother, and nephew were murdered in October 2008 by the estranged husband of Hudson's sister. Otunga refers to them directly, as well as to his late mother, when he mentions family members who have passed on. "Terrified" by the evil that was manifested in the house, Otunga says, "we had something more powerful. We had our own guardian angels in terms of our family that's passed on. . . . That is what saved us." By refiguring his dead family members not as victims but as all-powerful protectors, Otunga symbolically recuperates their deaths. They have not been destroyed but made stronger, as have the living, safeguarded by the spirits of the dead.

Although most first-person accounts presented on *Celebrity Ghost Stories* reaffirm the family as an institution characterized by love and support extending over multiple generations, living and dead, for some, the family as traditionally defined is more repressive than comforting. As we shall see, the series that challenge that institution open new and unsettling questions regarding children, difference, sexuality, and identity itself.

7

The Next Generation
Children of the Paranormal

Paranormal reality television is characterized by a persistent tension between disturbing the audience (by evoking fear) and reassuring them (containing threatening material within familiar formats peopled by familiar faces). Representations of children bring these conflicting tendencies into sharp focus, exposing complex cultural debates about the character, nature, and social position of society's youngest members. From an adult point of view, children are seen to be disturbing. Unfamiliar with cultural expectations, they disrupt the beliefs and routines adults take for granted. In the process of socializing them, parents must make explicit values that are otherwise left unspoken. Forced to explain or defend unexamined assumptions, adults can find themselves at a disadvantage. A child's very presence can expose problems within the family, especially if the child resists being molded or in any way fails to conform to expectations. This is particularly acute regarding issues of identity such as race, gender, and sexuality. Which aspects are innate and which socially mandated? When paranormal reality depicts children as having a preexisting character or temperament that is not determined by parental training (a nature that exceeds nurture), it tends to place them at one of two extremes: as angelic models of innocence or the epitome of evil.

The 1960s and '70s produced several iconic horror films about innocent-seeming children who come to personify evil. Some have uncanny powers

Psychic Kids: Children of the Paranormal

allowing them to control people's minds (*Village of the Damned* [1960]) or wish them into cornfields ("It's a Good Life," *The Twilight Zone* [1961]). Others are the spawn of the Devil (*Rosemary's Baby* [1968]), possessed by demons (*The Exorcist* [1973]), or the Antichrist (*The Omen* [1976]). In these films horror is produced by the dissonance between the adults' unquestioned faith that children are inherently innocent and overwhelming evidence to the contrary.

Because reality television purports to depict "real life," asserting that people appear as "themselves," it is impossible to imagine a weekly series built around a demon child. Consequently, children on paranormal reality television tend to fall toward the "innocent" end of the spectrum. At the same time, they maintain the capacity to disturb, challenging their parents' assumptions, undermining accepted categories, and generally freaking people out. The prototype for this approach is 1999's *The Sixth Sense*, revolving around a cherubic little boy who tries to persuade his mother and a male psychologist that ghosts exist and communicate with him, a claim the film resoundingly affirms. Using multiple perspectives, including that of a single parent, a medical professional, and, most important, the child himself, the film validates the child's view. The child becomes the teacher as, with gentle persistence, he breaks through his emotionally distraught mother's concern and the emotional detachment of a man fatally out of touch with his own experience. By privileging the child's perspective, paranormal reality series maintain *The Sixth Sense*'s balance between horror and happy endings, depicting children as both disruptors and guides.

The idea that children are naturally connected to spiritual or "otherworldly" realms is an offshoot of the nineteenth-century equation of childhood with innocence (i.e., moral goodness). A hallmark of Victorian literature, angelic child characters like Dickens's Little Nell or Harriet Beecher Stowe's Little Eva are literally too good for this earth. Dying young, they ascend directly to heaven. While contemporary paranormal programming does not go that far, it relies heavily on the association of children/childhood with positive moral qualities. Things associated with children/childhood are supposedly pure, unspoiled, innately good, and beyond reproach. Witnesses, mediums, and ghost hunters frequently locate their earliest paranormal experiences in childhood, relying on the presumption of children's innocence as a way to forestall accusations of trickery or deceit.[1] Young children on these shows are credited with being "more open," having an instinctive sensitivity to a wide range of paranormal phenomena. The younger the child, the more naïve, spontaneous, and free of calculation their claims seem. When footage from a baby-cam shows a child in a crib interacting with unseen entities in the middle of the night, the preverbal toddler can hardly be accused of perpetrating a fraud (*Ghost Nation*, "A Nightmare in the Nursery").[2] Those who present such actions as proof of the paranormal, however, can be.

Involving children with the paranormal has been a source of controversy since the advent of Spiritualism. In the mid-nineteenth century, there was considerable debate in Britain about allowing children to be mediums. If children were placed in a position where "they were open to exploitation—psychological or possibly even commercial," it could give rise "some sort of anti-spiritualist moral panic in which [Spiritualists] would be denounced for exploiting children."[3] Modern paranormal reality programs that involve children take steps to minimize criticism along these lines, most often by including the parents as guarantors that the children are present with their parents' permission. Rather than laying concerns to rest, the parents open themselves to accusations of commodifying their children, making them part of a spectacle. Exploitation, however, is not the only issue that arises in the episodes and series centered on children and psychic phenomena.

As soon as the question is raised as to whether parents can be assumed to be doing what is best for their children, the institution of the family is called into question. Portrayed as a source of multigenerational support in series such as *Celebrity Ghost Stories* (chapter 6), the family becomes instead a site of conflict, with parent pitted against child. Even though the youngest children do not recognize what it is in themselves that their parents find unsettling, their being "different" (i.e., psychic) throws their families into crisis. For teenagers, the adolescent struggle to come to terms with one's identity—as an individual, a member of society, and a member of a family—is compounded when they are bullied, ostracized, and even, in some religious contexts, condemned to hell. The family is depicted as an institution that pressures its youngest and least powerful members to conform to restrictive social norms by suppressing or containing anything that challenges traditional definitions of identity, including racial identification, gender, sexuality, or religious beliefs.[4] When the child disturbs those attempts and undermines those assumptions, s/he becomes a site where unaffected innocence and unnerving disruption meet.

In *The Ghost Inside My Child* (2013), a six-year-old boy unwittingly creates havoc by reporting memories of a previous life. In the process, he upends his parents' comfortable assumptions, redefining the world as a fluid space where different identities, different ways of being can be imagined.[5] Reincarnation is mentioned in passing in numerous paranormal reality shows where it is categorized as an aspect of the supernatural as opposed to a significant tenet of religious belief. (As with programs about exorcists, no series based on the subject of reincarnation has lasted more than a few of episodes.)[6] Little Luke says he used to be a woman named Pam who died in a fire. His mother wants to believe him but her husband tells her, "You're crazy." (Marital discord is strongly implied as husband and wife are interviewed separately, never appearing in the same shot or even the same room.) Mom is willing to entertain the possibility that reincarnation exists, but when she finds a newspaper account of a woman named Pam who died in a hotel fire, she is shocked to realize that not only might her blonde baby boy have once been a middle-aged woman, but s/he was African American. "It never *occurred* to me," she gasps repeatedly. Little wonder (the narrator informs us) that by the age of seven or eight, children "stop sharing such stories." While the six-year-old is completely at ease having multiple gender and racial identities, his parents are thrown into crisis when their rigid categories begin to dissolve.

The conflict between children and their elders—expressed in paranormal terms—is underscored in the A&E series *Paranormal State* (2007–2011). The college students who make up the Penn State Paranormal Research Society (PRS) are ideally positioned to act as intermediaries between teenagers and their parents. Defining their mission as helping others, the PRS team is made up of both men and women and integrates diverse approaches to the paranormal. The technological and research-based investigative techniques of ghost hunting are combined with respect for the mediums and demonologists who are invited in as guest experts on each episode. In the team's investigations it quickly becomes apparent that paranormal phenomena

Paranormal State *Paranormal State*

reflect rather than cause the domestic tensions the families are grappling with—something their teenage children try to resolve. As Karen Williams notes, in these shows paranormal phenomena "has come to figure private pathologies and traumas, and reality TV's camera is then endowed with the power of both revelation and recovery as it teaches 'real' people how to live with their very 'real' ghosts."[7] In "Do Bad Things" (2010), a teen named Heather contacts PRS, but when her mother suspects that the team might blame family members for what they are experiencing ("Someone in your family brought something supernatural into the mix"), she stops the investigation cold and banishes the team from the house. PRS does what it can to help Heather from a distance but her mother remains an unmovable obstacle. When parents require their children to conceal information, keep secrets, and stonewall, it makes the family a kind of fiction, or worse, a collection of falsehoods. To be a real family, as opposed to a conspiracy, the truth must come out. After a lifetime of being told to keep silent, these teenagers know they need all the help they can get.[8]

Another teen finds a way to break through parental intransigence with help from the PRS. In "Family Ties" (2008), Jimmy experiences things in his home that he cannot explain. Jimmy cannot tell the team much about his family's history because he has been kept in the dark. His mother does not want to discuss what has happened "'cause it's really painful," and his father refuses to talk. Seeing stoicism as his duty—the manly choice, the sacrifice he makes for his family—his father tells the producers, "To me, it's just my hell that I live with." The father's silence is what hurts his son the most. He "doesn't really understand how much this affects me," Jimmy protests. Finally persuaded to talk for his son's sake, Jimmy's father discloses that his mother

Chip Coffey, *Paranormal State*

killed herself upstairs, in the bathroom where Jimmy saw her ghost. The father has seen the spirit, too. Once everything is out in the open, Jimmy is happier and his father "satisfied" and "peaceful." Jimmy's greatest anxiety did not stem from seeing apparitions but from being kept in the dark by his family—the real "dark at the top of the stairs."

As we saw with little Luke/Pam, family tensions around the ongoing issue of identity are harder to resolve. In "The Sensitive" (2008), a teenaged girl is causing strain within her family, not because of anything she has done but because of who she is. From the outset, Liana is figured as a question. Are her symptoms the "early stages of demonic possession" or are they "psychological," team leader Ryan wonders? "Is she the target" of negative energies, medium Chip Coffey asks? Although Liana's mother reports that the family has "gone to all kinds of doctors for all kinds of testing," no one has been able to explain what her daughter is going through. It is the psychic medium who ventures that Liana herself is both the problem and its solution. Overwhelmed by paranormal phenomena, she attracts spirits because she has "got some mediumistic abilities." As an experienced psychic, Coffey can show her how to adapt to having such abilities, but it is up to Liana and her family to learn to accept her as she is. Most important, though, he advises her not to worry. Or, as Coffey puts it, "Don't kick your own butt too much, Miss Liana."

In the struggle between parents and children who are "different," terms associated with the paranormal take on a double meaning, their inherent ambiguity and metaphorical richness providing a valuable means for affirming the value of difference and articulating an oppositional stance to social pressures. Most striking is the way paranormal programs reiterate arguments used in support of LGBTQ rights, describing psychic sensitivity as something one is born with rather than something one has chosen. In "The Sensitive," Liana's mother accepts her paranormal abilities as a normal part of a teenager's emerging identity. Other young people police themselves, choosing carefully what to say and whom to trust. The double-voiced quality of paranormal terms resounds when Robbie Gilmore, a young African American man, identifies himself to the *Ghost Adventures* team as a voodoo priest.[9] The result of a spiritual calling, his relation to this religious tradition is profound. But given voodoo's occult status, Gilmore understands the fear and potential hostility his beliefs elicit: "It's not something that's really accepted." Wearing his long hair plaited in cornrows, his thinness accentuated by a loose blue shirt, Gilmore presents himself as an ordinary, somewhat vulnerable young man who has learned to keep this part of his identity hidden. "I'm not very public with the practice," he explains. What he is most troubled by, though, is his family's response which manifests as a kind of willful ignorance. "Even my parents. They—they know what I do. I've told them numerous times and they even block it out themselves." Like generations of young people, Robbie is fighting to develop, assert, and maintain an identity as an individual distinct from his family. If members of his family are at odds with what he considers an essential part of himself, he knows he can find support—a different community, a new kind of family—elsewhere. Despite what his parents might think, he insists, "there's some open-minded people around here who will say yes."

Whether one has a supportive parent like Liana or is forced to find support outside the family like Robbie Gilmore, employing the paranormal-as-metaphor allows speakers, in essence, to say what cannot be said. It also opens a path of resistance against socially sanctioned institutions including medical science, the Church, and ultimately the family itself.

Born This Way

Historians of American Spiritualism describe how the potentially transgressive nature of mediumship allowed members of socially devalued groups to subvert and redefine existing categories of identity.[10] One of the ways men and women used mediumship was "to skew codes of normative gender and sexuality" as they sought "to evade the limits placed upon the gendered body."[11] In doing so, both male and female psychics met with resistance. When one female medium communicated through a "main spirit control [who] was a vigorous young man," for instance, it was taken as an "indication of her sexual aberrance and tendency to undermine patriarchal authority."[12] Male mediums, in particular, "rarely escaped pathological classifications."[13] Accused of having "stereotypically feminine traits," male mediums were portrayed as "effeminate," "fragile, nervous," and "morbidly sensitive."[14] At the same time, the male psychic's very existence—his ability to amaze and confound, any commercial success—was proof that there were different ways of being. And different ways of being a man.

Because sexuality is rarely discussed openly in any paranormal reality series, the "gayness" of cast members is open to conjecture and relies on the reading of social codes. On *Paranormal State*, for example, frequent guest psychic Michelle Belanger has cropped hair and dresses in biker black. She wears pants (never skirts) and the occasional blindfold. In another episode ("Haunted Homecoming" [2010]), Ryan Buell announces that he has returned to his hometown in South Carolina to reunite "with my original investigative partner, Christina." Christina's self-presentation reaffirms classic signifiers of alternate sexuality: eschewing make-up, she wears wire-rim glasses, a short mannish hairstyle and, in the heat of South Carolina, a formal suit and tie.[15] One could say that members of the LGBTQ community might be coded on paranormal reality television but they are not hidden.

The careers of other paranormal TV personalities illustrate how the genre has adjusted to changing attitudes over time. Adam Berry, for example, was awarded a role on *Ghost Hunters* after a season-long competition on *Ghost Hunters Academy* (2010). Once he became part of the team, however, he was effectively segregated by being made the designated partner of the show's most prominent female cast member, Amy Bruni. After four years, Berry and Bruni left to create their own series, *Kindred Spirits* (2016), where the co-stars are both presented as tech-savvy investigators and as emotionally sensitive (to spirits, clients, and each other). As part of a generation that came of age following older mediums like Chip Coffey, Phil Jordan (*Psychic Detectives*), and James Van Praagh (*Monica the Medium*), Berry and others are comfortable identifying publicly as gay—though not on television.[16] Berry discusses his marriage and posts a picture of himself with his husband on his website.[17] Michelle Belanger identifies as "intersex" online, while Ryan Buell uses the term bisexual in a memoir published in 2010 (the last year

Amy Bruni and Adam Berry, *Kindred Spirits*

Paranormal State was in production). Only Tyler Henry, the youngest male medium on paranormal reality TV, openly voices enthusiastic support for gay rights on his television series. When he meets transgender activist Candis Cayne for a reading, Henry is in awe.[18] "For me, Candis Cayne represents a whole movement, the transgender movement, and equality for everyone. To meet the embodiment of everything I love is just incredible." "It's amazing," he gushes. "I'm, like, wow!"

A single series reflects these changing cultural attitudes and the work it takes to make change possible. A spin-off of *Paranormal State*, *Psychic Kids: Children of the Paranormal* (A&E, 2008–2010) stars medium Chip Coffey. Wearing flannel, an earring, and a bracingly unapologetic "don't f— with me" attitude, Coffey is neither fragile nor nervous. What he has to say comes through loud and clear. Blunt, practical, and to the point, he is a fighter. And he is ready to face down anyone or anything. As he did in "The Sensitive," Coffey here guides young people to embrace the ways they are different. When necessary, he gives their parents a good talking to. In the process, the series makes it clear that young people have options. If their families will not accept them, a welcoming community awaits, made up of people who are different too.

Each episode of *Psychic Kids* can be read as a "coming out" narrative. Children between the ages of eight and eighteen are encouraged to accept who they are, expressed here as coming to terms with their paranormal powers. The title sequence states that "countless children share an incredible secret": "they have psychic abilities." Given the social consequences of being different, this is not a blessing. "Feeling isolated and frightened, these kids," we are told, "have nowhere to turn." One child reports, "Kids at school think I'm crazy." Another has learned to keep his "secret" to himself: "It's not something I can talk about." There is, however, the chance that, with help, they will find acceptance where it matters most. And the person who can show them the way is Chip Coffey. Literally holding a light in the darkness, he proclaims loudly: "Don't run. Don't hide."

As in shows built around first-person testimony, the children featured on *Psychic Kids* are representative of small-town America. Highway signs establish rural locations in the Midwest (Lawrence, Kansas; Danville, Illinois; Norman, Oklahoma) or the nondescript outskirts of sprawling cities like Fort Lauderdale and Houston. Introductory shots of barren landscapes create a desolate mood: a lonely weather vane, a dusty farm, the stubble of cornfields in winter. Discovered playing alone in their yards, the children describe their secret psychic abilities. Twelve-year old Jillian has seen spirits "since she was two." Ahli, age eleven, is "highly empathetic" and "has predicted people's deaths by reading their auras." As they grow older, the children find it harder to conceal the truth about themselves. Like adolescents coming to terms with homosexual or transgender identities, psychic kids worry about being bullied or rejected at school. In the episode "Fear Management," fourteen-year-old Joel explains: "I'm really scared to tell anyone else 'cause, like, they won't believe me and they'll think I'm a freak. . . . They'd just—they'd try to avoid me more or just make fun of me." Twelve-year-old Brad has had psychic experiences all his life. Nevertheless, he says, "I'm not quite ready to tell my friends about stuff that happens to me. I don't know if I might be made fun of." When his mother worries about his increasing isolation from his peers, he insists, "I just wanna be a normal kid, kind of. I *am* normal." Above all, the children are desperate to be believed. "I want people to believe me," Ahli says, "and I want people to know that I'm not lying. These things are real and they're happening—every day."

On the whole, mothers believe their children—as one says, "This is very real"—but they are at a loss. Another says, through tears, "I don't know how to guide her. I don't know what to do with her. I don't know how to help her." Taking all the responsibility on her own shoulders, mother Alison explains, "You wanna help your child. It's my job to protect her. It's a helpless feeling." As with the people in first-person shows, they put little faith in experts. They agonize whether to turn to medical professionals for help. Teachers, counselors, and doctors have been of little use. Ahli has headaches, but her mother points out that "no doctor has been able to give me a diagnosis why she gets these migraines." Another wonders whether her daughter is schizophrenic: "I'm thinking, 'Okay, she's seeing things, she's hearing things.'

You just don't know what to do." Other mothers actively fear the medical/legal power of the state. In "The Demon House," a mother suspects that if she told anyone in authority about her daughter's "gift," "they might think you're crazy and then they might even try to take your kids away from you." Another mother, an older African American woman, bluntly explains to her daughter, "Psychiatrists—they'll just give you medicine and call you crazy. They have the authority to take you away from me and lock you up."

Then help arrives.

Wary of being labeled exploitative, *Psychic Kids* goes to great lengths to assure the audience that everyone is trying to do what is best for the children. Families in distress are provided with the services of "Chip Coffey, a psychic medium, and Dr. Lisa Miller, a clinical psychologist from Columbia University." As a title card informs us, these experienced and credentialed professionals are "dedicated to helping kids with psychic abilities." Although it is never explained how families are selected to appear on the program, when Coffey and Dr. Miller knock on the front door in one episode, they are literally welcomed with open arms: mother Alison embraces Dr. Miller while her daughter rushes up to give Chip a hug. The warm greeting makes it clear that what could be seen as an intrusive intervention in people's lives is happening at their invitation. The parents' voluntary participation speaks not only to their desperation but to their faith in the show's stated mission to be "inspiring, healing, uplifting."

Each episode has two goals: to validate the children to themselves and to their parents—in that order. After introductory segments, two or three children, each accompanied by a family member, meet at a small hotel or inn for a retreat. Over the course of a weekend, Chip guides the children through a series of paranormal exercises while a female mental health professional talks to family members in supportive one-on-one sessions. In the series' first season, Chip's partner is either psychologist Dr. Lisa Miller (who is also a producer of the series) or psychiatric social worker Edy Nathan (eight episodes, between 2009 and 2010). With their soft-spoken, kindly demeanors, the series' female professionals drain medical science of its frightening power. In fact, as active listeners offering patience, attention, and nonjudgmental reassurances, the women bear a strong resemblance to psychics. Instead of maintaining a distinction between science and faith, Dr. Miller fuses them, pointing out that her work assisting families may have a spiritual as well as a therapeutic dimension. "It feels as if our being brought together is purposeful," Dr. Miller tells the families, "that we've all been brought here for a reason."[19]

Chip Coffey and Lisa Miller, *Psychic Kids*

Chip, meanwhile, builds the children's confidence by inviting guests to demonstrate how psychic skills can be put to practical use. Ahli, for instance, is told that she has potential as a psychic healer. Instructed to hold her hands over an older woman to see if she can sense any underlying medical conditions, she diagnoses bronchitis, asthma, and a bad knee—all of which are immediately confirmed. In "The Missing Person," older teens assist the police by pursuing psychic leads in a case that has gone cold. When Lisa and Chip agree that "a *scientific* investigation would allay" some of the children's fears, an investigator is brought in to show them how to use voice recorders and EMF detectors ("Fear Management"). Validated by technology, the kids have what Chip calls their first real chance "to feel believed, empowered."

For the children themselves, the most transformative part of the experience is the chance to meet kids like themselves. Special attention is paid to the moments when the children meet each other, play together, laugh, or have solemn discussions about life. Friendships form quickly as the children open up with each other and start to come to terms with their abilities. As one girl says, "I want someone my age to talk to because they know what's going on. My mom's not going to know what's going on in a twelve-year old's life right now."[20] In "Angels and Demons," three teens united by their status as "outcasts" sit on a staircase in a psychic version of *The Breakfast Club* (1985). "Do you tell your friends?" Mallory asks. "No, I don't," Ashley replies. "They might, like, yell at you or call you a liar. I don't tell anybody." Dalton agrees with a terse, "Nope." Providing the children with peers and newfound friends (each show ends with the assurance that the children have stayed in touch), *Psychic Kids* succinctly handles the matter of social isolation. More intractable problems lie closer to home.

Ashley, Dalton, and Mallory, *Psychic Kids*

The stuff of domestic melodrama, fraught confrontations between parent and child expose the impossible position families find themselves in. Caught between conflicting demands, parents are expected to uphold the beliefs and standards of the community (values they genuinely embrace) even when doing so puts them at odds with the children they love and passionately want to support. Thirteen-year-old Ashley, for example, "embraces some of the spiritual beliefs of [her] Native American heritage" while her mother Alice is a Christian fundamentalist. "My trust is in the Lord," she declares. According to her religious beliefs, "psychics aren't speaking to the dead" but to demonic impostors. That is why "we need to stay away from that as Christians," she states unequivocally. Chip, in Chip-like fashion, is equally direct. "Big question for you, Mom. How would you feel if your daughter's belief system didn't mirror your own?" Alice remains adamant. "I would not feel good about it." But, she explains, being put in a position where she has to choose between her daughter and her faith "is really hard for me." Despite their avowed respect for Alice's beliefs, Chip and Lisa privately encourage Ashley to think about separating herself emotionally from her mother, recasting a standard phase of adolescent development in paranormal terms. When Ashley worries that her psychic abilities have come between her and her mother, Lisa gently suggests that Ashley's mother may never accept her daughter's beliefs (and daily lived experience). "Maybe it's too hard for your mother to hear it." Envisioning a time when Ashley will become more independent, Lisa proposes that she begin looking elsewhere to find the support her mother cannot provide. "You can lean on your mom and love your mom, but maybe learning about your psychic gifts can come from other people." In addition to herself and Chip, Lisa points to the other form of support *Psychic Kids* has supplied: "There are kids who you could share this with." Although sensitive to the parents' struggles, *Psychic Kids* is unambiguously weighted toward the children. It is this championing of the children's and teens' perspectives, privileging their emotional well-being, their sense of self-worth, and their freedom to be who they are, that gives the program its progressive political edge.

In *Psychic Kids*, if "family" does not always provide a loving, supportive environment, it must be reinvented. Serving *in loco parentis*, Chip and Lisa (or Edy) model a positive, accepting family unit that can accommodate difference. Unpretentious, unafraid, and unintimidated, Chip is a new kind of father figure: tough *and* gay *and* psychically "sensitive." Lisa and Edy suffuse the potentially cold figure of the medical professional with maternal warmth and kindness. Rather than dismissing the paranormal as superstition or countering religious faith with scientific fact, they are open to whatever people believe as long as it does not harm them or hamper others. By occupying the roles of surrogate parents, Chip and Lisa make it possible for children *and* their parents to see what a family that accepts difference might look like. While Chip and Lisa do not openly defy the parents, their very presence poses an implicit threat: If you are not there for your kids, we will be. If you drive them away, they will have somewhere to go.

Repeat, Recycle, Retrench

Opening (or reopening) questions about the way we understand the world and our place in it, paranormal reality television reveals contradictions in the culture, unresolved historical and social traumas, and the ongoing consequences of America's failure to deliver on its promises. Raising these questions does not amount, however, to a sustained political critique. Although appeals to the paranormal can be read as a form of resistance, it is not accompanied by any proposed plan of action, either radical or reactionary. Episodes and entire series are constructed in ways guaranteed to smooth over anger, grief, and disappointment. Mediums validate mourners (and are validated in return), countering loss with the promise that the dead are ever-present. Ghost hunters flirt with danger while surrounded by teammates who are their brothers and friends. Subjected to terror, first-person witnesses learn to trust themselves, and, coming into their own, find ways to survive. Traditional gender roles are reinforced as teams become pseudo-families, made up of older, fatherly male leaders, sensitive nurturing female psychics, and "younger brother" types who handle the technology (*Ghost Loop*, *The Holzer Files*). If social institutions such as the family or the police fail the people who depend on them, that can be fixed with the right kind of expert (occult) assistance. Problems on a scale that cannot be solved by the action of individuals (i.e., government policies that led to institutionalizing the sick, mass incarceration, racism, and genocide) are isolated geographically and temporally, positioned firmly and permanently "out there" and in the past. If our present-day surrogates find that the spirits haunting the scarred corridors threaten to make the crimes of the past too vividly real, they can simply jump in the SUV at the end of the hour and leave it all behind.

What began as horror is recuperated as hope as paranormal reality series, over time, bend toward reassurance. In 2019, fifteen years into the "paranormal trend," shows that had come and gone reappeared, modified in ways that made them more upbeat and less disturbing. A new *Ghost Hunters* debuted following a three-year hiatus, with Grant Wilson from the original cast serving as the paterfamilias of a team whose exclusive goal is to help others.[21] "Only with the truth can I help someone," Grant declares. He tells their first client, "We want to empower you with information. Fear is just a lack of knowledge, right?" *Ghost Brothers* (now subtitled *Haunted Houseguests*) returned with a new tag line that transformed their hobby into a mission: "We help the living find peace with the departed, one haunted house at a time." The series that underwent the most dramatic change was *Psychic Kids*, which, in its new guise, softened the potential transgressiveness of the original.

Nine years after the original ceased production, a revised version of *Psychic Kids* premiered on A&E. In the new series, the title takes on an extra meaning. Here the "psychic kids" are not only the clients but the adult psychics as well. The children featured on the original series have grown up. Happy and well-adjusted, they return to reality television eager to help children like themselves. Neither doctors nor social workers, the children of yesterday are now professional psychics, ready to pass along what they have learned to the next generation. Like the college-age team members on *Paranormal State*, youth makes these psychics ideal intermediaries between parents and children. When they tell the children that they went through something similar "when I was your age," it is immediately proved with clips from the earlier series, showing them when they were small, fearful, and overwhelmed. Like the online project begun in 2010 to support LGBTQ children and teens persecuted for being different, the young psychics present themselves as living examples that "It Gets Better."

Near the beginning of each episode, the young adult psychics pay obligatory tribute to the original show. These heartfelt statements are designed to refute any suggestion that being featured on a reality television show in any way harmed the children whose lives provided material for the original series. On the contrary, having participated in a show where they were encouraged to accept themselves as "different" is, it is implied, what made it possible for them to thrive. Other aspects of the original experience, however, are elided. When eleven-year-old Cassidy asks psychic Santana DeLeon, "How did [being on the earlier show] help you," DeLeon replies simply, "I had a really good mentor." A clip from the original series shows Santana as a teenager, receiving advice from Chip Coffey. Despite their centrality to the original series, Coffey and other well-known psychics glimpsed in these clips are never identified.[22] Directing credit for the children's positive experiences toward the show itself and away from any single mentor minimizes the contributions of potentially controversial figures like the prickly Coffey. Where the original series had a propensity to challenge parents while encouraging children to find support outside the family, on *Psychic Kids*, circa 2019, a child's place is in the home.

Unlike their predecessors, the young adults on *Psychic Kids* do not argue with parents because they don't have to. The tense confrontations between parents and psychics that characterized the first series are gone. In 2019, parents accept from the beginning that their children have psychic abilities. Unerringly supportive of their children and recognizing that they need help, the parents initiate contact with the series' producers. Each episode begins with a video made by the family/clients asking for help, followed by title cards that make it explicit that it is the parents who have reached out to the producers, not the other way around. When the children explore a haunted location with their psychic mentor, we see their parents nearby, vigilantly watching every step via video. Another family-produced video at the end of the episode confirms that all is well. In this idealized world, there is little doubt that parents know what is best for their children. Psychics, like pediatricians or Big Brothers/Big Sisters, are there to provide temporary specialist assistance. They help parents, not challenge them, as the new series reaffirms parents as the ultimate authority within the institution of the nuclear family.

In this vision of family, children are defined exclusively in relation to their parents and siblings. Unlike the original series, they do not make new friends by meeting people their own age. The only other children we see are their siblings. As a consequence, the family is depicted as complete in itself, self-sufficient, self-contained—and eerily isolated. Except for one occasion, no one engages with a larger community or is introduced to people whose points of view might differ from those of the parents. This picture of social isolation is partly assuaged by incorporating difference into "family" itself. The first four episodes of the new series feature various kinds of families: an upper-middle-class African American couple, a Hispanic lesbian couple, and a family whose community is identified specifically as "Navajo, Pawnee, and Seminole" rather than the broader but more generic "Native American."[23] This sensitivity to a diverse range of ethnic and cultural legacies as well as to new definitions of marriage reflects changes in society between 2008 and 2019 as America broadened its view of what "family" might look like. On the whole, however, the *Psychic Kids* of 2019 jettisons whatever edginess the original series had in favor of a feel-good show that reduces tensions all round. Children are not being exploited; they are being helped. They do not disturb their parents or undermine their values. In fact, parents have superior understanding which is demonstrated when they recognize that their child needs a little extra help. Any traits a child may have can be accommodated as long as that child learns to control and contain them. It is the parents' job to arrange the counseling necessary to insure that they do. In 2019's *Psychic Kid* family is everything—all-encompassing and not to be questioned.

The Future

At the beginning of the millennium, a one-hour special debuted on Halloween. Although no one knew it at the time, *The World's Scariest Ghosts: Caught on Tape* (1999) contained the seeds of nearly every paranormal reality show that would follow. Crisscrossing America from Illinois to Colorado to Connecticut, *The World's Scariest* brings us eyewitnesses who use cameras and tape-recorders to capture unexplained phenomena in their own homes. Surveillance footage similar to that seen in *My Ghost Story: Caught on Camera* or *My Horror Story* reveals a chair moving by itself when no one is around. Men put together an amateur ghost-hunting team to explore abandoned buildings à la *Ghost Hunters, Ghost Adventures* and *Ghost Asylum*. When a child reports seeing dead people, friendly adult psychic James Van Praagh (*Monica the Medium*) makes a house call to validate the little boy's abilities (*Paranormal State, Psychic Kids: Children of the Paranormal*). Demonologists Lorraine and Ed Warren use religious rituals to help the spiritually oppressed expel an evil force (*I was Possessed, The Demon Files*).[24] A family tells about moving into "what they thought was their dream house—but soon," we are informed, "their dream took a frightening turn" (*My Haunted House, Paranormal Witness, When Ghosts Attack!*). If not for the outmoded technology (VHS footage time-stamped "1993," film-based photographic negatives, and a mid-1990s computer terminal), any part of *The World's Scariest Ghosts* would fit right in beside any paranormal reality series produced between 2004 and 2019.

This is not to imply that the producers of the numerous series discussed above based their shows on (or even saw) the Halloween special, but that these templates were available, ready to be used. When circumstances were ripe, cable channels with firmly established brand identities, a dependence on reality television formats, and a 24/7 appetite for content could tweak their existing product by adding a little something supernatural to the mix. What they came up with was already waiting for them, bringing history with it.

The sudden surge in the popularity of paranormal reality TV at the start of the twenty-first century may have coincided with the nation-wide realization that the houses people lived in and the society they occupied were not what they had seemed, but such realizations are not limited to periods of national economic crisis. They happen regularly to individuals who have lost their jobs, towns that have lost factories, or victims of racism for whom life in America has rarely been safe or secure. As a consequence, we find familiar traces of populist distrust of "elites"—experts, authorities, or anyone who claims intellectual or institutional status. Perhaps the most unsettling paranormal programs are the ones that reveal what it feels like to be betrayed by the people you rely on for help. On *Ghost Bait* (2019), anxious homeowners are persuaded by a paranormal crew (led by an alpha-male leader and his "sensitive" female sidekick) to sit alone late at night in a haunted location with a burlap bag over their heads.[25] Having allowed themselves to be turned into literal bait for the hostile forces they fear most, the panicking clients are cajoled and bullied by the off-site team. As they shudder under their hoods, sobbing in terror, they are told that it is up to them to solve

Ghost Bait

their own problems. Conquer your own fears; confront the evil surrounding you. It is *your* responsibility to pull yourself up by your own bootstraps. The model/myth of rugged individualism is calcified into a political philosophy imposed on those who dare ask for assistance. In keeping with the logic of the format—the ideal final touch—the clients are required at the end of each episode to thank the team for what they have been put through.

The most popular and longest-lasting examples of paranormal reality television provide a metaphorical and conceptual framework in which "ordinary" people are shown voicing a lingering sense of unease when faced with forces they cannot define or experiences they cannot express. By enabling people to articulate an undeveloped but persistent sense that *something isn't right*, the paranormal performs a crucial function. As Kevin Glynn argues in his defense of tabloid culture, "occulted knowledges persist despite (or perhaps because of) their constant disavowal and marginalization by the truth-producing institutions of official culture."[26] For those disillusioned with, and resistant to, the empirical, logical, and mathematical explanations of scientific rationalism and its perceived inadequacy when it comes to describing the range and complexity of human experience, the paranormal can, like tabloid culture, be considered "a cultural resource well-suited to sustaining an oppositional popular stance toward the tastes, values, and 'standards' preferred by" the powerful.[27] By validating personal experience, emotion, faith, and ephemeral states that cannot be easily explained or proved by "hard" evidence, the paranormal as a category gives people a place to stand that is outside of and critical of "legitimate" explanations they find unpersuasive, reductive, or alienating. Consider *Celebrity Ghost Stories* (which itself serves as a model for a 2019 series, *Famously Afraid*). Reason would dismiss Della Reese's sense of her mother's presence as a neurological consequence of shock and blood loss, and Louis Gossett's and Debbie Allen's visions of their grandmothers as nothing more than dreams or hallucinations brought on by stress. Such explanations, however, would be inadequate for the people involved, patronizing in the attempt to define their experience for them, and incomplete when it comes to describing an experience that struck each of them with a force exemplified by the word "real."

If the answers proposed by psychic mediums or ghost hunters are never definitive, paranormal reality programs offer a steady supply of symbolic compensations. Ordinary people fight back and succeed where experts have failed. Psychics return joy to the faces of people in mourning and even secure justice by helping to solve crimes. Men find support from their teammates and the courage to face forces no one can be expected to surmount. At times, paranormal investigators speak for victims of the past, exposing the institutions that punished the poor and isolated the sick. Now and then there is even a glimpse of a more open, accepting, and diverse society where men and women work side by side as equals (*Kindred Spirits*, *Paranormal Lockdown*), children from every background can grow up to be publicly admired (*Celebrity Ghost Stories*) and even be celebrated for the ways they are different, despite having been set apart or misunderstood when they were young (*Psychic Kids*, *Paranormal State*). Sometimes, those who have been excluded are given the opportunity to tell their own story in their own words. These may all be illusions constructed by television, but the appeal of these illusions has sustained paranormal reality television for fifteen years and counting. Whether this particular iteration of interest in the paranormal is unique to this period or part of America's ongoing fascination with an alternate/resistant way of understanding the world, we are sure to encounter the paranormal again.[28]

What haunts America is never really gone.

Notes

Introduction: Viewer Discretion Advised

1. Jeffrey Weinstock, "Introduction," in *Spectral America: Phantoms and the National Imagination*, ed. Weinstock (Madison: Wisconsin University Press, 2004), 8.

2. Michael F. Brown, *The Channeling Zone: American Spirituality in an Anxious Age* (Cambridge, MA: Harvard University Press, 1997), 11.

3. Historically, each term has fallen out of favor due to scandal or revelations of fraud and been replaced by the succeeding term.

4. This study will focus on the spectral as opposed to fantastic physical creatures such as yetis, werewolves, hellhounds, the Loch Ness monster or selkies (Irish seal-sirens), Bigfoot, the "wampus beasts" pursued on *Mountain Monsters* (Destination America, 2013), or the "Japanese Water Monster and Icelandic Elves" featured on *Josh Gates Destination Truth* (2017).

5. Quoted in Martha Banta, *Henry James and the Occult: The Great Extension* (Bloomington: Indiana University Press, 1972), 24. He goes on to declare the "dynamic principle" of Spiritualism to be "general wonder-sickness."

6. Steven Connor, "The Machine in the Ghost: Spiritualism, Technology, and the 'Direct Voice,'" in *Ghosts: Deconstruction, Psychoanalysis, History*, eds. Peter Buse and Andrew Stott (New York: St. Martin's Press, 1999), 205.

7. Buse and Stott, 3. This position is similar to that of Kathryn Troy in her history of the "Indian spirit guide." "The actual presence of Indian spirits at nineteenth-century séances is neither accepted nor denied in this book. It is only relevant that Spiritualists accepted their experiences as truth. To assert at the onset that all Spiritualists were knowing frauds is risky and counterproductive" (*The Specter of the Indian: Race, Gender and Ghosts in American Séances, 1848–1890* [New York: SUNY Press, 2017], xiii–xiv).

8. María del Pilar Blanco and Esther Peeren, "Introduction: Conceptualizaing Spectralities," *The Spectralities Reader: Ghosts and Haunting in Contemporary Cultural Theory*, eds. Blanco and Peeren (London: Bloomsbury, 2013), 21; Buse and Stott, 3 (original italics).

9. Blanco and Peeren, 21.

10. Andrew McCann, *Popular Literature, Authorship and the Occult in Late Victorian Britain* (Cambridge, UK: Cambridge University Press, 2014), 27.

11. Misha Kavka, *Reality TV* (Edinburgh: Edinburgh Press, 2012), 167. Kavka also discusses the "grave sense of injustice" viewers feel when the "wash of supposedly talentless people" on reality TV become celebrities (157). "Reality TV participants" are dismissed "as fame-mongers, 'wannabes' and untalented nobodies looking for their fifteen minutes in the limelight" (145).

12. Mike Hale, "Consigning Reality to Ghosts," *New York Times*, December 13, 2009, AR26.

13. Hale.

14. June Deery, *Reality TV* (Cambridge, UK: Polity Press, 2015), 1. She also asserts that "to dismiss reality TV because of its often trivial content would be to miss its significance."

15. For concise histories of the development of reality television from an industrial/economic perspective, see Chad Raphael "The Political Economic Origins of Reali-TV," in *Reality TV: Remaking Television Culture*, second edition, eds. Susan Murray and Laurie Ouellette (New York: NYU Press, 2009), 123–40; Andrew Ross "Reality Television and the Political Economy of Amateurism," in *A Companion to Reality TV*, ed. Laurie Ouellette (Wiley Blackwell, 2017), 29–39; and Deery, 13–21.

16. Laurie Ouellette, *Lifestyle TV* (New York: Routledge, 2016), 5. See also Amanda Scheiner McClain's *Keeping Up the Kardashian Brand: Celebrity, Materialism, and Sexuality* (Lanham, MD: Lexington Books, 2014). Several key works on reality TV appeared before 2004 when the trend in paranormal reality programming began, including Jon Dovey's *FreakShow: First Person Media and Factual Television* (London: Pluto Press, 2000); Su Holmes and Deborah Jermyn's *Understanding Reality Television* (London: Routledge, 2004); and Annette Hill's *Reality TV: Audiences and Popular Factual Television* (London: Routledge, 2005) and *Restyling Factual TV* (London: Routledge, 2007).

17. Hill describes her approach as "popular culture ethnography . . . rooted in audience research" with "an emphasis on reception" (13).

18. Hill, 75. Despite audience's avowed skepticism, only one program has presented itself as dedicated to debunking paranormal claims. *Fact or Faked: Paranormal Files* (Syfy, 2010–2012) attempted to recreate alleged evidence of the supernatural such as sound recordings (EVPs), photographs of apparitions, mists or orbs, or video (a supernatural beast running across a field), and so on. When the crack team *cannot* reproduce the effects, it leaves open the possibility of a paranormal cause. Lasting two seasons (thirty-six episodes), the show has been the only one of its kind so far. Ironically, like nearly every paranormal series, *Fact or Faked* has been accused of falsifying evidence. See also Mary Roach, *Spook: Science Tackles the Afterlife* (New York: W. W. Norton, 2005).

19. Hill, 112, 113. Hill argues that viewers occupy "three positions simultaneously: paranormal skeptic, media critic," and a third position that allows them to momentarily "experiment with paranormal beliefs" (79, 83).

20. Ouellette 136, quoting John Corner, 45 ("Performing the Real: Documentary Diversions," *Television & New Media* 3, no. 3: 255–69).

21. Simone Natale, *Supernatural Entertainments: Victorian Spiritualism and the Rise of Modern Media Culture* (University Park: Pennsylvania State University Press, 2016), 1, 3.

22. Natale, 11.

23. Karen Williams, "The Liveness of Ghosts: Haunting and Reality TV," in *Popular Ghosts: The Haunted Places of Everyday Culture*, eds. Esther Peeren and Maria del Pilar Blanco (New York: Continuum, 2010), 149.

24. "Introduction," *Haunting Experiences: Ghosts in Contemporary Folklore*, eds. Diane E. Goldstein, Sylvia Ann Grider, and Jeannie Banks Thomas (Logan, UT: Utah State University

Press, 2007), 21. Goldstein describes "the effortless comingling of ancient tradition and contemporary mass and commodified culture" as a fundamental trait of the world we inhabit (6).

25. Williams, 154.

26. Sci Fi subsequently renamed itself "Syfy." The chart lists the series I will focus on; it does not list every paranormal reality program that has aired in the US since 2004. For a discussion of the first four years of the series, see Alissa Burger, "*Ghost Hunters*: Simulated Participation in Televisual Hauntings" in *Popular Ghosts* (Peeren and Blanco, 2010), 162–74.

27. Brian Stelter, "'Ghost Hunters' Seeks Spirits and Ratings," *New York Times*, November 11, 2009, C3.

28. James Hibberd, "A&E Reality Show Has Cops Chasing Ghosts," *Hollywood Reporter*, January 6, 2009, https://reporter.blogs.com/live_feed/2009/01/ae-announces-paranormal-cops.html. In their 1999 anthology *Ghosts*, Buse and Stott state that ghosts "have fallen on hard times in the late twentieth century," having become "a little dated . . . in comparison with such sophisticated other-worldly phenomenon" as "aliens, extra-terrestrials, conspiracy theories, [and] Martian landings" (1). Nevertheless, they conclude, "chances are, ghosts will make another comeback."

29. *Ghost Whisperer* ran from 2005 to 2010. *Medium* began on CBS (2005–2009) and was picked up by NBC for its final two seasons (2009–2011).

30. While traditional ratings have become less central in the era of cable, DVRs, and online viewing, raw numbers are still useful for publicity purposes. *Paranormal State*'s 2007 debut on A&E, for example, was reported as having been that channel's third-most watched show (Kimberly Nordyke, "Some Freaky Goings-On in A&E's 'Paranormal State,'" *Hollywood Reporter*, December 17, 2007). Social media traffic has become another metric for charting a show's impact. TLC's series *Paranormal Lockdown* was proclaimed to have "had a social media response unlike any other show of this type" ("Monroe House and Evidence Revealed Special" [2016]).

31. Both are 2014.

32. The Travel Channel's *Trending Fear* (2019) transformed a blogger's postings about his haunted apartment into a series where the blogger and a two-person team reach out to people who have contacted them online about their paranormal problems. Jettisoning the round-the-clock interactivity of social media in favor of a standard ghost-hunting format only highlights what have come to be perceived as limits of TV as a medium restricted by one-way communication, time slots, seasons, and weekly schedules. By the end of 2020, it was announced that new episodes of popular programs such as *Ghost Adventures* and *Kindred Spirits* would be moving to the streaming service Discovery Plus.

33. *Ghost Adventures*, "Missouri State Prison" (2016).

34. Other warnings are linked to specific scenes that have the potential to inspire questionable behavior. In *The Demon Files*, for example, a title appears in bright red letters in the middle of an episode: "Disclaimer: The exorcism you are about to witness is extremely dangerous. Do not attempt."

35. Blood dripping upward calls to mind Karen Beckman's definition of magic as "a suspension of disbelief that allows us to suppose . . . we are witnessing an astonishing event within a physical realm that nevertheless confounds the laws of physical bodies" (Karen Beckman, *Vanishing Women: Magic, Films and Feminism* [Durham, NC: Duke University Press, 2003], 8).

36. As Weinstock notes, "each generation puts this inheritance to use in different ways and with differing objectives," 8.

37. For discussions of the move from classical to modern horror in film, see Andrew Tudor, *Monsters and Mad Scientists: A Cultural History of the Horror Movie* (Oxford: Basil Blackwell, 1989).

38. Cory Franklin, writing for the *Chicago Tribune* ("Manipulation, Conflict of Interest, Plague Medical Research," reprinted *Upper Valley News*, June 15, 2015.)

39. Discussing similar reenactments on "tabloid television," Kevin Glynn explains how "the actors' performances are oddly 'authenticated' by the retrospective commentary given by the 'real' participants whose roles they play. Frequent intercutting between actor and original interrupts the program's verité effects and explicitly indicates its staged nature. Moreover, the actors themselves often bear little physical [or vocal] resemblance to the 'real' participants, the semiotics of which is to implicitly deny the significance of any difference between reality and representation" (*Tabloid Culture: Trash Taste, Popular Power and the Transformation of American Television* [Durham, NC: Duke University Press, 2000], 63).

40. The negative, even hostile, attitudes expressed toward people featured on reality shows often reflect a regional and class-based contempt. We can see this in the widespread criticism of the promiscuous working-class Italian American teens of *Jersey Shore*, the "white trash" extended family on *Here Comes Honey Boo Boo*, the bearded hillbilly millionaires of *Duck Dynasty*, the gaudy displays of sartorial excess on *My Big Fat Gypsy Wedding*, the catfights of the nouveau riche who have "more money than class" on *The Real Housewives of . . .* , etc. The alleged failure to adhere to middle-class standards is signified, to a great extent, through visual excess (clothing, make-up, hairstyles, body type) and verbally through the use of local slang, strong regional accents, and numerous acts of "bad behavior" (public drunkenness, fighting in public, talking behind a friend's back, etc.). The spectatorial position of watching others in order to ridicule them or feel superior is itself socially frowned on, contributing to the sense that fans of reality TV are indulging in a guilty pleasure.

41. Daniel Cottom, *Abyss of Reason: Cultural Movements, Revelations, and Betrayals* (New York: Oxford, 1991), 124.

42. Cottom, 124.

43. Cottom, 122 (original italics).

44. Hill, 15.

45. Blanco and Peeren, 16.

46. Zak Bagans is the central figure on both *Paranormal Challenge* and *Ghost Adventures*.

47. Zaffis is identified by this title in *The Demon Files*, "The Mirror" (2015).

48. Owen quotes George Bernard Shaw, who attended a meeting of the SPR and expected "to sleep in a haunted house with a committee of ghost hunters" (24).

49. Beth A. Robertson, *Science of the séance: Transnational Networks and Gendered Bodies in the Study of Psychic Phenomena, 1918–40* (Vancouver: UBC Press, 2016), 20.

50. Robertson, 40.

51. Michelle Hanks discusses the democratic and egalitarian motives of people who participate in British ghost hunts in *Haunted Heritage: The Cultural Politics of Ghost Tourism, Populism, and the Past* (Walnut Creek, CA: Left Coast Press, 2015), 89–91.

52. The term was first used in 2015. "Long-Term Trends in Deaths of Despair," Joint Economic Committee, US Congress, September 5, 2019, https://www.jec.senate.gov/public/index.cfm/republicans/2019/9/long-term-trends-in-deaths-of-despair; "Deaths of Despair"; Anne Case and Angus Deaton, "Mortality and Morbidity in the 21st Century," Brookings Papers on Economic Activity, Spring 2017.

53. Ann Case and Angus Deaton, "Rising Morbidity and Mortality in Midlife among White Non-Hispanic Americans in the 21st Century," PNAS (Proceedings of the National Academy of Sciences of the United States of America), December 8, 2015, https://www.pnas.org/content/112/49/15078, 2.

54. *Project Afterlife* (2015), for example, "seek[s] to solve the mysteries of resurrection." Each episode ends with a declaration that the team is getting closer to proving what happens after death. See Raymond A. Moody Jr., *Life after Life: The Investigation of a Phenomenon—Survival of Bodily Death* (New York: Bantam Books, 1975).

55. Other cable channels that built their programming exclusively around non-scripted series (HGTV, National Geographic, Travel Channel, and Animal Planet) have followed the daily lives of police officers, fishermen, farmers and "unusual" families or communities, e.g., *The First 48, The Deadliest Catch, Return to Amish, Sister Wives*, etc. Sometimes the "families" are animals (Animal Planet's *Meerkat Manor*, 2005–2008).

56. Ouellette, *Lifestyle TV*, 8, 132 (or 131, 138). She is referring to TLC's *The Little Couple*.

57. Ann Braude, *Radical Spirits: Spiritualism and Women's Rights in Nineteenth Century America*, second edition (Bloomington: Indiana University Press, 2001), 82.

58. Robertson, 55.

59. Robertson, 73.

60. Avery Gordon, *Ghostly Matters: Haunting and the Sociological Imagination* (Minneapolis: University of Minnesota Press, 1997), 23.

61. *The Dead Files*, "House of Horrors, Radford VA" (2014).

62. *Paranormal State*, "Spirits of the Slave Dungeon" (2010).

63. Gordon, 21.

64. Glynn, 10.

Chapter 1. Paranormal Survivors: Validating the Struggling Middle Class

1. Gordon, 4.

2. Marcia Eden, *When Ghosts Attack!*, "There's No Place Like Hell" (2013).

3. *When Ghosts Attack!*, "Beasts from the Beyond" (2013).

4. Jane Shattuc, *The Talking Cure: TV Talk Shows and Women* (New York: Routledge, 1997), 109.

5. Siegfried Kracauer, "Das neue Bauen" (1927), quoted in Blanco and Esther Peeren, 226.

6. Beverly Settle, *When Ghosts Attack!*, "There's No Place like Hell" (2013).

7. A woman named Christi expresses the identical sentiment in *Paranormal Witness: True Terror* (2015). After failing dramatically to cleanse her house of spirits, she says, "We're done. They can have that house. They can have everything."

8. Descriptions from "TV.com. Episode Guide," respectively: *The Haunted*, "Land of Misery" (2010); *Paranormal Witness*, "The Real Haunting in Connecticut" (2012); *When Ghosts Attack*, "Voices of the Dead" (2013).

9. For a discussion of HGTV, see Mimi White, "House Hunters, Real Estate Television and Everyday Cosmopolitanism," in *A Companion to Reality Television*, ed. Laurie Ouellette (Somerset: Wiley Blackwell, 2017), 386–401.

10. In the spring of 2016, reports began to appear documenting a marked increase in suicides for middle-aged white men. Sabrina Tavernise "Sweeping Pain as Suicides Hit a 30-Year High," *New York Times*, April 22, 2016, A1, A14; Dan Keating and Lenny Bernstein,

Washington Post, "Data: U.S. Suicide Rates on the Rise," April 23, 2016; Noam N. Levey, "Causes Cited for High Death Rates Among Middle-Aged Whites" *Tribune Washington Bureau*, January 30, 2016. Sociologists Jason N. Houle and Michael T. Light cite "theories of 'relative deprivation'" or "status threat" as a contributing factor for middle-aged white men who "experienced the foreclosure crisis as an individual failure, blaming themselves and 'going it alone'" ("The Harder they Fall? Sex and Race/Ethnic Specific Suicide Rates in the U.S. Foreclosure Crisis," *Social Science Medicine*, no. 180 [2017]: 120).

11. Now and then, one could catch glimpses of the dire housing sector on *House Hunters* whenever prospective buyers were shown a "short sale" where the bank had taken possession of a home and was hoping to recoup as much as it could of the property's former value.

12. Lori A. Trawinski, *Nightmare on Main Street: Older Americans and the Mortgage Market Crisis* (AARP Public Policy Institute, 2011), 3. In her essay "Paranormal Activity," Julia Leyda discusses how "possession and re-possession have become horrific concepts in the twenty-first century, defamiliarizing the home as haven to make it a site of terror and the uncanny" (*Jump Cut*, no. 56 [Fall 2014]).

13. Trawinski, 15.

14. Trawinski, 7–8.

15. Trawinski, 1.

16. Trawinski, 7.

17. Trawinski, 2. Trawinski defines middle class as people "with incomes ranging from $50,000 to $124,999." These "accounted for 53 percent of foreclosures of the 50+ population in 2011 [while] borrowers with incomes below $50,000 accounted for 32 percent." In the year 2011 alone, foreclosure rates were "23 times higher" than in 2007 (2).

18. It took until 2015 for economists to declare that home sales, prices, and levels of home ownership had become comparable to those in the previous peak year of 2007. Anyone looking to sell their home in the years immediately following 2008 was in the worst possible position. A new show on HGTV during this period was *Buying and Selling* (2012), an offshoot of *Property Brothers* that tried to address the realities of the housing market by featuring clients shopping for a new home while having their old one spiffed up so it could be sold in an admittedly difficult market. Shows built around renovating houses in order to sell them also predate the collapse (e.g., *Sell This House!*, 2003–2011).

19. Laurie Settle, *When Ghosts Attack!*, "There's No Place like Hell" (2013).

20. *When Ghosts Attack!*, "Beasts from the Beyond" (2013).

21. *Haunted Case Files*, "The Forbidding Funeral Home" (2016)

22. "TV.com. Episode Guide."

23. Marcia Eden, *When Ghosts Attack!*, "There's No Place Like Hell."

24. "The living present is scarcely as self-sufficient as it claims to be . . . we would do well not to count on its density and solidity, which might under exceptional circumstances betray us." Fredric Jameson, quoted in Blanco and Peeren, 54.

25. "Underwater Mortgage? Suze Orman Recommends Walking Away From Your Mortgage," Casey Bond, October 18, 2011, www.gobankingrates.com.

26. Orman recommended this step as early as August 2010: "You should continue to pay the mortgage as long as you can, ethically. But if you honest-to-God cannot pay for it, then stop paying for it." ("Interview: Suze Orman on Underwater Mortgages and Personal Finance," Hao Li, *International Business Times*, August 17, 2010, www.ibtimes.com/interview-suze-orman-underwater-mortgages.

27. Professor Brent T. White, quoted in Bond. A professor from the University of Arizona, White received widespread national attention when he advised homeowners to walk away as early as 2009 in a paper titled "Underwater and Not Walking Away: Shame, Fear and the Social Management of the Housing Crisis."

28. In *White Trash: The 400-Year Untold History of Class in America* (New York: Viking, 2016), Nancy Isenberg explores Americans' tendency when they experience economic problems to accept it as a personal responsibility rather than the result of national/global factors beyond their control.

29. John Langer, writing about local news programs, in Glynn, 41.

30. Gordon, 19.

31. Gordon, 24 (my italics). "The stories people tell about themselves, about their troubles, about their social worlds, and about their society's problems are entangled and weave between what is immediately available as a story and what their imaginations are reaching toward" (4).

32. Glynn, 157. "What is important, then, is to develop ways of understanding the role that power plays in determining *which* knowledges come to be treated as true and *whose* do not" (227, original italics).

33. Glynn, 227, 23.

34. Glynn, 10.

35. Glynn, 17. Cultural authorities tend to "to misinterpret (and therefore dismiss)" such "popular knowledges, antagonisms, and suspicions [because they] are expressed in very different social accents and a different idiom from those deployed by middle-class dissidents" (12). Glynn, 157.

36. Especially as capitalism is "a system that is utterly dependent on the repression of a knowledge of social injustice," Janice Radway, "Foreword," in Gordon, ix.

37. Blanco and Peeren, paraphrasing Jacques Derrida on Marx, 7.

38. Gordon, 7.

39. Blanco and Peeren, the editors of *The Spectralities Reader*, dismiss belief in actual ghosts as "a backward attitude" and "something of a fringe eccentricity," adding that "the widespread obsession with proving or disproving the reality of Spiritualist feats and related phenomena such as telepathy, clairvoyance *prevented the ghost's figurative potential from fully emancipating itself*" (3, original italics).

40. Gordon, 8 (my italics).

41. Marcia Eden, *When Ghosts Attack!*, "There's No Place Like Hell" (2013).

42. Featured in the series' first episode, a brick Queen Anne house serves as an iconic "haunted house" for *Paranormal Survivor*'s title sequence.

43. *Haunted Case Files*, "The Forbidding Funeral Home" (2016).

44. *Paranormal Survivor*, "Haunted Objects" (2015), "When Spirits Taken Over" (2016).

45. *My Ghost Story: Caught on Camera*, "Misery on the Missouri" (2013).

46. Tony Call (also billed as Anthony D. Call) narrates the series *A Haunting, Alaska Haunting, Amish Haunting*, and the specials *A Haunting in Connecticut* (2002) and *A Haunting in Georgia* (2002).

47. Buse and Stott, 4.

48. Glynn argues that the actors' lack of "physical resemblance to the 'real' participants," "implicitly den[ies] the significance of any difference between reality and representation,

fact and fiction" (63). I would argue that it underscores the fragmentation of identity and the atomization of individuals.

49. Rachel Pinkerton, *My Ghost Story: Caught on Camera*, "Misery on the Missouri" (2013). In "Scientific Rationalism and Supernatural Experience Narratives," Diane E. Goldstein discusses the way narrators of supernatural events rely on "modern scientific knowledge… in content and structure" when describing experiences that might not be believed (Goldstein, et al., 60–78).

50. Pinkerton.

51. *Paranormal Witness*, "The House on the Lake" (2005).

52. *Paranormal Witness: Pure Terror*, "Voodoo Preacher" (2016).

53. *A Haunting*, "Angels and Demons" (2012).

54. *Paranormal Witness: Pure Terror*, "Voodoo Preacher" (2016).

55. *Paranormal Witness: Pure Terror*, "Voodoo Preacher" (2016), features a similar dynamic. *A Haunting*, "Spellbound" (2007), features a husband who dismisses his wife's and stepson's concerns as "hocus pocus garbage." It is rare in these programs for one witness (usually a friend or family member) to be actively hostile toward the claims of the others.

56. *My Ghost Story: Caught on Camera*, "Misery on the Missouri" (2013).

57. The individuals who fail the witnesses are not portrayed as bad people usually; they have good intentions, but the scope of the problem is more than they can handle.

58. McCann, 34, 36 (quoting Emma Hardinge Britten).

59. McCann, 34, 33, 34.

60. McCann, 26.

61. *Ghostly Encounters*, "Refuge in Rosaries" (2006).

62. Even atheists are shown using a ritualized form of speech to establish a (paranormal) spiritual connection. In *When Ghosts Attack*, "Beasts from the Beyond" (2013), a woman tells of being frightened as a little girl. Her mother comforts her by saying, "White light, bright light, please protect me both day and night." This is identified explicitly as a mantra—not a prayer—though when the woman recites the words twenty years later they have an immediate, magical effect. Being choked in her bed by an unseen force, she repeats the mantra in her mind and is released instantly.

63. Sharon on *Ghostly Encounters*, "Play with the Occult, Pay the Price," also refuses to be a victim. When dark forces began to attack her children, she reports that she was "not scared—I was angry … so I just started fighting back." Like Cathy, she says, "I feel that I won that struggle and I'm much happier for it."

64. Glynn, 37.

65. Ouellette, *Lifestyle TV*, 130. She concludes, however, that we can't simply dismiss the representation of "ordinary people" as exploitative.

66. Ouellette, *Lifestyle TV*, 147.

67. Ouellette, *Lifestyle TV*, 146. "'Having a voice' is a social process, requiring the shared resources integral to recognition, interpretation, and validation" (147).

68. Graeme Turner, "Reality Television and the Demotic Turn" in Ouellette, *Companion*, 309–23, summarizing Nick Couldry, 315. Turner adds that participants are "relatively unconcerned by the fact they are donating their labor to a commercial enterprise—and surrendering their privacy along the way," concluding that "we need to find a way of explaining their

interest in this opportunity that does not simply assume naivety or gullibility or crassness of those seeking to participate" (315).

69. Buse and Stott, 4, referring to Spiritualism in Victorian Britain.

70. Ouellette, *Lifestyle TV*, 138.

71. Ouellette discussing Dovey, *Lifestyle TV*, 129.

72. Laura Grindstaff, "DI(t)Y, Reality-Style: The Cultural Work of Ordinary Celebrity" in Ouellette *Companion*, 332. Summarizing Sue Collins, she adds that "the increasing visibility of ordinariness" upholds "the higher values of 'real' celebrity by protecting it from clutter and sustaining scarcity as a measure of value."

73. Grindstaff, 332.

74. Julie Wilson, "Reality Television Celebrity: Star Consumption and Self-Production in Media Culture" in Ouellette, *Companion*, 421.

75. Glynn, 25.

76. Linda Blair hosted a paranormal series called *The Scariest Places on Earth* which ran for forty-one episodes between 2000 and 2006 on Fox Family. Episodes were set in locations familiar from numerous other shows such as the Lizzie Borden house, the *Queen Mary*, Magnolia Plantation, and Waverly Hills Sanitarium.

77. Hanks, 83.

Chapter 2. Ghost Hunters: Men on the Edge

1. John Leland, "Don't Say Ghostbuster, Say Spirit Plumber," *New York Times*, October 31, 2002, www.nytimes.com/2002/10/31/garden/don-t-say-ghostbuster-say-spirit-plumber.html.

2. The Sci-Fi Channel changed its name to "Syfy" in 2009.

3. Gretchen Stockdale, vice president and general counsel, Pilgrim Studios, interview, April 12, 2019.

4. Mike Nichols, executive producer, *Ghost Hunters*, 2012–2016, interview, April 12, 2019.

5. Craig Piligian, president and CEO, Pilgrim Studios, interview, April 12, 2019.

6. *Ghost Hunters*, "Angel of Death" (2016).

7. Hanks, 89.

8. Hanks, 90.

9. Milly Williamson, *CELEBRITY: Capitalism and the Making of Fame* (Cambridge, UK: Polity Press, 2016), 111.

10. Richard Dyer, *Stars* (London: BFI, 1980). Other shows that have made celebrities out of plumbers include *This Old House* (PBS, 1979–present), and *Dirty Jobs* (Discovery, 2003–2012). In the latter, also produced by Pilgrim Studios, host Mike Rowe visits people whose work is undervalued and overlooked, often due to the job's association with waste products, smells, and intense physical demands. Although he is a tourist in these areas, Rowe routinely testifies that the skills and hard work he has learned about in each episode are admirable and beyond him. In both shows, plumbing is presented as an interesting profession, requiring advanced training in various constantly evolving technologies (water, heating, cooling, waste) and creative problem-solving to pressing problems involving heating and cooling that could be a matter of life and death. As such, it is presented as a potential source of satisfaction and pride.

11. Graeme Turner, *Understanding Celebrity*, second edition (Los Angeles: Sage, 2014), 9.

12. Turner, 9.

13. Stelter.

14. Mike Hale, "Consigning Reality to Ghosts," *New York Times*, December 13, 2009, AR26.

15. Williamson, 111.

16. Williamson, 128. "The individual celebrity either displays or is constructed as possessing the values of individualism, entrepreneurialism and consumerism that are validated in neoliberal dominated culture" (125).

17. When the issue of the exploitation of "free labor" is raised in relation to reality TV scholarship, it often focuses on observational/contest programs such as *Big Brother*, *The Real World*, *Survivor*, or *The Bachelor*, series in which "monitoring transforms forms of leisure and domesticity into directly profitable activity" (i.e., producing a commodity that can be sold for the producers' profit) (Mark Andrejevic, "Real-izing Exploitation," in *The Politics of Reality Television: Global Perspectives*, eds. Marwan M. Kraidy, Katherine Sender [London: Routledge, 2011], 24). Andrejevic adds that "the comparison between celebrity and 'amateur' in reality TV" (for example in series that feature both recurring "stars" and one-time-only guests) "highlights … how the balance of power determines who benefits form the value-generating activity of being watched" (24).

18. Frances Kermeer quoted in Goldstein, 182.

19. Piligian, interview.

20. Nichols, Piligian, interview.

21. Burger cites the procedural structure as one of the ways *Ghost Hunters* encouraged fans to feel like participants, "creating a sense that viewers are positioned alongside the TAPS team members throughout pivotal moments in the investigation" (162). Producer Mark Stern adds that fans were particularly receptive to seeing "a team seeking answers rather than a narrator presenting information" (167).

22. As in first-person shows, investigators understand that one of the most helpful things they can do is to validate the witness's experience. "It actually reassured them that they weren't crazy. That what they were witnessing was, y'know, truly happening to them" (*Haunted Case Files*, "The Forbidding Funeral Home" [2016]).

23. This phrase is used in the title sequence for the first several seasons of the show. A revised title sequence debuted in spring 2014.

24. See Hanks. The strain of "tourism" is particularly evident when teams travel to Europe (e.g., *Ghost Adventures* in Transylvania).

25. *Ghost Adventures*, "Old Licking County Jail" (2014).

26. Roland Barthes, *Camera Lucida: Reflections on Photography*, trans. Richard Howard (New York: Hill and Wang, 1981), 79 (original italics).

27. *Ghost Asylum*, "Kuhn State Hospital" (2014). *Haunted History* (2013) focused on abuse at another former asylum in Pennsylvania in "Lost Souls of Pennhurst." As discussed in chapter 5, multiple shows have visited the same sites.

28. The longer a show runs, the more likely it is that there will be upgrades to more specialized technology. This move directly parallels the perception of the cast as more "celebrity/paranormal experts" than "ordinary" persons. "After they become familiar to an audience," *Ghost Hunters* producer Gretchen Stockdale said, after the show has "already been on for five, six, seven years, they don't recognize them as normal people anymore."

29. The "Vision X" is on *Ghost Adventures*, "Union Station" (2014). An investigator on an episode of *Paranormal Survivor* has "an app called Ghost Radar" ("When Spirits Talk," 2015).

30. *Ghost Adventures*, "Clovis Wolfe Manor" (2010).

31. *Ghost Adventures*, "Nopeming Sanitorium" (2015).

32. *Ghost Stalkers*, "Whispers Estate." Attending an opening night party for *Ghost Stalkers*, Neil Ginzlinger writes that he was open to belief in the paranormal. In fact, "I desperately wanted to be converted.... And I was buying in, until the wormhole detector turned up" ("The Creak in the Night is Music to their Ears," *New York Times*, October 11, 2014, C6).

33. *Ghost Asylum*, "Hayswood Infirmary" (2014).

34. In *Lifestyle TV*, Ouellette argues that the use of subtitles in reality series "positions lower-class whites (particularly in the South) outside the boundaries of mainstream America due to their inability to command proper English" (132–33).

35. "Nick asks countless questions ... but no audio evidence through EVPs is captured here" (*Ghost Adventures*, "Haunted Savannah" [2014]).

36. *Ghost Hunters*, "Angel of Death" (2016).

37. *Ghost Stalkers*, "Whispers Estate" (2014).

38. *Ghost Adventures*, "Mackey Mansion" (2016).

39. *Ghost Adventures*, "Union Station" (2014). The self of "my own eyes" is technologically mediated as Zak makes this statement while wearing a respirator mask and being photographed in green night-vision.

40. *Ghost Adventures*, "Nopeming Sanitorium" (2015).

41. Jeffrey Sconce, *Haunted Media: Electronic Presence from Telegraphy to Television* (Durham, NC: Duke University Press, 2000), 59.

42. Sconce 25. He warns that "each new communications technology seems to evoke ... a simultaneous desire and dread of actually making such extraordinary forms of contact" (83).

43. Sconce, 83.

44. Sconce, 59. As early as 1911, psychical researchers were already looking back to the days when "scientific apparatus ... came to play a central role in the spiritualistic séance" (James Coates, *Photographing the Invisible* [New York: Arno, 1973], quoted in Beckman 77).

45. Connor, 203–204.

46. For a discussion of the use of scientific terms and methods, see Goldstein "Scientific Rationalism and Supernatural Experience Narratives" (60–78).

47. *Ghost Adventures*, "Fear Factory" (2014).

48. The teams also occasionally double-check evidence gathered by other investigators. In an episode of *Ghost Asylum*, the team examines a video of the "Hayswood Ghost" and declare, "In our opinion, it's bogus" ("Hayswood Infirmary," 2014). When the *Ghost Hunters* team debunked a video from the *Queen Mary*, Mark Stern recalls, the team was "less accusatory, and a little more polite about it."

49. The siren spirit's attractive female voice is said to disguise its true evil nature (*Ghost Asylum*, "Old Cannon Memorial"). Investigators also deal with objects that are cursed, possessed or inhabited by spirits (e.g., *Haunted Collector* [2011], *Deadly Possessions* [2016]).

50. The use of humor in these shows makes parodies redundant.

51. Connor, 204–205. Connor makes his position clear when he states, "My argument is rooted at the deepest level on the presumption that no particle of such claims ... is in fact true" (206).

52. For example, the host of *Haunted Highway* is never convinced by the computer playback his teams show him when they return from their overnight camping trips.

53. Hale. This refusal to resolve the big question (what Hale calls "the teasing nature of the shows") can be especially frustrating.

54. *Ghost Adventures*, "Clovis Wolfe Manor" (2010). In "Rose Hall" (2011), Zak makes a similar statement when a voice-print of Johnny Cash is said to match that of a voice recorded by the team: "We cannot say that was the voice of Johnny Cash talking to us, but we cannot argue with this data either."

55. *Ghost Adventures*, "Haunted Savannah" (2014).

56. *Ghost Adventures*, "Black Dahlia House" (2016).

57. *Haunted Case Files*, "The Forbidding Funeral Home" (2016). In the reenactment the demon is played by an actor in a Minotaur costume.

58. In the 2016 "Angel of Death" episode of *Ghost Hunters*, Dustin and K. J. both identify themselves as "daddies" when trying to communicate with the ghost of a little girl.

59. John Fiske, *Television Culture* (London: Methuen, 1987), 214.

60. Aaron's status was upgraded in 2014 when he and Nick were identified as "fellow investigators."

61. Stelter.

62. Fiske, 221, 213.

63. Fiske, 213.

64. Fiske, 213.

65. *Ghost Adventures*, "Clovis Wolfe Manor" (2010).

66. *Ghost Adventures*, "Remington Arms Factory" (2009).

67. *Ghost Adventures*, "Mackay Mansion" (2016).

68. *Ghost Asylum*, "Old Cannon Memorial" (2014).

69. *Ghost Adventures*, "Heritage Junction" (2014).

70. *Ghost Stalkers*, "Whispers Estate" (2014).

71. *Ghost Adventures*, "Battle of Los Angeles" (2014).

72. *Ghost Adventures*, "Lizzie Borden House" (2011).

73. One of the most uncomfortable examples of the way women are positioned on *Ghost Adventures* takes place in the episode "The Mustang Ranch" (2013). The team invites married couple, psychics, and EVP specialists Mark and Debbie Constantino to accompany them during lockdown at the notorious Nevada brothel. Husband Mark tries to goad wife Debby into staying in one of the bedrooms in order to see if any ghostly "customers" show up. Debby's lack of enthusiasm at being cast as a paranormal prostitute is at odds with Mark and Zak's amusement at the "joke." The Constantinos' guest appearances on several *Ghost Adventures* episodes were rewritten by off-screen events in 2015 when Constantino murdered his wife and then killed himself in a standoff with police (Justin Wm. Moyer, "How Real-Life Horror Visited 'Rock Star' Ghost Hunters, Dead in Alleged Murder-Suicide," *Washington Post*, September 24, 2015). These events are referred to in "a very special episode" of *Ghost Adventures*, "The Washoe Club: Final Chapter" (2018), which ends with a number for people to call if they are victims of domestic violence.

74. *Ghost Adventures*, "Battle of Los Angeles" (2014).

75. Quoted in Banta, 23.

76. *Ghost Adventures*, "King's Tavern" (2013), "Mackay Mansion" (2016).

77. Exploring one house, Allan remarks to the camera "Yeah, this is bad s— here. . . . It's not something you wanna f— with" ("Battlefield: Flint, MI" [2013]). Unlike the men, when Allan curses (the language excised aurally while her mouth is blurred visually), instead of shouting suddenly in a loud, ejaculatory manner, she mutters to herself as if only "bad language" can express the inexpressible darkness she has found.

78. *Ghost Adventures*, "Overland Hotel and Saloon" (2014).

79. *The Velocity of Gary* (1999); *Ghost Adventures*, "Return to Linda Vista Hospital" (2012).

80. On *Ghost Adventures*, "King's Tavern," technical expert Billy also has heart problems when he becomes dazed inside the haunted house and has a dangerously rapid heartbeat.

81. *Ghost Adventures*, "Missouri State Prison" (2016). Similarly, on *Ghost Asylum* a team member asserts that there was a shadow figure: "[We] didn't pick it up on camera but I know what I saw" ("Old Cannon Memorial" [2014]).

82. *Ghost Adventures*, "Missouri State Prison" (2016).

83. Sconce, 26, 51.

84. Carl A. Wickland, MD, *Thirty Years Among the Dead* (Los Angeles: National Psychological Institute, 1924), 414. Madame Blavatsky, the founder of Theosophy, is the reputed speaker. See also Sconce, 28–31, 44–53, as well as illustrations of "the séance as 'spirit battery'" (29) and of a woman as a human radio antenna (68, 79).

85. Wickland, 414. The spirit of deceased writer Ella Wheeler Wilcox is credited with this observation.

86. In another episode (*Ghost Adventures*, "Bell Witch Cave" [2015]), Billy leaves in the middle of an investigation, admitting later, "I came out here because I was gonna cry. Honestly. But why would I be sad?"

87. On *Ghost Adventures: Aftershocks* (a 2014 clip-show spin-off in which Zak interviews people from earlier episodes), Zak argues that Aaron is in denial when he says he was never possessed, saying they all have been at one time or another. Aaron admits that, in the nine months following a 2013 episode that featured rituals performed by "a real-life warlock" and a "voodoo priestess," he had a "pretty hard-core depression," stopped driving, and did not want to leave his house. "I kept seeing my death."

88. *Ghost Asylum*, "Cannon Memorial Banner" (2014).

89. Fiske, paraphrasing Chodorow, 213.

90. As of 2019, *Ghost Adventures* alone has spawned six programs featuring members from its original cast: three shows with Zak Bagans (*Paranormal Challenge* [2011], *Ghost Adventures: Aftershocks* [2014], and *Deadly Possessions* [2016]), and three with Nick Groff (*Ghosts of Shepherdstown* [2016], *Paranormal Lockdown* [2016], and *Paranormal Lockdown UK* [2018]).

91. Nichols, interview.

92. *Ghost Asylum* ended when Chasey Ray left. The Tennessee Wraith Chasers regrouped for *Haunted Towns* (Destination America, 2017). Mike Goncalves replaced McKnight.

93. "A Message from Chasey Ray," https://www.youtube.com/watch?v=VHlYVrEuyDY.

94. As Clive Bloom says about our relation to ghosts: we "narrate them into 'life'" ("Angels in the Architecture: The Economy of the Supernatural" in Buse and Stott, 227).

Chapter 3. My Favorite Medium: Women's Work

1. Ann Braude, *Radical Spirits: Spiritualism and Women's Rights in Nineteenth Century America*, second edition (Bloomington: Indiana University Press, 2001), 102.

2. TLC's *The Healer* (2017) is the only series I know of that focuses on a psychic healer. The title figure of *Psychic Matchmaker* (2015) predicts which two people will make a good couple, and *Who Was I? My Past Lives* (2014) deals with reincarnation.

3. Other Biblical references to psychics (also referred to as witches, fortune tellers, and necromancers) include Leviticus 19:31, Exodus 22:18, Deuteronomy 18:10, 1 Samuel 28:3–9, 2 Kings 23:24, Jeremiah 27:9, and Acts 16:16–19.

4. Stanley Hall, "head of psychology at Clark University." Quoted in Deborah Blum, *Ghost Hunters: William James and the Search for Scientific Proof of Life after Death* (New York: Penguin Press, 2006), 305.

5. Lisa Held, "Psychic Mediums are the New Wellness Coaches," *New York Times*, March 19, 2019.

6. On October 28, 2018, "The Mediums of Lily Dale" (an episode of the documentary series *This Is Life with Lisa Ling* on CNN) presents a more nuanced view of psychics, including scenes where psychics alternately amaze and fail to impress clients during private readings.

7. *The Montel Williams Show*.

8. Natale, 3.

9. Natale, 3

10. Natale, 1.

11. Natale, 10.

12. Natale, 11.

13. Natale, 11.

14. Natale, 10.

15. See Braude; Logie Barrow, *Independent Spirits: Spiritualism & English Plebians, 1850–1910* (London: Routledge & Kegan Paul, 1986).

16. Robertson, 50.

17. Holzer is credited with writing over 100 books on supernatural subjects. He is cited as a pioneer in the field in *Ghost Adventures* episode "George Washington Ghost" (2014). In 2019, a paranormal reality series debuted based on letters, audio tapes, and film from Holzer's archives, *The Holzer Files* (TRV).

18. Albert A. Hopkins quoted in Beckman, "For British and American magicians, the 'Orient' . . . India in particular, was the birthplace of magic" (39). *Psychic Tia* (A&E, 2013) is an exception with star Tia Belle reading cards while dressed entirely in black.

19. Hans Holzer, *The Ghost Hunter* (New York: Fall River Press, 2014 [1963]), 126. This chapter is titled "Good Mediums are Rare."

20. Since 2004, the talk-show format has become associated with a genre even more disreputable than horror: the infomercial. These are usually half-hour sales pitches where an onstage host talks to a placid studio audience about weight loss, spiritual growth, or financing retirement. With titles like "Look Up to 2 Sizes Smaller Instantly!," "How to Tighten Crepey Skin," or "Do You Poop Enough?," these programs sell fitness, housewares, or health and beauty products on channels with no fixed identity (e.g., MALL, XTRA, BEST, REAL).

21. Edward's interaction with the audience is frequently cited as a model of "cold" reading.

22. Ouellette, *Lifestyle TV*, 8.

23. Ouellette, *Lifestyle TV*, 8. See also Deery, 53–56.

24. Dovey, 4.

25. Like Caputo and Cepero, Deborah Graham on *Psychic Matchmaker* (TLC, 2015) has a college-age daughter who tolerates her mother's compulsion to intervene in the lives of strangers. Graham is also a petite woman with a big personality, big hair, and big jewelry but the main difference between her and Caputo, et. al., is that she is a southerner working in the south. In accent, demeanor, and appearance, she resembles country singer/actress Reba McEntire. Graham uses her psychic abilities to establish a paranormally informed dating

service. Unfortunately, the clients who went on dates recommended by Graham evinced a marked lack of enthusiasm and the show lasted two episodes.

26. For a discussion of the evolution of TLC and its programs, see Ouellette, *Lifestyle TV*, 124–28.

27. The star of the series *Monica the Medium* introduces herself similarly: "Hi, I'm Monica. I'm just your typical college girl ... and, by the way, I talk to dead people."

28. Because the paranormal she deals with is more threatening than the one represented on *Long Island Medium* or *Angels Among Us*, Kim Russo occasionally gives someone a special crystal for their protection.

29. Ross, 35. For people appearing on reality TV competition shows, "the prospect of free self-promotion on a wide broadcasting platform is considered to be an adequate form of compensation," being "a potentially more lucrative asset in the attention economy than the fixed, or measurable, wages of industrialization" (35).

30. Kim Russo, for example, has appeared on TLC's *Say Yes to the Dress* (2013), helping her niece choose a wedding gown while assuring her that her late grandmother is present and approves.

31. This is consistent with Beth Robertson's description of psychics in North America between World War I and World War II. Seánces were frequently staged in "the living room of middle-class homes." "Marked with typically feminine crafts of embroidery and décor," these domestic spaces "commonly presented values of maternalism and the family" as they "asserted women's position as the moral and spiritual/authority within the home" (44–45).

32. In season eight, *Long Island Medium* sent Theresa on the road in her own special tour bus.

33. *Long Island Medium*, "Ugly Trucking" (2014).

34. For example, *The Haunting of . . . Pennhurst Revisited* (2014).

35. *Long Island Medium*, "There's a Lump" (2017).

36. According to the logic of the entertainment industry, success demands expansion. Originally a half-hour weekly show with occasional hour-long "specials," the series expanded to a full hour in season nine (2017).

37. Paula Deen has hosted several shows, including *Paula's Home Cooking* (2002–2013) on Food Network, *Paula's Party* (2006–2008), and *Paula's Best Dishes* (2008–2013). Deen's persona is that of a woman who, after a divorce, wrote a cookbook, hosted a TV show, and built a restaurant empire while working from her own kitchen. She has publically discussed being agoraphobic for twenty years following her father's death when she was nineteen. Caputo's anxieties are discussed in the episode "Panic Attack" (2017).

38. See Braude; Alex Owen, *The Darkened Room: Women, Power and Spiritualism in Late Victorian England* (London: Virago Press, 1989); Brown, 50–53.

39. Jill Galvan, *The Sympathetic Medium: Feminine Channeling, the Occult, and Communication Technologies, 1859–1919* (Ithaca: Cornell University Press, 2010), 12.

40. Galvan, 12. In 1924, a doctor and paranormal investigator noted that his wife "was easily controlled by discarnate intelligences" who would "take temporary but complete possession of my wife's body, without any injury to her" (Wickland, 17, 18).

41. In 2016, a private reading with John Edward (in person or on the phone) was listed on his website at $850. "All readings must be paid for at the time of booking by credit card, in person readings are to be paid in cash at time of reading but will be held with a credit card." A "private reading group" (defined as 20 people) costs $650. The large, two-hour "John Edward events" with several hundred people in attendance cost $150 per person, or $225

which includes a $99 membership in "Evolve" (an "on-line interactive John Edward community"), a password to his weekly podcast, "a signed book, two rose appreciation pins, an Evolve member pin, and a welcome letter."

42. Natale, 14. The prohibition on showing money is consistent with an Italian folk tradition which prohibits a client from putting money into the hand of a psychic. The client presents barter (food or goods) or gives money to the psychic's assistant, as seen in the film *Bicycle Thieves* (1948).

43. *Long Island Medium*, "On the Road: Niagara Falls" (2013).

44. The star of *Monica the Medium* also defines her job in therapeutic terms: "It's about the healing." *Crossing Over*'s title sequence depicts psychic work as a service, the narrator stating that John Edward found he "could reunite people in the physical world with those who have crossed over." The first episode of *Psychic Intervention* (2014) inadvertently reveals the pitfalls of shows dealing with grief. A woman is so distraught that she cannot stop crying and persistently resists Kim Russo's efforts to comfort her.

45. *Long Island Medium*, "Clearing the List" (2019).

46. *Psychic Matchmaker* Deborah Graham dates her first "premonitions" to the age of six.

47. Braude, 83.

48. Having left home, Monica is still defined in relation to her family. In one episode, she nervously anticipates a visit from her father while preparing for her first public reading with the celebrated psychic James Van Praagh. The reading goes well, she impresses her mentor, and her father sees her work for the first time (his appreciation of his daughter expressed as a growing belief in the paranormal).

49. Holzer, 7.

50. Holzer, 263, 171, 301. More than twenty similar assertions are made throughout the book.

51. *Ghosts in My House*, "Ghostly Vengeance" (2015).

52. Season 1, episode 6. Henry's assertion that this is "what makes me different than most mediums" again underscores his youth as he seems to be unaware that this is a ritual disclaimer used by nearly all paranormal reality television psychics.

53. The Boy George segment also makes explicit the conditions under which these sessions are arranged. At first, George refuses to cooperate and it seems that this is a reading where the medium will fail to elicit validation of his powers from a skeptical subject. The episode attempts to rectify the matter by cutting to George's manager watching on a monitor in another room. He verifies that Tyler's descriptions of a spirit coincide perfectly with someone he and George knew well, implying that George is just being difficult. Although this televisual construction of a three-way reading finds a way to validate Tyler's psychic connection with the dead, it is, at best, a partial solution. It is the celebrity's endorsement that matters. Eventually the manager storms in, interrupting the reading in order to dress down his client and insist that George acknowledge Tyler's gift. Reassured (primarily by Tyler's ignorance of his fame), George lightens up considerably for the remainder of the session.

54. Theresa Caputo, with Kristina Grish, *There's More to Life than This: Healing Messages, Remarkable Stories, and Insight About the Other Side from the Long Island Medium* (New York: Atria Books, 2013), 177.

55. *The Haunting of . . . Tito Ortiz* (2013).

56. When we see the production crew, it establishes television as the means by which the psychic and the person who "needs to hear" the message have been brought together.

57. For William James, psychologist and co-founder in 1884 of the American Society for Psychic Research, the value of the encounter between medium and client rests on the

undeniable power of this emotional connection. "The overwhelming sense of intimacy 'when your questions are answered, and your allusions understood, when allusions are made that you understand, and your own thoughts are met, when you have approved, applauded or exchanged banter, or thankfully listened to advice you believe in, it is difficult not to take away an impression of having encountered something sincere in the way of a social phenomenon'" (quoted in Blum, 299).

58. In the Lifetime series *Seatbelt Psychic* (2018), it is the taken-for-granted Uber driver who turns out to be a psychic, surprising riders with unsolicited readings.

59. *Psychic Investigators*, which ran for three seasons (2006–2009), is a close copy of *Psychic Detectives*, to the point of including many of the same psychic "guest stars" and retelling some of the same stories.

60. Male psychic Phil Jordan appears in five episodes.

61. Guest psychics include Micki Dahne ("Beauty and the Thief"), Ann Fisher ("Secrets of the Deep"), Jeanne Borgen ("Eyes of a Stranger"), Rosemarie Kerr ("Midnight Strangers"), Karen Prisant ("Hard Evidence"), Nancy Weber ("One Step Behind"), Elizabeth Joyce ("More than a Dream"), and Nancy Myer ("Bonds of Blood").

62. For the connection between old women and witches, see Carol F. Karlsen, *The Devil in the Shape of a Woman: Witchcraft in Colonial New England* (New York: Vintage Books, 1989); Sigrid Brauner, *Fearless Wives and Frightened Shrews: The Construction of the Witch in Early Modern Germany* (Amherst: University of Massachusetts Press, 1995); and Lyndal Roper, *Witch Craze: Terror and Fantasy in Baroque Germany* (New Haven: Yale University Press, 2004).

63. In the *Psychic Investigators* remake ("Who Killed the Flower Girl," 2009), the photographs are not face down and Pate's discussion of her choice is different. An accomplice's confession, obtained after the production of the 2006 *Psychic Detectives* episode, adds details about the woman's death that Pate does not know in the earlier episode.

64. *Psychic Detectives*, "The Flower Girl" (2006).

65. *Psychic Detectives*, "Prior Engagement." Noreen Renier appears in "In the Cards" (2004), "Prior Engagement" (2005), and "Lost in Transit," "Vanishing Visitors," "Sign of the Zodiac," and "Emergency Response" (all 2006). Carol Pate is in "A Psychic Warning" (2004), "The Flower Girl." (2006), and "While you were Sleeping" (2007). Pate also appears on an episode of *Forensic Files* ("Seedy Intentions," 2009).

66. *Psychic Detectives*, "Prior Engagement."

67. *Psychic Detectives*, "Psychic Warning."

68. *Psychic Detectives*, "Lost in Transit."

69. In *The Dead Files*, medium Amy Allan is often literally bent out of shape, her face contorted oddly and her shoulders twisted as she writhes under unseen pressures, listening to voices we cannot hear or squinting at things we cannot see. Unlike Theresa Caputo or Kim Russo, Allan is neither maternal nor overwhelmed by sympathy for others. She does not comfort the bereaved or reassure frightened people who have asked for her help. Like male ghost hunters, she risks not only physical pain but spiritual oppression/possession. At one point, she announces that a spirit has entered her body, something she describes afterward as a psychic crime: "I got jumped." Her matter-of-fact demeanor, though, precludes our seeing her as a victim. Even when she tells the audience that sometimes it takes her days to shake off the physical and spiritual effects of such an encounter, she comes across as tough and experienced.

70. *Psychic Detectives*, "Psychic Warning."

71. *Psychic Detectives*, "Psychic Warning."
72. *Psychic Detectives*, "Prior Engagement."
73. *Psychic Detectives*, "Lost in Transit."
74. *Psychic Detectives*, "Eyes of a Stranger."

Chapter 4. Confronting Evil: A Short Trip to the Dark Side

1. Illustration, *Demons expelled when confronted by the Eucharist*, Chapel of the Corporal, Orvieto Cathedral, Italy, painted 1357–1363.
2. On *Kindred Spirits*, "The Executioner" (2017), the investigators encounter a female ghost who lingers in the house she lived in for fifty years. The new owner's friends, styling themselves as ghost hunters, tried to terrorize the ghost to make her leave. Co-host Adam Berry is moved to tears thinking how confused and frightened the ghost must have been. He admonishes would-be ghost hunters severely: "You don't just run into houses and yell at ghosts."
3. Caputo, 21. The films *Ouija* (2014) and its sequel, *Ouija: Origin of Evil* (2016), are part of this trend rather than being precursors of the televised accounts.
4. Caputo, 81.
5. Caputo, 21.
6. Caputo, 81 (original italics).
7. Wickland, 17. Hanks also specifies a ban on Ouija boards as one of the few restrictions owners of haunted sites place on visiting ghost hunters: "A few sites requested that groups avoid using Ouija boards out of popular concerns about the association between Ouija boards and demonic possession" (180, n3). On *Paranormal Survivor*, "Don't Invite Them In" (2015), a paranormal investigator speculates that a house became haunted when "someone had opened a portal via a Ouija board." She suggests to the family that they move out as soon as it is "financially possible."
8. Harry Houdini, *A Magician Among the Spirits* (New York: Harper & Brothers, 1924), 190. He adds, "Not the least of the evils of Spiritualism is the insanity which it causes" (189).
9. Houdini, 189–90.
10. On *Celebrity Ghost Stories*, sitcom actor Michael Urie played with a Ouija board in his student days and made an unnerving connection with the ghost of a friend (2010).
11. Jonette Bekovic, *Women of Grace*, "Things that Go Bump in the Night," EWTN (2013). *Psychic Kids*, "Dangerous Games" (2019), also stresses the dangers of playing with Ouija boards.
12. *Haunted Collector*, "Firestarter; Haunted Museum" (2012); "nullifying" ("Priest Gun; Haunted Asylum," 2012).
13. "Things that Go Bump in the Night," part 5. The show's conservative views on women are visualized in its title sequence which features floating pairs of words: "Receptivity/trust," "surrender/motherhood," "spiritual maternity/authentic femininity."
14. People are also advised to "remove all non-Christian religious materials from your home." The definition of "non-Christian" is quite broad and includes anything to do with "Mormon[s], Christian Science, yoga, [or] transcendental meditation." Statues or images from "Oriental cultures" are suspect because they might contain hidden religious significance. Repeating affirmations "that allegedly lead to miracles" is also prohibited.
15. *Paranormal Witness* also has an episode about this figure ("Zozo," 2016).

16. This being is not necessarily what Christians would think of as a "devil" but an ancient force who is said to appear across multiple cultures.

17. Because seeing characters pushed to their breaking point is a highlight of melodrama, episodes that deal with extremes such as potentially overwhelming negative forces often occupy a special position in a series. "Zozo Demon" spawned extra episodes when "well-known demonologist" Darren, who took part in the "spirit board" session with Nick, is brought back for another episode in 2017 ("Samaritan Cult House"). On *Paranormal Lockdown*, when Nick Groff is personally tormented by bad dreams after an encounter with a demon at "Hinsdale House" it leads to a climactic confrontation in the season-ending episode "100 Hours at Black Monk House" (2016).

18. *Haunted Case Files*, "The Forbidding Funeral Home" (2016). A similar figure appears in the title sequence of *Paranormal Survivor* and in *Demon House* (2018), an offshoot of *Ghost Adventures*, written and directed by Zak Bagans.

19. The abandoned and repurposed factory can be seen as another example of the post-recession era, in this case the decline of American manufacturing.

20. Appearing as a guest on the news/talk show *The World Over Live* (on the Catholic channel EWTN), December 10, 2011, Father Lampert explains that Pope John Paul II decreed in 1999 that every diocese should have its own trained exorcist. The office of the Vatican exorcist was founded in 1614.

21. These shots recall horror films set in the Vatican such as *The Omen* (1976) and *The DaVinci Code* sequel, *Angels and Demons* (2009).

22. Gretchen Stockdale, interview.

23. Ex-detective Ralph Sarchie explains that, "even though I've now integrated scientific methods, the basis of my investigation is still of a religious vein and it is still done in the context of exorcism"—an explicitly Catholic ritual. In the title sequence of *The Demon Files*, we see Sarchie reading the rite while blessing a room with a crucifix. In the third episode, "The Trade," he commands the demons through "religious provocation," demanding in a loud voice, "I command you in the name of Jesus Christ to reveal your identity to us right now.... In the name and by the blood of our Lord Jesus Christ I command you to reveal yourself." In episode one, he declares "We're here to defeat Satan. That's the first order of business," as we see him kissing a crucifix.

24. As the *Women of Grace* are quick to point out, psychiatric evaluations are well and good but "we cannot psychologize away Satan."

25. *The Dead Files*, "Battlefield: Flint, MI" (2013).

26. "Tar" ("Triggered: Flint, Michigan," 2018); "fuzz" ("The Sacrifice: East Flat Rock, North Carolina," 2016); "looming ("Compelled: St. Charles, Michigan," 2016); "little creature" ("Burned Alive: Seattle," 2012).

27. *The Dead Files*, "House of Horrors: Radford VA" (2014).

28. *The Dead Files*, "Burned Alive: Seattle" (2012).

29. *The Dead Files*, "House of Horrors: Radford VA" (2014).

30. The advice to get a specifically male medium and the reference to a "chaos magician" are in "Triggered: Flint, Michigan"; the reference to a priest is in "The Sacrifice: East Flat Rock, North Carolina."

31. *The Dead Files*, "House of Horrors: Radford VA" (2014).

32. The program debuted on The Travel Channel in 2011 and remains in production.

33. Mikhail Bulgakov, *The Master and Margarita*, trans. Richard Pevear and Larissa Volokhonsky (New York: Penguin Books, 2016), 367.

34. In her essay "God, Capitalism and the Family Dog," Eileen R. Meehan discusses similar "prayer circles" in the reality show *Dog The Bounty Hunter* (in Ouellette, *Companion*, 171–88).

35. Donald Antrim, *The Afterlife* (New York: Farrar, Straus and Giroux, 2006), 105.

36. This prayer was written by Pope Leo XIII in the nineteenth century. Buell, like John Edward and Italian Americans Theresa Caputo, Rosie Cepero, and Kim Russo, is presumably Roman Catholic.

37. After using a Ouija board to summon a spirit called Vox, a family in *Paranormal Witness*, "The Dangerous Game" (2014), calls on a "Native American spirit guide" to help them cleanse their home.

38. Claud's team consists of his wife (identified as a "psychic-medium") and another woman described as a "medic."

39. *Ghost Adventures Aftershocks*, "Sedansville Rectory; Winchester Mystery House" (2014). At one point in "Letchworth Village" (*Ghost Adventures*, 2011), Bagans fears a negative energy has attached itself to him. A threatening gravelly male voice "captured on EVP" and subtitled for clarity warns him to "pray your god." Later, Bagans asks the spirit, "Is this where evil comes up and conquers good? We're here not to let that happen." The demon responds (as a printed title spells out several times): "Then come get me."

40. Caputo and Grish, *There's More to Life Than This*, xiii.

41. Caputo and Grish, xiii.

42. *Women of Grace*: "Things That go Bump in the Night," part I. *Women of Grace* is shown on EWTN (Eternal Word Television Network), identified on their website as the "Global Catholic Network."

43. *Sermons of Martin Luther*, vol. 2, ed. and trans. John Nicholas Lenker (Grand Rapids, MI: Baker Book House, 1906), 313. He goes on to say that the devils "amuse themselves thus either to deceive the people with false claims and lies or unnecessarily frighten and trouble them."

44. An overtly religious show, TLC's *Answered Prayers* (2015), featured first-person accounts of miracles. Hosted by Roma Downey (also a producer of Christian-themed scripted dramas), the series lasted for three episodes.

45. *Ghost Adventures*, "King's Tavern" (2013).

46. The short-lived *Project Afterlife* (three episodes in 2015) openly advocated a Christian view. Based on witness testimony about "near-death experiences," the series presented reenactments of people dying, meeting Jesus in Heaven, and being sent back to Earth because it was not their time to die. The concept of a "near-death experience" was first outlined by Raymond A. Moody Jr. in the best-selling book, *Life after Life: The Investigation of a Phenomenon—Survival of Bodily Death* (New York: Bantam Books, 1975).

Chapter 5. Abandoned Institutions: "It's in the Walls"

1. The prisons featured on *Ghost Adventures* include: Moundsville Penitentiary (2008), Idaho State Penitentiary (2008), Eastern State Penitentiary (2008), Ohio State Reformatory (2009), Castillo de San Marcos, St. Augustine (2009), Old Charleston Jail (2011), Central Unit Prison, Huntsville, Texas (2012), Wyoming Frontier Prison (2013), Missouri State Penitentiary (2013), Alcatraz (2013), Old Licking County Jail, Ohio (2014), Old Montana State Prison (2015), Hell Hole Prison (2016), and Nevada State Prison (2016). Hospitals include

an "Abandoned Psychiatric Hospital" in Cedar Grove, New Jersey (2008), Trans-Allegheny Lunatic Asylum, West Virginia (2009), Pennhurst State School (and asylum) (2009), Linda Vista Hospital (2009, 2012), Clovis Wolfe Manor (2010), Rolling Hills Asylum (2010), Waverly Hills Sanatorium (2010), Hill View Manor (2010), Yorktown Hospital, Texas (2011), Letchworth Village (2011), Ashmore Estates (2011), Tooele Hospital, Utah (2011), Tuolumne General Hospital (2013), Battle of Perryville, Field Hospitals, Kentucky (2013), Nopeming Sanatorium, Minnesota (2015), and Old Lincoln County Hospital, Tennessee (2015). By 2012, the show had accumulated enough material to create an hour-long special about prisons made up entirely of clips, titled "Dead Men Walking."

2. *Ghost Hunters*, "Waverly Sanatorium" (2006). On *Paranormal Lockdown*, Katrina says "Waverly Hills has been on my paranormal bucket list for ten years. This is *the* place. . . . If you wanna see activity, go to Waverly." Later, she tells Nick, "I am beyond excited to be here. I've been waiting ten years to get here." In 2007, *Ghost Hunters* had a special live Halloween episode at Waverly Hills and an episode revealing the results of the investigation a week later (November 7, 2007).

3. Also the subject of the third episode of The Travel Channel's *Portals to Hell* (2019).

4. "America's Most Historic Prison," http://www.easternstate.org.

5. Robin Evans, *The Fabrication of Virtue: English prison architecture, 1750–1840* (Cambridge, UK: Cambridge University Press, 1982), 407.

6. Janet Semple, *Bentham's Prison: A Study of the Panopticon Penitentiary* (Oxford: Clarendon Press, 1993), 11, quoting Roy Porter (*Mind-Forg'd Manacles*).

7. See Semple.

8. Over 300 prisons were based on variations of this concept including Eastern State (aka Cherry Hill) in Philadelphia. The prime example that exists today is Dublin's Kilmainham Gaol. From its spectacular east wing, built in 1861, "it is possible to see all 96 cells from a central viewing area" Abandoned in 1924, Kilmainham Gaol was reopened as a museum in 1966 and attracts 300,000 visitors a year (Kilmainhamgaolmuseum.i.e./timeline/).

9. Semple, 10, quoting M. Ignatieff, *A Just Measure of Pain*.

10. Michel Foucault, *Discipline and Punish: The Birth of the Prison*, trans. Alan Sheridan second edition, (New York: Vintage Books, 1995), 233.

11. Semple, 9.

12. Foucault, 233, 242, quoting E. Danjou, *Des Prisons* (1821).

13. Foucault, 236.

14. Foucault, 236.

15. Evans paraphrasing St. Paul to the Corinthians ("evil communication corrupts"), 333. Combining science with religious zeal, penal reformers used modern technological advances to explain the metaphysical progress of evil. According to John Burt, assistant chaplain at Pentonville, "demoralizing and criminalizing ideas" were said to "play upon the soul like a galvanic battery of vice"; Magistrate Benjamin Rotch thought that "moral contamination" resulting from communication was "almost electrical . . . so rapidly does it take effect" (Evans, 333).

16. Foucault, 249.

17. Foucault, 231.

18. Nick Groff, *Paranormal Lockdown*, "Shrewsbury Prison" (2016).

19. Evans, 4.

20. Evans details how, in 1823, when New York's Auburn Prison experimented with "complete seclusion," prisoners "died or went mad." As a consequence, "unmitigated solitude" was

replaced by a system of "hard labour in 'silent association'" (318). Convicts stayed in their cells at night and worked in groups in the daytime but were forbidden to speak.

21. Evans, 349.
22. Evans, 354.
23. Foucault, 239.
24. Evans, 335.
25. Evans, 335–37.
26. Evans, 337 (my italics).
27. Evans, 337.
28. Evans, 337.
29. Evans, 337.
30. Evans, quoting August Demetz and Albert Blouet, *Rapports sur les Penitenciers des Etats Unis* (Paris, 1837), 91.
31. Evans, 337.
32. Evans, 337.
33. Evans, 337, quoting Henry Mayhew and John Binney, *Criminal Prisons of London* (London, 1862), 163. An early code is described in Rev. John T. Burt, *The Results of the System of separate Confinement* (London, 1852) beginning on p. 271. In Nicole Krause's novel *The History of Love* (New York: W. W. Norton, 2005), two elderly neighbors agree to check on each other every day to make sure they are still alive: knock twice for yes, once for no.
34. The concept of "residual energy" circulated in the Spiritualist milieu at the end of the nineteenth century. In 1904, novelist Rosa Praed "speculate[d] that past events, all of history in fact, is '*imprinted on the circumambient ether of any locality.*'" Praed, who was influenced by her close relationship with a female medium that began in 1899 and lasted for thirty years, used an analogy with another technology to explain how traumatic events created an "imperishable photograph of an event which has taken place on that spot." She warns, however, that the "picture-gallery provided for us in space" is only "accessible to those who possess its key." ("Epilogue to *Nyria*," quoted in McCann, 143.)
35. Benjamin D'Harlingue, "Specters of the U.S. Prison Regime: Haunting Tourism and the Penal Gaze," in Peeren and Blanco, *Popular Ghosts*, 136.
36. Such questions are part of the pseudo-interactivity discussed by Burger in regard to *Ghost Hunters*.
37. Foucault, 237, quoting Charles Lucas, *On the Reform of Prisons*.
38. Semple, 117. Communicating through the tubes was also useful in "constantly enforcing a clockwork regularity on the administration of the prison" (118). This idea carried over into the twentieth century with the introduction of radio. "Radio headsets installed in Sing Sing's cells in the late twenties brought in the outside world and served as a strategic ally for Warden [Lewis E.] Lawes, whose fireside chat radio programs piped directly into the cells on Sunday evenings" (Alison Griffiths, *Carceral Fantasies: Cinema and Prison in Early Twentieth-Century America* [New York: Columbia University Press, 2016], 8).
39. Foucault, 237.
40. Sean Kelley, senior vice president, director of interpretation and public programming, Eastern State Penitentiary Historical Site, interview, October 16, 2016.
41. Castle, 17.
42. Castle, 15, 16.
43. Adam Smith, *An Inquiry into the Nature and Causes of the Wealth of Nations*, vol. 2 (1776, 1801), 314.

44. Terry Castle, *The Female Thermometer: Eighteenth-Century Culture and the Invention of the Uncanny* (New York: Oxford, 1995), 7. The paranormal is another way of thinking of the uncanny—something that cannot be pinned down or proven, the apprehension of which is derided as mere superstition, the product of dreams, or nothing but a vague, persistent feeling. From the tangible proofs of positivism, we are thrown back onto unassuageable ambiguity. For Castle, the attempt to impose a univalent meaning through the absolute control of space and time (as the penal reformers did in the eighteenth and nineteenth centuries) reveals the "paranoia, repression, and incipient madness" inherent in their designers' "implacable logic (7).

45. Castle, 7. She defines the uncanny as "when the primitive beliefs which have been surmounted seem once more to be confirmed" (quoting Freud, standard edition [1955], xvii, 249).

46. Castle, 7.

47. "Denice," Sherwin-Williams customer support, September 23, 2016.

48. *Ghost Hunters*, "Waverly Sanatorium" (2006).

49. William Faulkner, *Requiem for a Nun* (1951).

50. *Ghost Hunters*, "Waverly Sanatorium" (2006).

51. When *Portals to Hell* visits Eastern State Penitentiary in 2019, the cast points out that they are the first investigators allowed to visit the prison's death row.

52. *Ghost Hunters*, "Waverly Sanatorium" (2006).

53. The phrase "bloodiest forty-seven acres in America" serves as the title of the 2011 *Ghost Hunters* episode set at Missouri State Penitentiary. *Ghost Asylum*, "Missouri State," describes the prison as the site of "one hundred and sixty-eight bloody years" of "nonstop violence" (2016).

54. The former Northern Michigan Asylum is in Traverse City, Michigan.

55. See D'Harlingue.

56. According to Kelley, 200,000 people take the daytime tours each year.

57. D'Harlingue, 137.

58. Kilmainham Gaol Museum in Dublin is an example of a former prison that has undergone extensive renovation.

59. *Ghost Hunters*, "Waverly Sanatorium" (2006).

60. Austin Reed, *The Life and Adventures of a Haunted Convict*, ed. Caleb Smith (New York: Random House, 2016), 198–205.

61. *Ghost Hunters*, "Waverly Sanatorium" (2006).

62. The most extreme version of using photographs of subjects who cannot consent appears in a *Hauntings and Horrors* episode on Edgar Allan Poe (2014). In its discussion of grave robbers who supplied medical schools with bodies to dissect, the episode presents several nineteenth-century photographs that seem to be of actual flayed bodies flanked by young men in lab coats.

63. Pennhurst Asylum, Spring City, Pennsylvania, originally known as the Eastern State Institution for the Feeble Minded and Epileptic (1908–1987), has been featured on *Ghost Hunters* (2011) and *Ghost Adventures* (2009).

64. This is different than the effect on programs about psychic-mediums where family members provide photographs as evidence that the dead were once alive and well and happy.

65. Sean Kelley points out that the museum called "Cell Block 7" in Jackson, Michigan, is beside "the active Michigan State prison. They opened up one of their cell blocks for tours

and … you can actually see [inmates] walking around." This raises the question of "how to handle the ethics and the legality of being around men who are incarcerated."

66. *Paranormal Lockdown*, "Shrewsbury Prison" (2016).

67. *Paranormal Lockdown*, "Shrewsbury Prison" (2016).

68. Quoted in Semple, 132. To avoid the extreme effects of solitary confinement, Bentham eventually suggested having between two and four inmates in each cell. Because "this species of punishment … may overthrow the powers of the mind and produce incurable melancholy," Bentham argued, it should only be used for brief periods. "If greatly prolonged, it would scarcely fail of producing madness, despair" (130).

69. John Sears, *Sacred Places: American Tourist Attractions in the Nineteenth Century* (New York: Oxford, 1989), 88–89. Some institutions even charged admission (84). *Buried Alive* is the title of a memoir written in the nineteenth century by a former inmate as noted in the Missouri State Penitentiary episode of *Ghost Adventures*. *Buried Alive (Behind Prison Walls) for a Quarter of a Century: Life of William Walker*, ed. Thomas S. Gaines (Saginaw, MI: Friedman & Hynan, 1892). Like Austin Reed, Walker had been enslaved.

70. "Images of the tomb and resurrection occur frequently in the accounts of prisons and asylums and suggest that these institutions symbolized, for some visitors at least, the fear of spiritual death" (Sears, 97).

71. Semple, 129. Prisoners were hooded when they left their cells, ostensibly to prevent recognition by others inside the prison and those they might meet outside after their release.

72. Semple, 16, quoting Browning.

Chapter 6. In America There Is Real Evil: Excluded Americans

1. This line is featured over the title sequence of *A Haunting* and can be heard in the episodes "Angels and Demons," "Haunted Victorian," and "Back from the Grave." In other episodes, the narrator says, "In this world there is real evil."

2. It is important to note that almost every program assumes that "America" and the United States are synonymous. A handful of episodes are set in Europe, but most are either explicitly located in the US or presumed to take place there. Canada serves as an occasional substitute, presenting an English-speaking, all-purpose North American image that blurs national distinctions if you don't look too closely. In *Ghostly Encounters*, for example, the northern city seen outside the loft where genial host, Lawrence Chau, introduces each episode is never identified as Toronto, though segments that take place in St. John, New Brunswick, or Halifax, Nova Scotia are clearly identified as such ("Kids Who See Ghosts," 2011). *Hauntings and Horrors* visits locations in the US (Waverly Hills Sanatorium in Louisville, Kentucky) but at least one segment per episode is situated in a named Canadian city or town. The program did disguise its national origins when it changed its title, having aired originally as *Creepy Canada*.

3. Sears argues that the link between land and culture is fundamental to the self-identification of US citizens as Americans, though by using the term "American" to refer to Europeans, he elides the experience of Native Americans (4).

4. Ulrich Baer, "To Give Memory a Place: Contemporary Holocaust Photography and the Landscape Tradition," in Blanco and Peeren, 427.

5. "Haunting, as a conceptual metaphor, can elucidate the way architecture, landscape, geography and tourism mediate particular presences and absences, both material and in

the less apprehensible form of dealing with traumatic or oppressive pasts" (Blanco and Peeren, 20).

6. Sears, 6.

7. John Canup, *Out of the Wilderness: The Emergence of an American Identity in Colonial New England* (Middletown CT: Wesleyan University Press, 1990), 42.

8. Increase Mather, "A Discourse Concerning the Uncertainty of the Times of Men, and the Necessity of being Prepared for Sudden Changes & Death" (1696).

9. Canup, 39–40.

10. Canup, 33.

11. Canup, 30.

12. Canup, 38.

13. Canup, 88.

14. Canup, 5, 4.

15. Canup, 62. "As Indians are made to vanish into the psychic spaces of America's citizens, the psychic space within each citizen is itself transformed into American territory, and each citizen comes to contain an America, to be *homo Americanus*" (Renée L. Bergland, *The National Uncanny: Indian Ghosts and American Subjects* [Hanover, NH: UPNE, 2000], 4).

16. Canup, 79; Mather, 1699.

17. Canup, 78, Cotton Mather, *The Present State of New England* (Boston, 1690), 35.

18. Troy, 55. Not everyone lauded this creation of the Spiritualist movement. In *The Principles of Psychology*, William James dismisses Native American "spirit guides" or "controls" as "grotesque, slangy, and flippant personage[s] ... calling the ladies 'squaws,' the men 'braves,' the house a 'wigwam,' etc. etc." (New York: Henry Holt 1890), 394.

19. Caputo, 65. She describes him as "serious, disciplined, and structured—a little like Sitting Bull" (65).

20. Troy, xi.

21. Troy interprets the figure of the Indian spirit guide differently, arguing that "the purpose of the haunting was to force recognition of the ghost.... Spiritual enlightenment thus required ... bringing the forgotten Indians back into the foreground" (70).

22. Judith Richardson, *Possessions: The History and Uses of Haunting in the Hudson Valley* (Cambridge: Harvard University Press, 2003), 209.

23. Richardson, 5–6. She adds, "haunting is by definition an intervention, an occupation, a claim of priority and possession" (174) and this makes "belonging and possessing issues that perennially trouble American minds" (8).

24. Buse and Stott, 9.

25. National Geographic's *Haunted History*, "Ghosts of the Mississippi."

26. The 2006 horror film *The Woods* is set in New England and features foliage that kills at the command of a group of witches.

27. *Paranormal Lockdown*, "Oliver House" (2016).

28. A football team in Ireland suggested that its losing record was due to the fact that their stadium in County Mayo was unwittingly built on an Indian burial ground—a satiric nod to the ubiquity (and geographic fluidity) of this trope.

29. On an episode of *Celebrity Ghost Stories*, singer Jermaine Jackson begins his story by announcing dramatically: "My mother had told us our home was built on Indian burial grounds"—though this detail (as we see in other programs) turns out to be irrelevant (2010).

30. On *Long Island Medium*, "Haunted Houses" (2016), Theresa meets a client on her doorstep and asks, "Do you ever hear, like, drumming?" The client replies, "It's funny that

you would say that because up in the back of our property is a Native American burial ground." Lest the sounds be mistaken for something angry or negative, Theresa is quick to clarify that the chanting sounds "more like ceremonies and celebrations."

31. This episode is recycled in *The Dead Files Revisited* (2012), which is made up of two half-hour condensed versions of previous episodes. In this episode, the second half hour is "Fear at the Family Tree." Both half-hours are about grandmothers who are worried about their grandchildren. The 2019 series, *Psychic Kids*, also visits Leslie's Family Tree Restaurant.

32. Jill Lepore, *The Name of War: King Philip's War and the Origins of American Identity* (New York: Knopf, 1998), 193.

33. *The Other Side*, a Canadian series that ran from 2014 to 2018, seems to have been designed to explore the different attitudes of Canadian First Peoples toward spirits. As far as I know, it has not been shown in the US. Episodes are available on YouTube.

34. *Paranormal State*, "The Fury" (2009), also has a shaman visit to discuss "the mound builders" in West Virginia, whose burial mounds are in "proximity to a stream which has been dammed"—a disruption that the shaman is sure will provoke a reaction. The client family (whom Ryan calls "not the first to unintentionally violate the land on which their home stands") uses sage too, though no Native Americans are present when they do. Ryan tells them "Native Americans all revere sage as a cleansing element" because it "stinks" to spirits.

35. Some of Danielson's dialogue is subtitled and some not. This is.

36. In another *Ghost Adventures* episode that consults the Chippewa ("Dakota Sanatorium of Death"), interviews with local Native Americans are summarily dropped when someone brings up the issue of satanic rituals, a topic which dominates the rest of the episode. *Ghost Adventures* opened its fourteenth season (2017) with two episodes focusing on paranormal questions associated with the Navajo and shot on Navajo land. Later episodes also show more engagement with and respect for Native American culture.

37. Jack Blades, *Celebrity Ghost Stories* (2012).

38. Other *Ghost Adventures* episodes that focus on the slavery era include "Kentucky Slave House" (2011) and "Myrtle Planation" (2014).

39. An electronic device displays the words "unjust" and "malicious."

40. Catherine R. Squires, "The Conundrum of Race and Reality Television" (Ouellette, *Companion*, 268). She attributes the term "mirror show" to B. Haggins.

41. In "Old City Jail" (2017), Juwan Mass mentions attaining the rank of Eagle Scout.

42. Ouellette, *Lifestyle TV*, 136.

43. Ouellette, *Lifestyle TV*, 130, summarizing Vicki Mayer's work on casting.

44. William Thomas Jr. (Buckwheat) and Lincoln Perry (Stepin Fetchit) were actors whose names were overshadowed by the characters they played.

45. Mike Nichols, executive producer of the first six episodes of *Ghost Brothers*, interview, April 12, 2019.

46. *Ghost Adventures*, "Magnolia Plantation" (2009).

47. In a 2019 episode of *Kindred Spirits* ("Dying Regrets"), Amy and Adam are uncomfortable being polite to the spirit of the former overseer at a Virginia plantation.

48. In *Ghost Adventures Aftershocks*, "Bobby Mackays; Brookdale Lodge" (2014), Zak calls himself "a dumbass" for having taunted spirits earlier in his career. "I didn't have the knowledge." He promises to stop.

49. The stereotype of the hard-talking, cigarette-smoking aunt fits right in with comedies such as *Boo! A Madea Halloween* (2016), selected skits on the television series *Key and Peele*, and the *Scary Movie* franchise (five films between 2001 and 2013 featuring multiracial casts),

all of which offer African American comedians the chance to find humor in paranormal subjects.

50. *Ghost Asylum* does something similar at Missouri State Prison (2016). A collage on one wall shows pictures of the people executed there. Although more than half are African American men, the team focuses on a white couple they call "Bonnie and Carl" (exploiting the obvious echo with Bonnie and Clyde).

51. The series' tag line is: "They investigate in the areas of Los Angeles that other teams won't."

52. *Ghosts in the Hood*, "Scared Straight Outta Compton," "Menace 2 South Central."

53. Della Reese, *Celebrity Ghost Stories* (2012). Like Gossett, Reese, at age eighty-one, is one of the older featured speakers on *Celebrity Ghost Stories*. In keeping with the diversity of its participants, this series represents people from a greater age range than seen on other programs.

54. Scripted shows with overtly Christian identities were most notable in the 1980s and 1990s, including *Highway to Heaven* (1984–1989), *Seventh Heaven* (1996–2007), and *Promised Land* (1996–1999), the last a *Touched by an Angel* spin-off.

55. Debbie Allen, *Celebrity Ghost Stories* (2012).

56. Pam Grier, *Celebrity Ghost Stories* (2014).

57. Craig Piligian, Gretchen Stockdale, Mike Nichols, interview, April 12, 2019.

58. As "Lisa Lisa," Velez was part of the singing group Lisa Lisa and Cult Jam (*Celebrity Ghost Stories*, 2013).

59. David Otunga, *Celebrity Ghost Stories* (2014).

Chapter 7. The Next Generation: Children of the Paranormal

1. During a reading for a family, Theresa Caputo meets a girl of about eight or ten who sees spirits; she comments in the voice-over that the girl reminds her of herself at that age (*Long Island Medium*, "Larry Returns," 2019).

2. *Ghost Nation*, "A Nightmare in the Nursery" (2019).

3. Barrow, 263. This debate focused in particular on "whether children should be allowed to be mediums," regardless of any innate abilities (262).

4. In extreme cases, those who do not, or cannot, conform have been subjected to incarceration and/or coercive hospitalization. See chapter 5.

5. *The Ghost Inside My Child*, "Orphan Trains and Hotel Flames" (2013).

6. *The Ghost Inside My Child* and *Who Was I?: My Past Lives* (2014) deal exclusively with reincarnation.

7. Williams, 151.

8. In *A Haunting*, "The Shadowman" (2014), domestic violence is a greater threat to the family than supernatural forces. Not knowing whether to be more afraid of a malignant being outside his window or of his volatile father pounding furiously on his bedroom door, a little boy becomes hysterical and runs into a wall, breaking several bones.

9. *Ghost Adventures*, "Myrtles Plantation" (2014).

10. Braude, *Radical Spirits*.

11. Roberston, *Science of the Séance*, 55, 50.

12. Robertson, 54.

13. Robertson, 55.

14. Robertson, 56; Galvan, 165. Consequently, some felt compelled to hide the "extraordinary secret" of their "sensitivity" from others (Galvan, 164). See Robertson's discussion of William Cartheuser, a medium in the 1920s and '30s. Late in his career, he abandoned his first spirit guide (a young girl characterized by a high voice) and developed a new spirit guide, an authoritative male doctor with "a very powerful voice." Nevertheless, even his supporters "did not find such displays enough to counter his allegedly frail body and childish, effeminate mind" (57). Alex Owen discusses the nineteenth century "impression that occultism attracted mannish women and effeminate men," and points to "the ambiguous gender persona of Madame Blavatsky," founder of the hugely influential Theosophical Society, whom a friend "affectionately called 'Jack'" (*The Place of Enchantment: British Occultism and the Culture of the Modern* [Chicago: Chicago University Press, 2004], 107).

15. Ryan Buell with Stefan Petruca, *Paranormal State: My Journey into the Unknown* (New York: It Books, 2010). On Belanger's website she describes herself as a "psychic vampire" and "intersex" (she defines both terms as undefinable) (www.michellebelanger.com/faq).

16. One of the few male mediums appearing on *Psychic Detectives* and *Psychic Investigators*, Phil Jordan is also the author of an autobiography with the title *I Knew This Day Would Come: A Personal Journey to Psychic Self-Awareness.*

17. After her show *Life Among the Dead* played on US television in 2007, British psychic Lisa Williams left her husband, became a single parent, came out as a lesbian, and assumed a role as a celebrity advocate for gay rights in England. Because of the show's limited availability, these events had little resonance in the US.

18. *Hollywood Medium with Tyler Henry* (2016).

19. *Psychic Kids*, "Fear Management."

20. *Psychic Kids*, "The Ghost of Freddie."

21. The 2019 revival of *Ghost Hunters* ran in direct competition with *Ghost Nation* which featured the original *Ghost Hunters* founder Jason Hawes and team member Steve Gonsalves.

22. Coffey appears in "Spirit in the Mirror." In episode "Make the Spirits Stay," we see a clip from 2008 featuring an unidentified Kim Russo.

23. "The Ghost in the Bed," "Awake and Afraid," and "Spirit in the Mirror," respectively. In the latter, the parents make a point of including their son in communal meetings with tribal elders.

24. As a sign of the hostility directed at paranormal celebrities, the *New York Times* obituary for Lorraine Warren described her as someone who "claimed to be a clairvoyant" and her husband as someone who "called himself a demonologist." Quoting the *Viking News* of Westchester Community College (possibly a first), the *Times* labeled the couple "audacious and unabashed frauds, capitalizing on the completely meritless superstition which is all too common in modern society" (Neil Genzlinger, "Paranormal Investigator Portrayed in *The Conjuring* Dies at 92," *New York Times*, April 19, 2019).

25. Images of terrified, hooded victims evoke the photographs of Afghan and Iraqi prisoners tortured by Americans at Abu Ghraib which were made public in April 2004.

26. Glynn, 157.

27. Glynn, 10.

28. Weinstock, 6.

Bibliography

Andrejevic, Mark. "Real-izing Exploitation." In *The Politics of Reality Television: Global Perspectives*, eds. Marwan M. Kraidy and Katherine Sender, 11–30. London: Routledge, 2011.

Antrim, Donald. *The Afterlife*. New York: Farrar, Straus and Giroux, 2006.

Bader, Christopher D., F. Carson Menchen, and Joseph D. Baker, eds. *Paranormal America: Ghost Encounters, UFO Sightings, Bigfoot Hunters, and Other Curiosities in Religion and Culture*. New York: New York University Press, 2010.

Baer, Ulrich. "To Give Memory a Place: Contemporary Holocaust Photography and the Landscape Tradition." In *The Spectralities Reader: Ghosts and Haunting in Contemporary Cultural Theory*, eds. María del Pilar Blanco and Esther Pereen, 415–43.

Banta, Martha. *Henry James and the Occult: The Great Extension*. Bloomington: Indiana University Press, 1972.

Barrow, Logie. *Independent Spirits: Spiritualism and English Plebians, 1850–1910*. London: Routledge & Kegan Paul, 1986.

Barthes, Roland. *Camera Lucida: Reflections on Photography*, trans. Richard Howard. New York: Hill and Wang, 1981.

Beckman, Karen. *Vanishing Women: Magic, Films and Feminism*. Durham, NC: Duke University Press, 2003.

Bergland, Renée L. *The National Uncanny: Indian Ghosts and American Subjects*. Hanover, NH: UPNE, 2000.

Blanco, María del Pilar, and Esther Peeren, eds. *The Spectralities Reader: Ghosts and Haunting in Contemporary Cultural Theory*. London: Bloomsbury, 2013.

Blanco, María del Pilar, and Esther Peeren. "Introduction: Conceptualizaing Spectralities." In *The Spectralities Reader: Ghosts and Haunting in Contemporary Cultural Theory*.

Bloom, Clive. "Angels in the Architecture: The Economy of the Supernatural." In *Ghosts: Deconstruction, Psychoanalysis, History*, eds. Peter Buse and Andrew Stott.

Blum, Deborah. *Ghost Hunters: William James and the Search for Scientific Proof of Life after Death*. New York: Penguin Press, 2006.

Bond, Casey. "Underwater Mortgage? Suze Orman Recommends Walking Away from Your Mortgage." October 18, 2011. http://www.gobankingrates.com.

Braude, Ann. *Radical Spirits: Spiritualism and Women's Rights in Nineteenth Century America*, second edition. Bloomington: Indiana University Press, 2001.
Brauner, Sigrid. *Fearless Wives and Frightened Shrews: The Construction of the Witch in Early Modern Germany*. Amherst: University of Massachusetts Press, 1995.
Brown, Michael F. *The Channeling Zone: American Spirituality in an Anxious Age*. Cambridge, MA: Harvard University Press, 1997.
Buell, Ryan, with Stefan Petruca. *Paranormal State: My Journey into the Unknown*. New York: It Books, 2010.
Bulgakov, Mikhail. *The Master and Margarita*, trans. Richard Pevear and Larissa Volokhonsky. New York: Penguin Books, 2016.
Burger, Alissa. "*Ghost Hunters*: Simulated Participation in Televisual Hauntings." In *Popular Ghosts: The Haunted Places of Everyday Culture*, eds. Esther Peeren and María del Pilar Blanco, 162–74.
Buse, Peter, and Andrew Stott, eds. *Ghosts: Deconstruction, Psychoanalysis, History*. New York: St. Martin's Press.
Canup, John. *Out of the Wilderness: The Emergence of an American Identity in Colonial New England*. Middletown, CT: Wesleyan University Press, 1990.
Caputo, Theresa, with Kristina Grish. *There's More to Life than This*. New York: Atria Books, 2013.
Castle, Terry. *The Female Thermometer: Eighteenth-Century Culture and the Invention of the Uncanny*. New York: Oxford, 1995.
Coates, James. *Photographing the Invisible*, reprinted edition. New York: Arno, 1973.
Connor, Steven. "The Machine in the Ghost: Spiritualism, Technology, and the 'Direct Voice.'" In, *Ghosts: Deconstruction, Psychoanalysis, History*, eds. Peter Buse and Andrew Stott.
Cottom, Daniel. *Abyss of Reason: Cultural Movements, Revelations, and Betrayals*. New York: Oxford, 1991.
D'Harlingue, Benjamin. "Specters of the U.S. Prison Regime: Haunting Tourism and the Penal Gaze." In *Popular Ghosts: The Haunted Places of Everyday Culture*, eds. Esther Peeren and María del Pilar Blanco, 133–46.
Deery, June. *Reality TV*. Cambridge, UK: PolityPress, 2015.
Dovey, Jon. *FreakShow: First Person Media and Factual Television*. London: Pluto Press, 2000.
Evans, Robin. *The Fabrication of Virtue: English Prison Architecture, 1750–1840*. Cambridge UK: Cambridge University Press, 1982.
Fiske, John. *Television Culture*. London: Methuen, 1987.
Foucault, Michel. *Discipline and Punish: The Birth of the Prison*, second edition, trans. Alan Sheridan. New York: Vintage Books, 1995.
Franklin, Cory. "Manipulation, Conflict of Interest, Plague Medical Research." *Chicago Tribune*, reprinted *Upper Valley News*, June 15, 2015.
Galvan, Jill. *The Sympathetic Medium: Feminine Channeling, the Occult, and Communication Technologies, 1859–1919*. Ithaca: Cornell University Press, 2010.
Ginzlinger, Neil. "The Creak in the Night is Music to their Ears." *New York Times*, October 11, 2014, C6.
Ginzlinger, Neil. "Paranormal Investigator Portrayed in *The Conjuring* Dies at 92." *New York Times*, April 19, 2019.

Glynn, Kevin. *Tabloid Culture: Trash Taste, Popular Power and the Transformation of American Television*. Durham, NC: Duke University Press, 2000.

Goldstein, Diane E., Sylvia Ann Grider, and Jeannie Banks Thomas, eds. *Haunting Experiences: Ghosts in Contemporary Folklore*. Logan, UT: Utah State University Press, 2007.

Gordon, Avery. *Ghostly Matters: Haunting and the Sociological Imagination*. Minneapolis: University of Minnesota Press, 1997.

Griffiths, Alison. *Carceral Fantasies: Cinema and Prison in Early Twentieth-Century America*. New York: Columbia University Press, 2016.

Grindstaff, Laura. "DI(t)Y, Reality-Style: The Cultural Work of Ordinary Celebrity." In *A Companion to Reality TV*, ed. Laurie Ouellette, 324–44.

Hale, Mike. "Consigning Reality to Ghosts." *New York Times*, December 13, 2009, AR26.

Hanks, Michelle. *Haunted Heritage: The Cultural Politics of Ghost Tourism, Populism, and the Past*. Walnut Creek, CA: Left Coast Press, 2015.

Held, Lisa. "Psychic Mediums are the New Wellness Coaches." *New York Times*, March 19, 2019.

Hibberd, James. "A&E Reality Show Has Cops Chasing Ghosts." *Hollywood Reporter*, January 6, 2009, https://reporter.blogs.com/live_feed/2009/01/ae-announces-paranormal-cops.html.

Hill, Annette. *Paranormal Media: Audience, Spirits, and Magic in Popular Culture*. London: Routledge, 2011.

Hill, Annette. *Reality TV: Audiences and Popular Factual Television*. London: Routledge, 2005.

Hill, Annette. *Restyling Factual TV*. London: Routledge, 2007.

Holmes, Su, and Deborah Jermyn, eds. *Understanding Reality Television*. New York: Routledge, 2004.

Holzer, Hans. *The Ghost Hunter*. New York: Fall River Press, 2014 [1963].

Houdini, Harry. *A Magician among the Spirits*. New York: Harper & Brothers, 1924.

Isenberg, Nancy. *White Trash: The 400-Year Untold History of Class in America*. New York: Viking, 2016.

James, William. *The Principles of Psychology*. New York: Henry Holt, 1890.

Karlsen, Carol F. *The Devil in the Shape of a Woman: Witchcraft in Colonial New England*. New York: Vintage Books, 1989.

Kavka, Misha. *Reality TV*. Edinburgh: Edinburgh Press, 2012.

Keating, Dan, and Lenny Bernstein. "Data: U.S. Suicide Rates on the Rise." *Washington Post*, April 23, 2016.

Leland, John. "Don't Say Ghostbuster, Say Spirit Plumber." *New York Times*, October 31, 2002. http://www.nytimes.com/2002/10/31/garden/don-t-say-ghostbuster-say-spirit-plumber.html.

Lepore, Jill. *The Name of War: King Philip's War and the Origins of American Identity*. New York: Knopf, 1998.

Levey, Noam N. "Causes Cited for High Death Rates Among Middle-Aged Whites." *Tribune Washington Bureau*, January 30, 2016.

Leyda, Julia. "Paranormal Activity." *Jump Cut*, no. 56 (Fall 2014).

Li, Hao. "Interview: Suze Orman on Underwater Mortgages and Personal Finance." *International Business Times*, August 17, 2010. http://www.ibtimes.com/interview-suze-orman-underwater-mortgages.

Luther, Martin. *Sermons of Martin Luther*, vol. 2, ed. and trans. John Nicholas Lenker. Grand Rapids, MI: Baker Book House, 1906.

Mather, Cotton. *The Present State of New England*. Boston, 1690.
Mather, Increase. "A Discourse Concerning the Uncertainty of the Times of Men, and the Necessity of Being Prepared for Sudden Changes & Death." 1696.
McCann, Andrew. *Popular Literature, Authorship and the Occult in Late Victorian Britain*. Cambridge, UK: Cambridge University Press, 2014.
Moody, Raymond A., Jr. *Life after Life: The Investigation of a Phenomenon—Survival of Bodily Death*. New York: Bantam Books, 1975.
Moyer, Justin Wm. "How Real-Life Horror Visited 'Rock Star' Ghost Hunters, Dead in Alleged Murder-Suicide." *Washington Post*, September 24, 2015.
Murray, Susan, and Laurie Ouellette, eds., *Reality TV: Remaking Television Culture*, second edition. New York: NYU Press, 2009.
Natale, Simone. *Supernatural Entertainments: Victorian Spiritualism and the Rise of Modern Media Culture*. University Park, PA: Pennsylvania State University Press, 2016.
Nordyke, Kimberly. "Some Freaky Goings-On in A&E's 'Paranormal State.'" *Hollywood Reporter*, December 17, 2007.
Ouellette, Laurie, ed., *A Companion to Reality TV*. Oxford, UK: Wiley Blackwell, 2017.
Ouellette, Laurie, ed. *Lifestyle TV*. New York: Routledge, 2016.
Owen, Alex. *The Darkened Room: Women, Power and Spiritualism in Late Victorian England*. London: Virago Press, 1989.
Owen, Alex. *The Place of Enchantment: British Occultism and the Culture of the Modern*. Chicago: Chicago University Press, 2004.
Peeren, Esther, and María del Pilar Blanco, eds. *Popular Ghosts: The Haunted Places of Everyday Culture*. London: Bloomsbury, 2010.
Radway, Janice. "Foreword." In Gordon, *Ghostly Matters*.
Raphael, Chad. "The Political Economic Origins of Reali-TV." In *Reality TV: Remaking Television Culture*, eds. Susan Murray and Laurie Ouellette.
Reed, Austin. *The Life and Adventures of a Haunted Convict*, ed. Caleb Smith. New York: Random House, 2016.
Richardson, Judith. *Possessions: The History and Uses of Haunting in the Hudson Valley*. Cambridge, MA: Harvard University Press, 2003.
Roach, Mary. *Spook: Science Tackles the Afterlife*. New York: W. W. Norton, 2005.
Robertson, Beth A. *Science of the Séance: Transnational Networks and Gendered Bodies in the Study of Psychic Phenomena, 1918–40*. Vancouver: UBC Press, 2016.
Roper, Lyndal. *Witch Craze: Terror and Fantasy in Baroque Germany*. New Haven: Yale University Press, 2004.
Ross, Andrew. "Reality Television and the Political Economy of Amateurism." In *A Companion to Reality TV*, ed. Laurie Ouellette.
Sagers, Aaron. "'Ghost Hunters' Amy Bruni, Adam Berry Exit: Fall Out, Feuds, Predictions Begin." *Huffington Post*, May 30, 2014. http://www.huffingtonpost.com/aaron-sagers/ghost-hunters-amy-bruni-a_b_5419842.html.
Scheiner, Amanda McClain. *Keeping Up the Kardashian Brand: Celebrity, Materialism, and Sexuality*. Lanham, MD: Lexington Books, 2014.
Sconce, Jeffrey. *Haunted Media: Electronic Presence from Telegraphy to Television*. Durham, NC: Duke University Press, 2000.
Sears, John. *Sacred Places: American Tourist Attractions in the Nineteenth Century*. New York: Oxford, 1989.

Semple, Janet. *Bentham's Prison: A Study of the Panopticon Penitentiary*. Oxford: Clarendon Press, 1993.
Shattuc, Jane. *The Talking Cure: TV Talk Shows and Women*. New York: Routledge, 1997.
Sinclair, Upton. *Mental Radio*. New York: Albert and Charles Boni, 1930.
Smith, Adam. *An Inquiry into the Nature and Causes of the Wealth of Nations*, 1776, 1801, vol. 2.
Squires, Catherine R. "The Conundrum of Race and Reality Television." In *A Companion to Reality TV*, ed. Laurie Ouellette.
Stelter, Brian. "'Ghost Hunters' Seeks Spirits and Ratings." *New York Times*, November 11, 2009, C3.
Tavernise, Sabrina. "Sweeping Pain as Suicides Hit a 30-Year High." *New York Times*, April 22, 2016, A1, A14.
Trawinski, Lori A. *Nightmare on Main Street: Older Americans and the Mortgage Market Crisis*. AARP Public Policy Institute, 2011.
Troy, Kathryn. *The Specter of the Indian: Race, Gender and Ghosts in American Séances, 1848–1890*. New York: SUNY Press, 2017.
Tudor, Andrew. *Monsters and Mad Scientists: A Cultural History of the Horror Movie*. Oxford: Basil Blackwell, 1989.
Turner, Graeme. "Reality Television and the Demotic Turn." In *A Companion to Reality TV*, ed. Laurie Ouellette, 309–323.
Walker, William. *Buried Alive (Behind Prison Walls) for a Quarter of a Century: Life of William Walker*, ed. Thomas S. Gaines. Saginaw, MI: Friedman & Hynan, 1892.
Weinstock, Jeffrey. "Introduction." In *Spectral America: Phantoms and the National Imagination*. Madison: Wisconsin University Press, 2004.
Wickland, Carl A., MD, *Thirty Years Among the Dead*. Los Angeles: National Psychological Institute, 1924.
Williams, Karen. "The Liveness of Ghosts: Haunting and Reality TV." In *Popular Ghosts*, eds. Esther Peeren and María del Pilar Blanco, 149–61.
Williamson, Milly. *CELEBRITY: Capitalism and the Making of Fame*. Cambridge, UK: Polity Press, 2016.
Wilson, Julie. "Reality Television Celebrity: Star Consumption and Self-Production in Media Culture." In *A Companion to Reality TV*, ed. Laurie Ouellette, 421–36.

Index

Adams, Dave, 150–51
Addams Family, The, 133
African American representation, 23, 152, 153, 161–62, 175–76, 179–80, 183, 186–92, 196, 202, 205, 209, 215, 244n49, 245n50
Allaire, Brent, 172–73
Allan, Amy, 23, 78, 126–28, 170–71, 175, 230n77, 235n69
Allen, Debbie, 194–96, 218
Alonso, Maria Conchita, 192
American Idol, 6
American Super/Natural, 9
Amityville Horror, The, 168
Andrejevic, Mark, 228n17
Angels Among Us, 19, 93, 94, 233n28
Angels and Demons, 237n21
Answered Prayers, 238n44
Antrim, Donald, 129
Apache, 176

Bagans, Zak, 60, 63, 64, 67, 68, 69–81, 84, 121–22, 124, 130, 141, 142, 148, 153, 157, 158, 160, 169–70, 173–74, 178–79, 187–89, 222n46, 229n39, 230n54, 230n73, 231n87, 231n90, 237n18, 238n39, 244n48
Barbershop, 185
Baywatch, 106
Beaumont, Gustave de, 159
Beckman, Karen, 221n35
Bekovic, Jonette, 130

Belanger, Michelle, 16, 23, 180–83, 206, 246n15
Bell, Tia, 232n18
Bentham, Jeremy, 137, 142, 159–60, 242n68
Bergland, Renée L., 243n15
Berry, Adam, 15–16, 20, 84, 206–7, 236n2, 244n47
Best, Willie, 186
Beverly Hills Housewives, 6
Bewitched, 18–19
Bicycle Thieves, 234n42
Blades, Jack, 244n37
Blair, Linda, 47, 227n76
Blair Witch Project, The, 63
Blanco, Maria del Pilar, 5, 225n39, 242n5
Blavatsky, Helena, 231n84, 246n14
Bloom, Clive, 231n94
Boo! A Madea Halloween, 244n49
Borden, Lizzie, 77, 227n76
Borgen, Jeanne, 116, 235n61
Boy George, 106, 234n53
Breakfast Club, The, 210
Breaking Amish, 95
Brinkman, Sue, 121
Brown, Ken, 188, 189
Bruni, Amy, 15–16, 84, 206, 207, 244n47
Buell, Ryan, 74, 79, 123, 126, 128, 129, 172–73, 180–83, 203–4, 206–7, 238n36, 244n34
Buffalo Soldier, 176
Bulgakov, Mikhail, 128

Burger, Alissa, 221n26, 228n21, 240n36
Buse, Peter, 36, 166–67, 221n28, 227n69

cable television, 5, 7, 9–10, 26, 29, 51, 83, 89, 216, 221n30, 223n55
Call, Anthony D. (Tony), 225n46
cameras, 4–5, 11, 14, 17, 21, 25, 34, 36, 37, 52, 54, 60, 63–65, 67–69, 71–73, 75–76, 78–81, 84, 86, 95, 97, 99, 107, 110, 113, 121, 141, 144, 146, 147, 153, 158, 160, 161, 167, 170, 181, 183, 186, 189, 191, 194, 203, 215, 230n77, 231n81
Canada, 242n2, 244n33
Cancelmi, Jennie Marie, 19, 93, 94, 95, 96, 107, 109
Caputo, Larry, 18, 95, 97–99
Caputo, Larry, Jr., 95, 97
Caputo, Theresa, 18–19, 93–110, 115, 117, 119, 121, 130, 164, 165, 166, 232n25, 233n32, 233n37, 235n69, 238n36, 243n19, 243n30, 245n1
Caputo, Victoria, 95, 97, 121
Case, Anne, 17
Cash, Johnny, 230n54
Castle, Terry, 143–44, 241nn44–45
Cayne, Candis, 207
celebrity, 13, 15, 45–49, 50–51, 56–57, 84, 88, 92, 96, 100, 104, 106–7, 109–10, 192, 196, 220n11, 227n72 (chap. 1), 227n10 (chap. 2), 228nn16–17, 228n28, 234n53, 246n17, 246n24
Celebrity Ghost Stories, 9, 13, 18, 26–27, 46–50, 107, 122–23, 191–98, 201, 218, 236n10, 243n29, 245n53
Cepero, Rosie, 19, 93, 94, 95, 96, 101, 104, 107, 109, 232n25, 238n36
Chau, Lawrence, 119, 242n2
Cherokee, 174
Chippewa, 173–74, 244n36
Cho, Margaret, 192
Christianity, 43, 119, 129, 130–31, 194, 211, 236n14, 237n16, 237n23, 238n46, 245n54
Christie, Agatha, 111–12
Claud, Dwayne, 124, 129, 238n38
Cloverfield, 63
Coffey, Chip, 20, 204, 206–12, 214
Comanche, 175

Connor, Steven, 69, 71, 229n51
Constantino, Debbie, 230n73
Constantino, Mark, 230n73
contempt, 4, 5, 14, 48–49, 57, 222n40, 226n55
Creepy Canada, 242n2
Crossing Over with John Edward, 91–93, 103, 234n44
Culkin, Macaulay, 104

Dahne, Micki, 235n61
Danielson, Bob, 173–74, 244n35
Daoism, 43
DaVinci Code, The, 237n21
Dead Files, The, 9, 23, 40, 78, 126–28, 170–71, 175, 230n77, 235n69, 237n30, 237n32, 244n31
Deadly Possessions, 229n49, 231n90
Deaton, Angus, 17
Deen, Paula, 100, 233n37
Deery, June, 5, 6, 220n14
DeLeon, Santana, 214
Demon Exorcist, 124, 129
Demon Files, The, 16, 125, 216, 221n34, 222n47, 237n23
Demon House, 237n18
demons/demonic, the, 16, 20, 28, 42, 43, 44, 70, 73, 80, 82, 121–27, 129–30, 146, 175, 188, 193, 194, 200, 202, 204, 209, 211, 216, 230n57, 236n1, 236n7, 237n17, 237n23, 238n39, 246n24
Destination Fear, 15
D'Harlingue, Benjamin, 141
Dickens, Charles, 159, 201
direct address, 5, 14, 25, 36, 60, 81, 84, 95, 97, 107, 113, 121, 141, 158, 161, 186, 189, 191, 194, 230n77
DiSchiavi, Steve, 127, 170–71, 175
disclaimers, 10–11
Dog the Bounty Hunter, 238n34
Donahue, Phil, 91
Downey, Roma, 238n44
Driver, Katherine, 25
Dr. O, 180–83
Dr. Phil, 185
Duck Dynasty, 222n40
Dyer, Richard, 56

INDEX

Eastern State Penitentiary, 55–56, 135–46, 149–50, 153–55, 159, 239n8, 240n40, 241n51, 241n63
Eden, Marcia, 38
Edward, John, 91–93, 103, 107, 232n21, 233n41, 234n44, 238n36
Electra, Carmen, 106
Esposito, Giancarlo, 192
Estrada, Erik, 192
Evans, Robin, 239n15, 239n20
EVPs (Electronic Voice Phenomena), 52, 65, 67, 72, 79, 86, 142, 187, 220n18, 229n35, 230n73, 238n39
exorcism, 15, 20, 40, 44, 124–26, 127, 128, 129, 202, 221n34, 236n1, 237n20, 237n23
Exorcist, The, 47, 200

Fact or Faked, 220n18
Famously Afraid, 218
Faraday, Michael, 140
Farley, T. J., 113
femininity, 18, 20, 73–74, 77, 79, 80, 82, 85, 96–103, 105, 111–12, 114–16, 178–79, 206, 209, 212–13, 216, 229n49, 233n31, 236n13
Fisher, Ann, 235n61
Fiske, John, 75
Fixer Upper, 29
Flip or Flop, 29
Flores, Susan, 43, 123
Fond du Lac, 173
Forensic Files, 111, 235n65
Foucault, Michel, 137–38
Fox sisters, 86

Galvan, Jill, 100, 246n14
Get Out, 12
Ghost Adventures, 9, 10, 15, 16–19, 21, 35, 59, 60–83, 121–24, 131–34, 136, 141–42, 156–57, 164, 169–73, 178–80, 186–89, 205, 216, 221n32, 228nn23–24, 228n29, 229n35, 229n39, 230n54, 230n60, 230n73, 231n80, 231nn86–87, 231n90, 232n17–18, 238n39 (chap. 4), 238n1 (chap. 5), 241n63, 242n69, 244n36, 244n38
Ghost Adventures: Aftershocks, 231n87, 244n48

Ghost Asylum, 9, 15, 16, 22, 59, 62, 63, 66, 70–71, 73, 74–76, 81, 82, 84–85, 128–29, 133, 134, 147–48, 153, 156, 158, 183–84, 185, 216, 228n27, 229nn48–49, 231n81, 231n92, 241n53, 245n50
Ghost Bait, 216–17
Ghost Brothers, 15, 73, 161, 162, 185–90, 213, 244n45
ghost hunters, 15, 17, 20, 50–70, 73–77, 84, 99, 117, 134, 146, 178, 201, 212, 218, 222n48, 222n51, 235n69, 236n2, 236n7
Ghost Hunters, 7, 15, 16, 20, 53–60, 63–68, 74, 79, 82–83, 84, 125, 133–34, 136, 146, 147, 152, 161, 176–78, 186, 196, 206, 216, 221n26, 228n21, 228n28, 229n48, 230n58, 239n2, 240n36, 241n53, 241n63, 246n21
Ghost Hunters (2019), 213, 246n21
Ghost Hunters Academy, 15, 84, 206
Ghost Hunters International, 15, 84
Ghost Inside My Child, The, 202
Ghost Lab, 15, 75
Ghost Loop, 213
Ghost Nation, 16, 201, 246n21
Ghostly Encounters, 26, 29, 42–43, 119, 123, 131, 226n63, 242n2
Ghostly Matters, 32
ghosts, 3–4, 6–7, 11, 13, 15, 21, 28, 33, 37–38, 47–49, 55, 58–61, 68, 70–71, 76–77, 79, 81, 85, 105, 108–9, 117, 127, 130–31, 134, 142, 146, 149, 159, 161–63, 166–67, 180, 182, 184–85, 192–95, 200, 203–4, 221n28, 225n39, 230n57, 230n73, 231n94, 236n2, 236n10, 243n21
Ghosts in My House, 105, 115
Ghosts in the Hood, 191–92, 245n51
Ghosts of Shepherdstown, 84, 106–7, 231n90
Ghost Stalkers, 16, 59, 63, 66, 67, 73–74, 76, 78–79, 138, 147–48, 150–51, 164, 174–75, 229n32
Ghost Stories, 11
Ghost Whisperer, 9, 221n29
Gilmore, Robbie, 205
Ginzlinger, Neil, 229n32
Glee, 48
Glynn, Kevin, 33, 46, 217, 222n39, 225n32, 225n35, 225n48

Goldstein, Diane, 6, 220n24, 226n49, 229n46
Goncalves, Mike, 231n92
Gonsalves, Steve, 56, 60, 74, 83, 246n21
Goodwin, Aaron, 71, 76, 80, 157, 179, 188–89, 230n60, 231n87
Gordon, Avery, 21, 23, 25, 32, 33, 225n31
Gossett, Louis, Jr., 192–94, 196, 218, 245n53
Graham, Deborah, 232n25, 234n46
Greer, Pam, 195–96
Griffiths, Alison, 240n38
Grindstaff, Laura, 227n72
Groff, Nick, 16, 64, 74, 76, 78, 80–81, 83, 84, 122, 130–32, 141–42, 147, 151–52, 155, 157–58, 160, 167–68, 175–76, 229n35, 230n60, 231n90, 237n17, 239n2

Hale, Mike, 57, 229n53
Hanks, Michelle, 17, 56, 59, 222n51, 228n24, 236n7
Harnois, Brian, 83
Harris, Youree Dell, 89
Harvey, Marcus, 185–90
Haunted, The, 9, 26, 28, 29, 31
Haunted Case Files, 73, 123, 228n22, 230n57, 237n18
Haunted Collector, 16, 59, 74, 120, 229n49
Haunted Highway, 59–60, 74, 229n52
Haunted History, 9, 228n27
Haunted Houseguests, 213
Haunted Towns, 231n92
Haunting, A, 9, 11, 13, 16, 26, 29, 31, 35–37, 41–43, 120, 163, 164, 168, 175, 226n55, 242n1, 245n8
Haunting of . . . with Kim Russo, The, 19, 88, 93, 102–3, 106–9
Hauntings and Horrors, 134, 146, 241n62, 242n2
Hawaiian Life, 29
Hawes, Jason, 54–58, 60–61, 67, 74, 79, 83–84, 152, 246n21
Hayward, Sharon, 119, 131, 226n63
Healer, The, 231n2
Henry, Tyler, 20, 104–7, 109, 117, 207, 234nn52–53
Here Comes Honey Boo Boo, 222n40
HGTV, 29, 223n55 (intro.), 223n9 (chap. 1), 224n18

Hill, Annette, 6, 14, 71, 220n17, 220n19
History of Love, The, 240n33
Hollywood Medium with Tyler Henry, 9, 20, 88, 103–7
Holzer, Hans, 90–91, 105, 232n17, 232n19, 234n50
Holzer Files, The, 91, 213, 232n17
Home Alone, 104
hoods, 153, 184, 216, 242n71, 246n25
Hopkins, Albert, 232n18
horror genre, 3, 10–14, 26–27, 29–30, 35, 42, 49–50, 60, 63, 71, 73, 91, 108, 121, 123, 136, 146, 147, 156, 157, 163, 168, 174, 176, 178, 185–86, 198–200, 213, 222n37, 232n20, 237n21, 241n62, 243n26
Houdini, Harry, 120, 236n8
House Hunters, 29, 224n11
housing crisis, 12, 29–32, 34
Hudson, Jennifer, 197–98

Imperioli, Michael, 48
Income Property, 29
Indian burial grounds, 161, 164, 168–69, 243nn28–30, 244n34
infomercials, 232n20
Isenberg, Nancy, 225n28
I Was Possessed, 125, 216

Jackson, Jermaine, 243n29
James, Thomas, 20
James, William, 4, 77, 234n57, 243n18
Jameson, Fredric, 224n24
Jersey Shore, 222n40
Joan of Arc, 44
John Paul II (pope), 237n20
Johnson, Aberdeen, 183–84
Johnson, Beverly, 122–23
Johnson, Lorie, 105–6
Jon and Kate Plus Eight, 95
Jones, Dot, 48
Jordan, Phil, 20, 206, 235n60, 246n16
Joyce, Elizabeth, 235n61

Kavka, Misha, 5, 6, 220n11
Kazan, Lainie, 48
Keeping Up with the Kardashians, 6

Kelley, Sean, 149–50, 155, 156, 240n40, 241n56, 241n65
Kemble, Fanny, 159
Ken-Tae, Monica, 103–4, 107, 109, 233n27, 234n44, 234n48
Kerr, Rosemarie, 235n61
Key and Peele, 244n49
Khan, Chaka, 192
Kilmainham Gaol, 239n8, 241n58
Kindred Spirits, 15–16, 20, 84, 134, 206–7, 218, 221n32, 236n2, 244n47
Kirkland, Kenny, 113–14, 116
Klinge, Barry, 75
Klinge, Brad, 75
Kracauer, Siegfried, 27
Krause, Nicole, 240n33

Lampert, Father Vince, 125, 237n20
Last Week Tonight with John Oliver, 87–88
Leland, John, 55
Leonard, Sugar Ray, 192
Lepore, Jill, 171
Leviticus, 87, 232n3
Leyda, Julia, 224n12
Life Among the Dead, 97, 103, 246n17
Lindberg, Chad, 67, 78–79, 148, 150–52, 175
Little Couple, The, 95
Little People, Big World, 95
Lizzie McGuire, 48
Long Island Medium, 3, 18–19, 20, 88, 93–105, 110, 112, 116, 130, 165, 233n28, 233n32, 233n36
Love It or List It, 29
Luther, Martin, 130–31, 238n43

Magic Mike, 185
Mama Medium, 19, 93
Martineau, Harriet, 159
masculinity, 17–18, 20, 39, 51–53, 72–79, 82, 90, 116, 216
Mass, Juwan, 185–90, 244n41
Mather, Cotton, 166
Mather, Increase, 165
McBride, Chi, 192
McCann, Andrew, 41
McCann, J. W., 153

McCormick, K. J., 177–78, 230n58
McDougal, Steven "Doogie," 84
McEntire, Reba, 232n25
McKnight, Chasey Ray, 67, 70, 84–85, 184, 185, 231n92
Medium, The (opera), 91
Medium (television series), 9, 221n29
mediums (psychics, sensitives, etc.), 15, 18, 20, 22, 40, 42, 50, 59, 68–69, 72, 74, 77, 79–80, 82, 85–117, 120, 124, 127, 130, 164, 166, 171, 174, 197, 201, 202, 204–6, 209, 212, 218, 232n6, 232n19, 234n52, 234n57, 238n38, 241n64, 245n3, 246n16
Meehan, Eileen R., 238n34
Méliès, Georges, 123
Melrose Place, 48
Mencia, Carlos, 48, 192
Menotti, Gian Carlo, 91
Mercey, Nadine, 105, 115
Miles, Buddy, 113
Miller, Lisa, 209–12
"Miss Cleo," 89–90
Monica the Medium, 20, 103–4, 206, 216, 233n27, 234n44
Morris, Nathan, 48
Most Haunted, 134, 136, 148
Muldoon, Patrick, 48
Mummy Returns, The, 185
Munsters, The, 133
Murch, Robert, 122
Murder, She Wrote, 112
Music, Eilfie, 203
My Big Fat Gypsy Wedding, 95, 222n40
Myer, Nancy, 235n61
My Ghost Story: Caught on Camera, 10–11, 35, 40, 46, 65, 171, 215
My Haunted House, 9, 11, 30, 216
My Horror Story, 215

Natale, Simone, 6, 88–89, 234n42
Nathan, Edy, 209, 212
Native Americans, 23, 43, 127, 161, 162, 164, 166–72, 174–76, 191, 211, 215, 238n37, 242n3, 243n18, 244n34, 244n36
Navajo, 215, 244n36
Newhart, Bob, 125

Nichols, Mike, 66, 244n45
Nightmare on Elm Street, 12
night vision cameras, 4, 17, 52, 64–65, 71, 81, 86, 185, 229n39
Nineteen Kids and Counting, 95

Ojibwe, 174
Oliver, John, 87–88, 116
Omen, The, 200, 237n21
Orman, Suzie, 224n26
Ortiz, Tito, 107–8
Osborne, Jack, 74
Other Side, The, 244n33
Otunga, David, 197–98
Ouellette, Laurie, 6, 18, 45, 46, 93–94, 186, 226n65, 226n67, 229n34, 233n26
Ouija (film), 236n3
Ouija boards, 20, 112, 119–22, 236n7, 236nn10–11, 237n17, 238n37
Our Gang, 186
Owen, Alex, 222n48, 246n14

Pantoliano, Joe, 48
Paranormal Activity, 63
Paranormal Challenge, 15, 84, 134, 231n90
Paranormal Lockdown, 16, 63, 130, 134, 138–39, 141, 145–47, 151–52, 153, 155, 157, 164, 167, 218, 221n30, 231n90, 237n17, 239n2
Paranormal Lockdown: UK, 231n90
Paranormal State, 10, 11, 16, 20, 23, 59, 61, 74, 79, 123, 125–26, 128, 129, 164, 172–73, 180–83, 190, 192, 195, 202–7, 213, 216, 218, 221n30, 244n34
Paranormal Survivor, 11, 13, 19, 21, 26, 35, 41, 120, 225n42, 228n29, 236n7, 237n18
Paranormal Witness, 9, 13, 26, 28, 30, 35, 36, 39, 120, 124, 216, 223n7, 236n15, 238n37
Pari, Dustin, 177–78, 230n58
Pate, Carol, 112–16, 235n63, 235n65
Paula's Home Cooking, 100
Pawnee, 215
peeling paint, 21, 144–45
Peeren, Esther, 5, 225n39, 242n5
Penobscot Nation, 172–73
Piligian, Craig, 53–55
Pinkerton, Rachel, 40
Plana, Tony, 192

plumbers, 55–58, 227n10
Poberezhny, Sergey, 182
Poe, Edgar Allan, 139, 140, 241n62
Poltergeist, 12, 168
Portals to Hell, 239n3, 241n51
Porter, Scott, 84, 183–84
possession, 20, 80–82, 117, 124–26, 204, 224n12, 231n87, 233n40, 235n69, 236n7, 238n39
Powers, Bernard, 180–81
Praed, Rosa, 240n34
prayer, 41–44, 128–30, 172–73, 193–94, 226n62, 238n34, 238n36, 238n39
priests, 15, 41–44, 89, 124, 126–29, 175, 180, 205, 231n87, 237n30
Prisant, Karen, 235n61
Project Afterlife, 222n54, 238n46
Property Brothers, 29
Property Virgins, 29
Psychic Detectives, 20, 111–16, 206, 235n59, 235n63, 235n65, 246n16
Psychic Intervention, 102, 234n44
Psychic Investigators, 235n59, 235n63, 246n16
Psychic Kids (2019), 213–15, 236n11, 244n31, 246nn22–23
Psychic Kids: Children of the Paranormal, 20, 192, 195, 207–12, 216, 218
Psychic Matchmaker, 231n2, 232n25, 234n46
Psychic Readers Network, 89–90
Psychic Tia, 232n18
Puritans, 165–67, 173–74

Radway, Janice, 225n36
Real Exorcist, The, 125
Real Housewives of . . . , The, 222n40
reality television, 3–7, 10, 12–14, 16–17, 42, 45–46, 53–54, 57, 83–84, 94, 186, 200, 203, 213–14, 216, 220n11, 220nn14–16, 222n40, 226n68, 228n17, 233n29
Reed, Austin, 152, 242n69
Reese, Della, 193–94, 196, 218, 245n53
reincarnation, 202, 231n2, 245n6
Reiner, Noreen, 114–16, 235n65
Richardson, Judith, 166, 243n23
Robertson, Beth, 233n31, 246n14
Rockwell, Norman, 163
Roman, Alex, 43

Roman Catholicism, 43, 124, 129, 130, 237n20, 237n23, 238n36, 238n42
Rosemary's Baby, 12, 200
Ross, Andrew, 233n29
Rowell, Victoria, 47
Russo, Kim, 19, 93, 95, 96, 102–3, 106–9, 115, 117, 164, 233n28, 233n30, 234n44, 235n69, 238n36, 246n22

Sacagawea, 166
sage (smudging), 43, 95, 121, 164, 165, 172, 191, 244n34
Salem witch trials, 3
Sarchie, Ralph, 237n23
Say Yes to the Dress, 233n30
Scariest Places on Earth, The, 227n76
Scary Movie, 244n49
Sconce, Jeffrey, 68–69, 229n42, 231n84
séances, 6, 86, 88, 101, 120–21, 140, 219n7, 233n31
Sears, John, 163–64, 242nn69–70, 242n3
Seatbelt Psychic, 20, 235n58
Seminole, 175, 215
Settle, Lori, 25, 27–28, 30, 31, 38
sexual identity, 20, 75, 78, 205–8, 212, 240n34, 246nn14–15, 246n17
Sheets, Cathy, 36–44, 49, 194, 226n63
Shining, The, 168
Short, Elizabeth, 62
Sitting Bull, 243n19
Sixth Sense, The, 95, 200
slavery, 161, 175–83, 187–90, 192, 193, 195, 242n69, 244n38
Smith, Adam, 144
Smith, Brannon, 70, 81–82, 129
Smith, Chris, 70–71, 74–76, 81–82, 84, 128–29, 158, 183–84
Society for Psychical Research (SPR), 16–17, 68, 234n57
Spera, Tony, 130
spiritualism, 3, 4, 14, 41, 46, 69, 71, 80, 86, 88, 93, 120, 140, 166, 201, 205–6, 219n5, 219n7, 225n39, 227n69, 229n44, 233n31, 236n8, 240n34, 243n18
Sprague, Achsa, 86
Spratt, Dalen, 185–90
Stepford Wives, The, 12

Stepin Fetchit, 186
Stern, Mark, 53–55, 58, 69, 82–83, 228n21, 229n48
Stockdale, Gretchen, 66, 125, 228n28
Stott, Andrew, 36, 166–67, 221n28, 227n69
Stowe, Harriet Beecher, 201
Strongheart, Ron, 172–73
Supernatural Entertainments, 88–89
Survivor, 53
Sympathetic Medium, The, 100

Tango, Dave, 64, 83
technology, 10, 11, 15, 17–18, 40, 51–53, 60, 62–73, 77–80, 82, 84–85, 89, 95, 117, 134, 141, 191, 210, 213, 216, 228n28, 229n42, 240n34
Tenney, John E. L., 16, 76, 78–79, 138, 147–48, 150–52, 175
Thayer, Tom, 53
There's More to Life than This, 130
Thirty Years among the Dead, 80
This Is Life with Lisa Ling, 232n6
Tocqueville, Alexis de, 159
Tolley, Billy, 64, 68, 81, 83, 231n80, 231n86
Tornado Alley, 9
Touched by an Angel, 194, 245n54
Trawinski, Lori, 29–30, 224n17
Trending Fear, 221n32
Trip to the Moon, A, 123
Troy, Kathryn, 166, 219n7, 243n21
Turner, Graeme, 45–46, 57, 226n68
Twilight Zone, The, 200

uncanny, 19, 60, 139, 142–44, 146, 151, 160, 199, 224n12, 241nn44–45
Urie, Michael, 236n10

Van Praagh, James, 20, 206, 216, 234n48
Velez, Lisa Lisa, 197, 245n58
Velocity of Gary, The, 231n79
Village of the Damned, 200
voodoo, 36, 127, 175, 188–89, 205, 231n87

Walker, William, 242n69
Wampanoag, 167
Warren, Ed, 216, 246n24
Warren, Lorraine, 16, 216, 246n24

Wasley, Jay, 64, 83, 169–70
Weber, Nancy, 235n61
Weidman, Katrina, 16, 138, 141, 147, 151–52, 157–58, 160, 167–68, 175–76, 239n2
Weinstock, Jeffrey, 3, 221n36
Wen, Ming-Na, 192
When Ghosts Attack!, 11, 25, 26, 27–28, 30, 38, 42, 216, 226n62
White, Brent, 225n27
Who Was I? My Past Lives, 231n2
Wickland, Carl, 80, 120, 231nn84–85, 233n40
Wilcox, Ellie Wheeler, 231n85
Williams, Billy Dee, 192
Williams, Karen, 6
Williams, Lisa, 97, 100, 103, 246n17
Williamson, Milly, 57, 228n16
Wilson, Grant, 16, 55–57, 66, 74, 83, 84, 134, 147, 213
Winfrey, Oprah, 91
Women of Grace, 120, 121, 126, 130, 131, 236nn13–14, 237n24, 238n42
Woods, The, 243n26
World's Scariest Ghosts: Caught on Tape, The, 215–16

Yoruba, 180–81

Zaffis, John, 16, 74, 120–21, 222n47

About the Author

Photo by Terry Lawrence, by permission

Amy Lawrence is professor emerita of film and media studies at Dartmouth College. She is the author of *The Passion of Montgomery Clift*, *The Films of Peter Greenaway*, and *Echo and Narcissus: Women's Voices in Classical Hollywood Cinema*. She has written on women's voices in film, radio, and recordings (Helen Morgan, Marlene Dietrich); masculinity, acting and stardom (Valentino, James Stewart, James Mason); and on experimental animation. She also makes short animated films.

www.ingramcontent.com/pod-product-compliance
Lightning Source LLC
Chambersburg PA
CBHW030616230426
43661CB00053B/2014